HARVARD STUDIES IN COMPARATIVE LITERATURE

1 Three Philosophical Poets: Lucretius, Dante, and Goethe. By George Santayana *
2 Chivalry in English Literature: Chaucer, Malory, Spenser, and Shakespeare. By William Henry Schofield *
3 The Comedies of Holberg. By Oscar James Campbell, Jr.*
4 Mediaeval Spanish Allegory. By Chandler Rathfon Post *
5 Mythical Bards and the Life of William Wallace. By William Henry Schofield *
6 Angevin Britain and Scandinavia. By Henry Goddard Leach *
7 Chaucer and the Roman Poets. By Edgar Finley Shannon *
8 Spenser and the Table Round. By Charles Bowie Millican *
9 Eger and Grime. By James Ralston Caldwell *
10 Virgil the Necromancer. By John Webster Spargo *
11 Chaucer's Use of Proverbs. By Bartlett Jere Whiting *
12 English Literature and Culture in Russia (1553–1840). By Ernest J. Simmons *
13 D'Edmond Spenser à Alan Seeger: Poèmes Anglais Traduits en Vers Français. By Fernand Baldensperger *
14 Proverbs in the Earlier English Drama. By Bartlett Jere Whiting *
15 Catullus in Strange and Distant Britain. By James A. S. McPeek *
16 Jean Racine. By Alexander F. B. Clark *
17 Un Voyageur-Philosophe au XVIIIe Siècle: L'Abbé Jean-Bernard le Blanc. By Hélène Monod-Cassidy *
18 A Bibliography of the Theophrastan Character in English with Several Portrait Characters. By Chester Noyes Greenough and J. M. French *
19 The Testament of Werther in Poetry and Drama. By Stuart Pratt Atkins *
20 Perspective of Criticism. Edited by Harry Levin *
21 Vissarion Belinski, 1811–1848. By Herbert E. Bowman *
22 Contexts of Criticism. By Harry Levin
23 On Translation. Edited by Reuben A. Brower *
24 The Singer of Tales. By Albert B. Lord
25 Praisers of Folly: Erasmus, Rabelais, Shakespeare. By Walter Kaiser
26 Rogue's Progress: Studies in the Picaresque Novel. By Robert Alter
27 Dostoevsky and Romantic Realism: A Study of Dostoevsky in Relation to Balzac, Dickens, and Gogol. By Donald Fanger
28 The Icelandic Family Saga: An Analytic Reading. By Theodore M. Andersson
29 Roman Laughter: The Comedy of Plautus. By Erich Segal
30 Pan the Goat-God: His Myth in Modern Times. By Patricia Merivale

* Out of print

Harvard Studies in Comparative Literature
Founded by William Henry Schofield

22

CONTEXTS OF CRITICISM

CONTEXTS
of CRITICISM

by Harry Levin

HARVARD UNIVERSITY PRESS

Cambridge, Massachusetts

© Copyright 1957 by the President and Fellows of Harvard College

Third Printing, 1969

Distributed in Great Britain by
Oxford University Press, London

Library of Congress Catalog Card Number 57-7613
SBN 674-16700-7
Printed in the United States of America

For

RENATO POGGIOLI

Preface

This is a book by courtesy of the Harvard Studies in Comparative Literature, a welcome haven for a series of papers which have led a scattered existence through the past ten years. Most — but not all — of them have been published before, under professional or literary auspices more far-flung than widely circulated. All have in common the fact of having been spoken before they were printed, sometimes even before they were written out. Occasional essays, in the literal sense of both words, they have been framed to meet various occasions, and in each case have attempted to deal with subjects proposed or suggested by the provisions of an academic invitation. Since I cherish my contact with the original audiences, and am far from certain upon what plane I might expect to encounter further readers, I have made no effort to erase the marks of oral presentation. Instead, I have simply indicated the circumstances of delivery, in the hope that these would sufficiently account for variations of tone or of presupposition. My headnotes, which also endeavor to keep the record of previous publication and of other relevant detail, will provide an appropriate place for acknowledging my specific obligations to sponsors and editors.

A consecutive reading, which I do not recommend, would certainly uncover repetitions and possibly inconsistencies. In moving back and forth from any position, one is bound to re-cross familiar territory, as well as to observe the same landmarks from different angles. Indeed a slight overlapping of subject-matter, from one paper to the next, has helped me to find a sequence through the miscellany. This ranges freely afield, but in cyclical fashion, between the general and the particular: between problems of definition, formulation, and method, on the one hand, and analyses of style, structure, and technique, on the other. *Context*, the operative word in my title, stands as the locus where these two concerns come together, where precept may be tested by example, and where

the image stimulates the idea. The text itself, put under the
closest scrutiny, must always be the point of departure and the
point of return for criticism. Yet we cannot appreciate its significance, or fully understand it, unless we are willing to pursue its connotations into the broader areas of artistic practice
and human experience. A contextual approach, since it centers
upon the exact relation between form and meaning, constantly
looks in both directions and then turns back to the immediate
intersection.

Relativity, if not relativism, conceived not as the disappearance of standards but as the discernment of relationships, must
be a premise whenever we consider literature, if we would
trace any order in its complexities. The historical and the
comparative approaches enable us to place a given work precisely by relating it to other works and to other manifestations
of culture. We cannot, of course, take all of world literature
for our province; the most we can do is to view it as the horizon
against which our own traditions may be finally measured.
But, just as the anthropologists discover similar processes working through diverse cultures, so — through our peculiarly spe-
calized branch of the science of man — underlying patterns are
to be found. The effect of convention in shaping them, and
the extent to which literature may be conceived as an institution, I have ventured to discuss elsewhere. Here the theoretical
questions touch the methodology of humanistic scholarship,
with regard to other disciplines, and the status of art, with
regard to other modes of knowledge. With regard to the changing schools of critical thought, I have relied considerably on
semantics as a precision instrument for defining concepts in
the terms of those to whom they were most meaningful.

Thus we are brought back to the texture of language, and
especially to the practical devices by means of which it can act
is a surrogate for reality. That is the sphere of prose fiction,
which — under one aspect or another — is the theme of half
the essays in this volume. These in turn are by-products of a
long preoccupation with the history of the novel, and with certain French and American novelists. Suggestion will not take
the place of demonstration; but the instances and issues now

before us will fit into a more general line of interpretation, which follows the curve of modern development from realism to symbolism, and from the social and scientific actuality that some writers reflect to the psychological and philosophical nature of the reflection as conveyed by others. The shift of emphasis, which brings us close to the problem of the imagination itself, registers the emergency of our time. This is not primarily a crisis of criticism, and I hope that one of my titles will not be misconstrued. It is a cultural crisis. Obviously, criticism is ancillary to culture; but culture, at its present stage, seems to need whatever attendance it can still command; and it may now be the function of criticism to articulate what could be left unsaid in the past and what can be no longer taken for granted.

HARRY LEVIN

Cambridge, Massachusetts
September 1, 1956

CONTENTS

WORKING DEFINITIONS

New Frontiers in the Humanities

A graduate school of arts and sciences was inaugurated on January 5, 1954, at the recently founded Brandeis University in Waltham, Massachusetts. The occasion was marked by a symposium on "Frontiers of Knowledge." Four visiting speakers were asked to present their respective views on behalf of the Sciences, the Social Sciences, the Creative Arts, and — in the present instance — the Humanities. This address was published in The Harvard Library Bulletin, X, 2 *(Spring, 1956),* and is reprinted here with the permission of the President and Fellows of Harvard College.

▼▲▼

Looking toward this highly propitious occasion, looking out of my study window in the general direction of Waltham, I might have looked to a source of inspiration which has quickened many an American scholar. It so happens that my house in Cambridge is no more than a stone's throw from Divinity Hall, where Emerson delivered his famous address on that very theme — no less a theme than man himself, the whole man, thinking and acting in a world where nature and idea are at one, and where yesterday emerges into today. But if I were to throw a proverbial stone, it would crash against the plate-glass windows of the more modern Biological Laboratories, which impede my view of the old Emersonian structure by surrounding it on three sides. On the fourth side it is confronted and, of course, overshadowed by the Peabody Museum of Archaeology and the Agassiz Museums of Natural History. I sometimes wonder what Emerson, who was so fond of parables, would make of this object-lesson in containment, which outflanks and exhibits the fragile shell[1] of his dream for humanity — and for the humanities — as if it were a fossil preserved from some prehistoric epoch. The missing link in that scientific quadrangle, a new botanical building, is now under construction; and, as a consequence, Divinity Avenue has become a dead-end street. I refrain from pursuing the further implications of that impasse all the more willingly because, at the moment, it seems to be under public litigation.

Our common concern is with frontiers, not barriers: not limiting but extending the boundaries of knowledge. This is what the scientist seems to be doing, with an almost supersonic rapidity. The social scientist, just as soon as he calls himself by that name, has his work cut out for him. Whereas the humanist's field is so vast and vague, so centrally located and tangentially defined, that he can never be absolutely sure where its frontiers lie — or if indeed they are, or should be, new. "Make it new," said the venerable Confucius; but novelty is a relative matter in time, as frontiers are relative matters in space. It is now two generations since our American frontier, as Frederick Jackson Turner then pointed out, ceased to be a domain of action and became a concept of history. Perhaps we are less like the pioneering frontiersmen than our metaphor flatters us into assuming. We like to think we cultivate the virtues of independence, as they truly did in shifting for themselves and in mastering their elements. Actually we grow more and more dependent, not merely on services or even luxuries, not merely on labor-saving but thought-saving devices. In principle, we still consider ourselves a hardy mixed breed of rugged individualists. In practice we Americans get smoother every day, and so intolerant of nonconformity as to become our own worst enemies. Our only hope is our basic intermixture: the tolerance that pluralism inspires, the endless contribution of minorities. What, then, could be more hopeful than such an undertaking as we are here to welcome? What could be more Emersonian in its hopefulness?

Such a discussion as this, pushing through the methodological limits toward the speculative horizons of the various disciplines represented, seeks common ground in that No Man's Land of *Grenzwissenschaft* which we categorically term the love of wisdom, "philosophy." It presupposes an equal belief in the unity of knowledge and in the division of labor. It presses somewhat beyond the usual subdivision, when it separates the arts from the humanities. But it does well to give special recognition to the serious artists — musicians, painters, writers — who maintain their standards by joining our faculties, and thereby make the academy a conservatory, a studio, a haven for artistic creation. How creative they will remain, whether the advance-guard has turned academic, what the artist may hazard in turning professor, it is not for a mere professor to say. Clearly we stand to profit from daily collaboration with those who practice the skills we endeavor to analyze. Our endeavors, on the other hand, are occasionally sidetracked by a frustrated impulse to create: a kind of Stanislavsky method in criticism which identifies the critic too naïvely with his subject, a rhapsodic mode of subjective interpretation which encourages the interpreter to recreate works by others in his own image. Hence, with all mutual good will, we can avoid contradictions and confusions by distinguishing the practical from the analytic approach. So far as the practitioner is engaged in innovation or experimentation, he comes closer to the scientist; but art cannot claim a continuous progress, as science can; it can only change, with every permutation making the next step more difficult.

Yet, so far as it accumulates, that accumulation — the very exhaustion of obvious rhymes and reëchoing chords and probable combinations — increases our knowledge; our systematic study of the arts can thus be progressive and, for whatever the term may be worth in this connection, scientific. At this point, when we should be securely settled within our assigned terrain, one other distinction is likely to supervene. This is the largely gratuitous issue raised, by their extreme partisans, between criticism and scholarship — or rather, under these two titles of respect, the intramural quarrel between an ill-informed estheticism and a narrow-minded antiquarianism. Fortunately for the rest of us, there are signs that both sides are conducting a rear-guard action. That learning and judgment are interdependent processes, rather than mutually exclusive viewpoints, I trust, is one of our premises this afternoon. There must, and will, be differences of emphasis; but they are no sharper than those which fruitfully exist between fundamental research and applied science, or — in that science regarded as an art — between theoretical medicine and medical practice. The practicing critic is a sort of clinician, diagnosing, prescribing, and from time to time consulting his colleagues, the pathologists — that is to say, the scholars. To speak more directly, he must greet and evaluate what is new as it comes along; so should all interested and educated persons, albeit to a lesser degree. Their education will best have prepared them for the challenge of novelty by according them full access to what is old, to the rich backlog that has already accumulated and that is most appropriately housed in our universities.

Though it may seem unduly paradoxical to take this backward glance at a moment when we should be looking forward, that paradox is firmly built into this institution, the latest development of Western man's longest tradition. Moreover, it is embodied in our country, the youngest child of civilization's old age, the rather callow heir of all the ages lately come into maturity. The great migrations, which have been the animating forces of culture, have never stopped since the days of Babylon; particularly during the last generation, out of the very agonies of the old world, America has been able to naturalize many of Europe's finest minds; and our educational institutions have reaped incalculable benefits from the new Diaspora. One may attest these circumstances without stepping from this platform. The metamorphosis of the United States, from a provincial to a cosmopolitan role, has been completed by the mid-twentieth century. However, there is a provinciality in time which is even more constricting than provinciality in space. Its archetypal spokesman, Monsieur Homais, made so frantic an effort to "keep up with his century" — the nineteenth — that he survives as a byword for all that has dated since then. Montaigne, a more up-to-date thinker, reminds us that human nature is diverse and undulating. Alas, we do not need to be reminded that personal experience, even at its widest and deepest, is limited. To break through the limitations, to widen our own perspectives, to deepen our understanding of ourselves, we must share the crystallized experiences of mankind, as humanism has handed them down to us.

Viewed in that prospect, which is our retrospect, we are posterity. By addressing us, the poets of bygone periods have outspanned those periods; in reading them, we bring the dead to life. But we, after all, are simply another phase in the collective consciousness of humanity — an interim which we, in turn, may transcend by what we communicate to the unborn. Thus art is a conquest, as André Malraux has argued. For Malraux, who has acted and suffered so poignantly through the political and military defeats of our time, art is man's victory over time itself. And Malraux has grandly conceived our culture as a timeless and placeless museum, *le musée imaginaire,* where the masterpieces of every school and style are ranged simultaneously. Scientific techniques, collaborating with humanistic researches, have made possible this state of mind through restoration, reproduction, and dissemination. Let me add one recent example to the many that Malraux has collected with such discriminating eclecticism. The mosaics of Saint Sophia, the Christian temple consecrated to Wisdom, have been covered during the greater part of the five hundred years since the fall of Constantinople. A few years ago their Turkish whitewash was expertly removed by a Boston archeologist, the late Thomas Whittemore. A book has just been published in which these glories of Christendom shine forth as colored photographs have never done before. Furthermore the editor, André Grabar, a Russian-born Byzantinist jointly attached to the Collège de France and Dumbarton Oaks, has sent his technicians over six thousand miles to reproduce the other major examples of Byzantine mural decoration. To have them, collocated for the first time within the compass of a single volume, is more than a recovery; it is a discovery.

The sages of Byzantium, standing "as in the gold mosaic of a wall," were — to William Butler Yeats — the poet's singing masters. Comparably, in transcribing the vision of classical antiquity, the humanist-teachers of the Renaissance awakened the genius of their artist-pupils. Ordinarily the chance of survival, whether by evolution or resurrection, has been better for ideas than for images, since words have not had to await the invention of photography — or, for that matter, printing — in order to be duplicated and circulated. If our mental sphere now seems to be a museum without walls, it has long been a library without shelves, where all books coexist in an ideal order which such fastidious librarians as T. S. Eliot are constantly rearranging. "For literature," Ernst Robert Curtius has written, "all the past is present, or can become so." It does become so, when Professor Curtius demonstrates the continuity of European literature from Homer through the Latin Middle Ages to Dante. The ancient and the medieval author have both been profoundly studied; but to achieve a panoramic overview of so much that lies between them, to trace the inter-cultural relationship in its temporal dimension and its spatial orientation, to correlate each documentary or monumental artifact against the vertical axis of chronology and the lateral axis of structure, this — I believe — is something new under the sun. Just as the historical method liberates us from history by enabling us to stand outside a given situation, perceiving its lines of connection with larger events, so the comparative method enables us to follow an individual process of develop-ment by bringing together different manifestations which have taken similar forms.

Both of these methods, singly and together, seem to char-acterize the massive syntheses of our leading contemporary humanists. They are adumbrated in Sir James Frazer's pro-tracted footnote to Vergil, *The Golden Bough,* and elaborated in Arnold Toynbee's *Study of History,* that free-hand sketch of nothing less than the morphology of civilization. These two infinitely sugestive and necessarily hypothetical works have been subjected to extensive questioning: it seems proper for more cautious men to refine upon the tactics pioneers have used in covering a broad extent of ground. It is their breadth of outlook, their wealth of exemplification, which should be noteworthy; and here we often have to recross the line that today connects, instead of dividing, the humanities and the social sciences. We are realizing again that many phenomena, which we have tended to view as purely esthetic, cannot really be comprehended unless they are seen in a functional context. One may instance the epic, and the solution to the Homeric problem that Milman Parry found by living among the Serbo-Croatian bards. Anthropology has focused our attention upon the ritual origin and the quasi-magical function of the arts; psychology has taught us that fantasy is not falsehood but significant distortion of the truth; and mythology, as now we recognize, comprises not only outmoded fictions but the ideologies by which men continue to live. Explorations of poetic imagery by the Sorbonne philosopher, Gaston Bachelard, point the way toward a vocabulary of symbolism. That indeed would help us to fulfill one of Bacon's most neglected projects for *The Advancement of Learning*: a science of the imagination.

These instances should indicate, at least, that the imaginary museum or universal library need not be a static or dryasdust conception. What Bacon called the custody of knowledge is no mean responsibility, and the custodian is no mere caretaker; he is rather, in Biblical idiom, a Scribe. He must keep up the inventory of extant monuments, as well as the catalogue of surviving archives; he must even make room, in his cobwebbed storehouses, for the discarded hypotheses of yesterday's science. Only the mind of Spinoza's God perhaps, under the aspect of eternity, could take full cognizance of the whole encyclopedic conglomeration of miscellaneous lore. Scholarship is therefore a coöperative record, which is always being augmented and corrected. Here and there experts apply their respective modes of analysis, and little by little this unwieldy collection undergoes a continual revaluation. It is the obligation of custodianship to put certain works on exhibition, as it were, to put relevant books into circulation. But the stored embarrassment of riches complicates the business of selection. So much has been thought and said, and our criteria are so variable, that Matthew Arnold himself might falter in picking out the best. It was simpler to choose, from Hebrew scriptures or Greek translations, a Pentateuch or a Septuagint than it is for latterday Scribes to agree on the Hundred Best Books of the world. Happily, no canon is immutable: only the other day the irrefragable doctors of Saint John's College, Annapolis, announced that *Huckleberry Finn* had been promoted to classical status — which presumably means that one of the previous hundred has been demoted to the Apocrypha.

Since the perennial question "What is a classic?" will elicit varying responses, we must be ready to raise it again and again; and since there are unquestionably more than a hundred great books, it does not make too much difference which are canonized, so long as the others are kept available. This is the heyday of reprints and anthologies, not to speak of digests and abridgments. But the literary market is likewise flooded with what may be neutrally described as subliterature; and since that condition is basically an economic one, it is subject to the operation of Gresham's Law. It may be that a commendable zeal for widespread literacy has somehow ended by spreading it too thin, with a resulting cultural inflation. The consequences, for better or worse, may be temporary; for we are moving so quickly into the audio-visual epoch that the reading habit itself is seriously jeopardized. The fact that picture-magazines are superseding word-magazines may prove to be a blessing in disguise, to the extent that the photographs in *Life* are superior to the articles in *Time*. Television, by catering to demands for popular entertainment, journalistic reportage, and domestic utility which have been served too exclusively by publishers, may well reduce the effectual reading public to the proportions of those audiences whom the greatest writers were content to address. Meanwhile it is characteristic of our technological style of life that even its artistic amenities come in the guise of mechanical appliances: notably the phonograph, which has so multiplied appreciation heretofore reserved for connoisseurs and musicologists. Whatever our problems of cultural production may be, we are certainly accomplished consumers.

Educators have shown a proper interest in the fanfares and flickers of these crucial media; some of them have braved those appalling conventions, without undue compromise and with moderate success. Some of the complexities involved in mass communication, linguistic interchange, and pedagogical semantics have been faced by such ingenious experimentalists as

I. A. Richards. The university, far from becoming a cloister, is all too keenly preoccupied with mundane affairs; scholars, under the mounting pressures of anti-intellectualism, apologize for their commitments to purer learning; yet their fellow citizens seldom hesitate to accuse them of irresponsibility. Their answer should be that they are doubly — if not triply — responsible. They are answerable to the present, yes, both as citizens and as pedagogues, justifying their existence to their contemporaries. But they are peculiarly answerable to the past and — we must not forget — to the future: their job is the strategic link in that chain of transmission whereby the past is brought into the present and whence the present is relayed to the future. In this sense, precisely, their post is at the frontier. Too often, it must be confessed, those long-range duties are slighted in favor of timeliness, popularity, and other more immediate distractions. As between the needs of teaching and the claims of research, of course, the balance is subtle. We shall not upset it if we concede that, on elementary levels, the student comes first; whereas the higher we advance in the educational scale, the more the subject-matter is given priority. The pedagogue gradually makes way for the expert.

We are concerned with higher aims, with the highest. They run counter to that current tendency which levels downward, and which has so undermined the secondary curriculum that the college must teach what students have failed to learn at school: the program sometimes known as General Education. Then, because our colleges must do what in Europe has previously been done by the *lycée* or the *Gymnasium*, it is our graduate schools which can most aptly be designated as our universities. There, at long last, we must not flinch from specialization; nothing else, nothing but obstinate rigor, guarantees professional competence; shortcuts are few and prerequisites are many. Most specifically, a command of languages, both classical and modern, is quite as essential for a humanistic background as mathematics is for a scientific one. Such a command can no longer be taken for granted, and that is a loss which goes far beyond any particular field. It is part of the penalty our society pays for failing to place the same high

value on intellectual attainments that they hold in European
or Jewish tradition. On the whole, education follows the
patterns set by a nation's typical institutions: in our case, set
largely by corporate enterprise, along lines inherently less
adaptable to the humanities than to other fields. The names
of powerful industrialists, which once carried predatory overtones, now convey philanthropic reverberations; and their
foundations patronize research with the lavishness of Maecenas
and the discernment of Lord Chesterfield; yet their well-meant
attempts are understandably dogged by such industrial habits
as competition, advertisement, and — to cite Louis Dembitz
Brandeis —"the curse of bigness."

In the humanities, if nowhere else, man is still the measure
of things. His judgment cannot be delegated to committees or
teams; his opinions cannot be derived from questionnaires or
polls; his observations cannot be confined to reports or sur-
veys. He can — protean creature that he is — assimilate his
personality to his environment; hence he can masquerade, in
an age of cybernetics, as an International Business Machine.
A case in point is the so-called "Chaucer Laboratory" sponsored by the University of Chicago, where photostats of the
eighty-odd manuscripts of *The Canterbury Tales* were as-
sembled and collated by several generations of graduate students under the supervision of two professors. I would not
deprecate the validity of recording somewhere, for the sake of
the record, all the variants of so important and inaccessible a
text. But a text needs to be edited in order to be read; and the
task of editing involves choices, which require not only technique and training but taste and — let us be candid — also
talent. A single editor, F. N. Robinson, working independently
for almost forty years, managed to produce what is still our
most satisfactory Chaucer. With access to no more than a dozen
manuscripts, Professor Robinson anticipated most of the
Chicago readings; now, revising his Cambridge edition after
twenty years, he finds himself obliged to make about two
hundred changes out of nearly twenty thousand lines; this
minimal one per cent, a margin rather of doubt than of
error, is more than counterbalanced by other interpretations

in which he has guided the later editors. In a word, a word of tribute to my old teacher, there are no synthetic substitutes for the devotion and the perception of a trained intelligence.

One of the scholar's compensations is the privilege of belonging to a community of minds, of associating with his intellectual peers. But he should not forget that investigation is, by nature, a lonely pursuit; that few men, as Melville noted, are comfortable about crossing frontiers; that the purest satisfaction is the unshared awareness of having approached a little nearer to some elusive segment of reality — and even this is alloyed by the possibility that it may all turn out to be paranoia. Small wonder that so few investigators venture far alone, and that so many return to easier assignments and time-serving rewards. If the academic profession is an honorable career, that honor is conferred upon it by those to whom it is essentially a calling, a vocation, or — in Shakespearean phrase —

> a wild dedication of yourselves
> To unpath'd waters, undream'd shores.

If I may shift back from Shakespeare to Bacon — and, in spite of all the arguments by scholarly paranoiacs, it is a genuine shift — I should like to quote one of Bacon's warnings: "Whereas the more constant and devout kind of professors of any science ought to propound to themselves to make some additions to their science, they convert their labors to aspire to certain second prizes . . . and so the patrimony of knowledge cometh to be sometimes improved, but seldom augmented." Some of the ways by which these second prizes can be attained, as Bacon lists them, have a familiar aspect: hasty compilation, labored interpretation, championship of fashionable causes. We are prompted to remember the literary activities that attached themselves to the reputation of Henry James upon his centennial a decade ago. At that date Leon Edel was in the army; though he had already devoted some fifteen years to the disinterested study of James's life and work, though he was characteristically generous in sharing his detailed information with those who were hustling into print, he did not begin to publish his own biography until last year. Its first volume is enough to establish the clear authority of patient documentation, experienced insight, and a respect for the nuances of human individuality worthy of James himself. If the second and third volumes live up to this standard, Mr. Edel will have gained a rare first prize. He will have expounded anew the lesson of his master: "Be generous and delicate and pursue the prize."

That ultimate goal, I suspect, is not knowledge but wisdom — a matter which is obviously beyond my scope. Though we are told by Job that the price of wisdom is above rubies, rubies would seem to be more highly valued in this world. But not in the long run: in the grimly pragmatic tests of the European nineteen-thirties, intellect proved more transportable than property. One of the world's great centers of erudition, the Warburg Institute, was transplanted from Hamburg to London University. There, in the Imperial Buildings at South Kensington, I had the pleasure of visiting last spring. I was taken through the four enormous rooms that shelter the Institute's Faustian library, vastly enlarged but according to plans laid out for the original Kulturwissenschaftliche Bibliothek of that brilliant polymath, Aby Warburg. The books in the first room deal with the religions, the philosophies, the dawning sciences, the systems invoked by mankind to explain the universe to itself. The next three rooms, in overwhelming succession, contain history, the chronicle of man's secular behavior; then literature, the testament of his many-sided introspection; and finally the plastic arts, the mirror of his sensuous apprehension. One feels, in traversing this sequence, like a neophyte undergoing an initiation into the aggregate memories of a ubiquitous tribe. One witnesses, in the gifted group of cultural historians who have accompanied and animated this far-ranging project, the survivals, the continuities, the transmigrations of culture itself. And the emergent reaction is a renewal of our confident belief that images persist and ideas endure, just as the Law and its commentaries outlive the Ghetto and the concentration camp.

Art as Knowledge

This paper was submitted to a panel discussion of "Methods of Knowledge," in one of a series of conferences held to celebrate the Columbia University Bicentennial at Arden House on October 29, 1954. It is reprinted from the proceedings of that conference, The Unity of Knowledge, *edited by Lewis Leary and published by Doubleday and Company (1955), with grateful acknowledgment to the publishers and to the Trustees of Columbia University.*

▼▼

1. Fact and Fantasy

When the modern mind plays Hamlet, surveying its own potentialities and limitations, we may not find it untimely to pause for a moment over a skull. The most striking object that suggests itself for such melancholy contemplation is one which may have once belonged to a jester; but the name is not Yorick in this context; the specimen I have in mind has been scientifically labeled as Piltdown Man. Quite recently, like many another venerated relic, it has been unmasked as a pious fraud — or rather, a pseudo-scientific artifact masquerading as a natural phenomenon. Hamlet indeed has come a long way from Piltdown, historically speaking; but chronologically, it now appears that distance is far less impressive than the anthropologists had surmised. I do not call up this grinning apparition in order to cause them any embarrassment, nor to obtrude a *memento mori* upon a festive occasion. Nor do I presume to remind distinguished colleagues, whose researches have penetrated so much farther than mine, that the pursuit of knowledge sometimes encounters misleading clues as well as missing links. The object-lesson that cannot really be overstressed at this point, it seems to me, is how man's continual effort to know himself is complicated by man's habitual tendency to deceive himself.

Perforce we are all of us bound to believe, with Pascal, that the heart has certain reasons of its own which the reason seldom — if ever — knows. Nevertheless to probe them, to illuminate their enveloping obscurity, to establish a rationale of the emotions as it were, has been the daring venture of psychology, and especially of psychoanalysis. The very advance of reason has brought us into closer cohabitation with the irrational. Freud himself, predisposed to be rationalistic, was just as shocked as anyone else might be when first confronted with the revelations of infantile sexuality. Though he was right to pay attention to them, he was wrong to accept them at face value; and yet it was that preliminary mistake which led him to the genuine discovery, as Ernest Jones shows in his current biography. Most of the shocking episodes revealed to Freud by his patients, as it was discovered afterward, had never actually taken place; in other words, they were not facts but fantasies; and this became the crucial distinction that shaped the Freudian approach — though it might have undermined Dr. Kinsey's. Thus Freud, in recognizing material claims, threw new light on imaginative processes; he advanced the cause of self-knowledge by following its detours through the areas of self-deception.

Now the terms of the present discussion presuppose both unity of knowledge and diversity of methods: and method, etymologically considered, is simply a way of getting somewhere. No further presupposition should be necessary for the various sciences, which proceed along their parallel courses with an unhesitating directness. That the arts, however deviously, can also be methods of knowledge — this is a very hospitable but more problematic assumption, which requires at least a word of justification. Here I would not forego the rare advantage of sharing our problems, admitting with equal candor that science is not always attended by certainty and that apologists for the humanities all too often surround their subjects with vagueness. Scientists may begin by direct observation, yet they continue through inference and deduction. Though they explore the unknown, their exploration largely remains uncharted for the layman; often it is not to be apprehended except by abstract formulation or crude analogy; and when the data are apprehensible, they are so voluminous and specialized that they can only be canvassed by legions of experts who scarcely speak one another's professional languages. Each of them, each of us, possesses a little learning and professes a great deal of faith in the aggregate wisdom of our colleagues.

We are all, to extend a phrase of T. S. Eliot's, "expert beyond experience." We can never, by definition, know too much; the dangerous thing, of course, is not knowing enough; and today, in this respect as in others, we live dangerously. More is probably known than at any previous time — but to whom is it known at first hand? Ideally ordered, the sum of it may subsist in the mind of God — but where, for human beings, is it available? Alphabetically indexed, it swells the bibliographies and outdates the encyclopedias. But mere accumulation is not advancement, any more than the Library of Congress is a constitutional guarantee that every member of the United States Senate will behave like a civilized individual. Nor is humane knowledge to be confounded with "know-how," much as we may rely upon contrivances or profit from by-products. The fundamental question is still "What do I know?" Yet if we search the contemporary conscience, its answers may well seem guarded, more limited, less self-reliant than the response of Montaigne's humanism four hundred years ago. If the *what* has increased, the *I* has diminished. Insofar as the free use of knowledge involves assimilation, integration, and mastery, insofar as it implies a personal relationship between the knowable and the knowers, we are comparatively benighted. Our *expertise* has outrun our experience.

Into that bleak and incomplete state of affairs, art brings the possibility of enlargement. The kind of experience it offers, to be sure, is not quite the real thing; if we want to be ontological about it, we must admit, it is notoriously second-hand. But reality is so many-faceted, and our apprehension of it so single-minded, that we are lucky to have this intersubjective means of keeping in touch with the curiosities and the sympathies of our fellow men. Every mode of inquiry is symbolic, in that it faces particular complexities and reduces them to quantitative, syllogistic, linguistic, or graphic generalizations; for an intractable and elusive whole it substitutes some convenient and typical part. But artistic symbols — being at once less rigorous and less arbitrary than other types — are all the more significant, in that they connote personalities and situations which have the widest appeal and the most immediate meaning. Although universality is itself a relative concept, here it may help to distinguish the esthetic from the more technical phases of experience. The latter may be valid or not, as the appropriate specialists determine, according to their objective criteria and independently of what others may think. The former owes its degree of validity to the reactions of whoever is willing to participate in it, on a basis of nothing more nor less than common humanity.

Each participant will react according to his lights, implicitly comparing his own observations with those which the artist has been conveying to him. He will be convinced to the extent that he finds what in classical criticism is termed "verisimilitude." But that is incidental; for if the artist's outlook coincided entirely with his own, he could look for little in it that was new to him; and it is this, primarily, that interests him. He and the artist engage in a twofold process, involving the recognition of norms on the one side and the introduction of novelties on the other. Classicism would favor the one, and romanticism the other; but in practice both, the universal and the unique, seem interdependent. The concrete instance is given a wider application and a normative interpretation; the hypothetical example is empirically tested and experimentally verified. The veracity of art, however, has been called into question just as frequently as it has been confirmed. The very word *poetry,* broadly construed to cover works of the imagination, literally means something which is made up; while the word *fiction,* which carries similar connotations, passes as a synonym for falsehood. The compound *make-believe* is apt in linking this sense of poetic artifice with "that willing suspension of disbelief" which the poet requests from his audience.

Poets at best can merely claim, with Pindar, to utter "things like truth." Dismissing these as fabrications, moralists can emulate Plutarch in calling poets liars. Undeniably, many of their poems would be nothing but more or less beautiful lies, if we held them to a strict correspondence with literal fact; it is through their expression of feeling that they attain that paradoxical significance which we are willing to accept as poetic truth. Truth itself, when it is not a philosophic abstraction or a mathematical tautology, rarely figures anywhere complete or unembellished; yet other disciplines are measured by their approximations to it, rather than by their defections from it. When poetry was originally defined as an imitation of nature, two opposing views were possible: Plato's, which emphasized the difference, and Aristotle's, which emphasized the resemblance between the imitation and its object. Aristotle had much more to contribute in this field, and was much less bemused by an aprioristic conception of reality; but perhaps, in defending poetry against the Platonic condemnation, he came to overemphasize its relation to life at the expense of its formal properties. Though he points out the source of art in the interplay between two instincts, *mimesis* and *harmonia*, he has nothing more to say on the tantalizing subject of harmony. Nonetheless he warrants us, if warrant we need, to assume that art is equally concerned with reproducing life and with arranging it into a pattern.

Puritans have argued from age to age that poetry is untrue, that fiction is false, that art is immoral. Philistines, coming later and staying longer, have charged that artistic activity serves no useful purpose; that it is impractical. Truly it is a game, in the sense that it goes through certain motions disinterestedly and with enjoyment. For the stolid utilitarian, it is not less childish than other games; hence, for Jeremy Bentham, pushpin was as good as poetry. History gives a twist to this argument by reminding us that the origins of poetry were not only didactic but also functional. Verse was developed in a preliterate period, apparently as a mnemonic technique for handing on information, the deeds and the observances of the tribe. Even after writing was introduced, the Greeks consulted Hesiod's poems on husbandry; and the Romans studied the structure of the universe as described in the hexameters of

Lucretius. Prose, which took over such informative functions, gradually superseded many of the metrical forms; the epic was outmoded by the novel, which in its turn has been yielding ground to journalism. No sort of fiction can keep up with the facts, when they are popularly accessible. When documents were lacking, on the other hand, the imaginative faculties took their place. With the march of civilization, in the Hegelian view, poetry outlives its usefulness and subsides into techno-logical obsolescence. Against this, the rear-guard defense would depend upon Shelley's affirmation that only poets can save a mechanized world from itself.

Is the *Iliad* compatible with the printing press? asked Marx. And Marx, despite his own commitment to material progress, went on to predict that it would prove incompatible with that mythological worldview which had stimulated the arts to their highest achievements in the past. The sacrifice was worth conceding, he seems to have believed, since it heralded a millennium of enlightenment which would make imagina-tion superfluous. But, among the winds of doctrine now con-flicting, the truth has yet to prevail; the Marxist ideology has turned out to be another mythology, and one which acts less as a stimulus than as a deterrent to the Muses. With recent years we have come to doubt whether the printing press is necessarily more truthful than Homer. Though our century may look prosaic to the reader of novels, for the newspaper reader it is fantastic. The forces of irrationality, banished from their traditional shrines, have been practicing mischief underground. Myth and prophecy now return disfigured to haunt us; they invade our lives in the guise of propaganda and advertising. Instead of offering us the guidance of ethical insight, they seek to manipulate our suffrage and our patron-age. Instead of helping to set our emotions in order, they ex-cite unsatisfied appetites and promote unappeased hostilities. To put it summarily, all our matter-of-factness has not suc-ceeded in releasing us from the power of fantasy; on the con-trary, it has released that power from responsible control and legitimate fulfillment.

Artistic discipline, which controls and fulfills those psycho-

logical energies, therefore has its uses; and though the verities
it formulates and circulates may not be immutable, they have
a widespread and continuing relevance. They invite the individual consciousness to take its own bearings through con-
sultation with an endless sequence of models and parables,
archetypes of behavior and angles of vision. This wealth of
examples, amid the confusion of precepts and in the absence
of more systematic categories, constitutes a frame of reference
which educated men invoke to characterize their circumstances
and temperaments. Thus, when a basic mental condition is
currently diagnosed as an "Oedipus complex," the phraseology
is an acknowledgment that a psychoanalyst's acumen was long
ago anticipated by a tragedian's. More casually, whenever we
designate an acquaintance or an occurrence as Gargantuan or
Quixotic, the epithet is more than a characterization; in either
case, it is an attitude toward reality, a *modus vivendi*. The
knowledge acquired through the intensive study of such cases
is the theme of Melville's tribute to the creator of Falstaff and
Hamlet:

> No utter surprise can come to him
> Who reaches Shakespeare's core;
> That which we seek and shun is there —
> Man's final lore.

Let us pass over the third and fourth lines of the stanza; the
phrase "seek and shun" expresses an ambivalence which we
shall be considering soon enough; and I would not propose,
least of all to a body of scholars, that anyone — even Shakespeare — had said the last word about anything. There is perhaps a hint of question-begging in the second line: if we
get to the core, and if the core is a microcosm, naturally we shall
then know everything — just as Tennyson's flower in the
crannied wall will teach us the secrets of the universe. The
opening proposition is the one that seems most fraught with
implication for us: it attests not only that the reading of
Shakespeare is an emotional preparation for later experience,
but that experience will prove to be a corroboration of

Shakespeare, and consequently that the relations of art and
life are reciprocal.

2. A Science Pertaining to the Imagination

Properly enough, the creative process is known by its fruits.
Critics may examine the special devices of the various media,
or compare a given imitation with its particular object. Estheticians, insofar as they are interested in the work of art, focus
their attention upon its impact. Scholars do much to reconsti-
tute its background, which usually includes the biography of
the artist, and is frequently documented by his testimony and
— what is more significant — his apprenticeship and experimentation. But what actually takes place within his mind, of
course, remains opaque. We still lack — and, as Bacon pointed
out, we need — "a science pertaining to the imagination." We
have made so little progress toward this goal since Bacon's day
that his very phrase may seem surprising to those who now
think of science and imagination as a pair of eternal opposites.
As a consequence of that misunderstanding, which stems from
the problem I have just been discussing, utterly primitive notions of artistic creation are still prevalent today. If we believed that the work emerged full-armed from the head of the
artist, parthenogenetically, we would not need to speculate
further about its origin. In speaking of *inspiration*, as most
people do, we go so much further that we transpose the whole
question into the sphere of the supernatural. And when we
talk about *genius*, we presumably mean that some attendant
spirit waits on the artist and does his job.

Artists have found it advantageous to cultivate these quaint
metaphors, wrapping themselves and their activities in an aura
of mystery. Their position is equivocally supported by another
ancient belief: that genius is very closely allied to madness.
This is confirmed by the modern view that insanity, with its
free associations, illuminates other intensified states of emotion: "The lunatic, the lover, and the poet. . ." Poetic frenzy
is still mysterious, when reduced to a function of the nervous
system, because it is so much more complex and unpredictable
than those functions which can be traced by neurology. But

because it is also more distinctive and more explicit, there are other means for gauging its causes and noting its effects. The systematic study of imagery, the stuff of imagination, can trace it back to its visual and literary sources and analyze the characteristic imprint it leaves upon style. Ingenious procedures have been developed for testing the imaginative bent of the average person, through what psychologists call "thematic apperception." The analysis of dreams, beyond the light it may throw upon other phases of the unconscious, is especially revealing in this connection, since it watches the behavior of uncontrolled fantasy. We learn too, from folklore, how similar habits of the collective mind reach the level of consciousness as myths.

We need not try, then, to penetrate the brain. We only need to observe the manifestations of an inherent and universal tendency which, with no pretense to anatomic precision, we might describe by Bergson's term, "fabulation." That faculty, as Bergson conceives it, is neither rational intelligence nor brute instinct; it occupies a middle place and mediates between cognition and intuition. Fabulation can thus be a method of knowledge, in our particular terms, since it can plunge into depths too obscure for the reason and bring irrationalities up to the surface of awareness. This corresponds somewhat to the psychoanalytic conception of the *ego*, in its dual relationship with the *id* and the *superego*. The subdivision of the mind into three related faculties, however, is one of the oldest traditions of psychology; and the imagination is traditionally conceived as mediating between the memory and the reason. For the thoroughgoing materialist, imagination is not much more than memory; for Hobbes it was "decaying sense" — that is to say, the imagination combines such impressions as the memory retains from previous sensory experience. The Greek word, *phantasia*, first meant something made visible, with the connotation of having been seen at one time but no longer present. Synonymously, the Latin *imaginatio* was a sort of mind's eye envisaging things past, putting the mental pictures together in different ways, associating and compounding images, but introducing nothing wholly new.

It has never been assumed, by any who have given thought to the subject, that the imagination created *ex nihilo*. Originality would seem to depend, after the accumulation of experiences, upon the aptness with which they are recombined. "I do not believe that the human imagination has ever invented anything which might not be true, either in this world or some other one," wrote Gérard de Nerval. Just as it can be said that mistakes are meaningful, or that abstractions have content, or that nonsense has a logic of its own, even so the most wayward caprices of fancy can be regarded as having some basis in fact. The facts of this world weighed so heavily on the poet, in the case of Gérard, that he himself escaped into the fantastic worlds of opium and hallucination — but not without realizing that there could be method in madness, and that the poet's self-induced delusions were the most potent of anodynes. Bacon, when he included imagination in his methodology of the sciences, has suspected it of providing a means of escape from reality. Poetry, for him, was a fictitious version of history; and because it was not bound to the factual truth, it was free to improve upon actuality; but this amelioration was dangerous because, taken literally, it was untrue. At all events, in Bacon's resonant words, fiction brought mankind what history had denied, and satisfied the mind with shadows when the substance could not be enjoyed.

That, for better or worse, is wish-fulfillment. It can be incidentally elevating; it "raises the mind by accommodating the images of things to our desires, and not, like history and reason, subjecting the mind to things." Though Bacon was more of a historian than a poet, and obviously more committed to things as they are than to what they should be, for a moment here the realist gave passing recognition to the ideal. In this he followed the critical theory of the Renaissance, which transcended Aristotle in maintaining that art was no mere imitation of nature but indeed the creation of a golden world. The implication, so poignantly exemplified by *Don Quixote*, might have been drawn that ideals and realities were drifting farther apart. Every recorded epoch has harked back to an earlier and happier dispensation, a golden age, just as every civilization has dreamed of reverting to a simpler and more natural condition, a pastoral state. But mankind's visions of felicity, instead of dwelling in an idyllic past, may also look ahead to a technological future, a utopia — or, alternatively, an afterlife. This outlook, in whatever direction, foresees a happy ending; the curtain will fall on virtue rewarded and vice punished here and now; or else the last act will round out a divine comedy, where poetic justice prevails hereafter. Yet the prologue, we recall, was a scene in a garden — the old, the oldest idyll, interrupted when the fruit was plucked from the tree of knowledge.

And without the other half of the fable, the sudden shift from innocence to experience, any account of life would be irredeemably one-sided and superficial. It would limit itself to the assumption that art was no more than a technique of flattering man's desires. It would emphasize pleasures and ignore responsibilities. The realization of pain is the very fruit of the tree, the discovery that is reënacted over and over in tragedy. Life itself, as Dr. Johnson insisted, is much too large to be either tragic or comic; it is both and more. To view it as the one or the other is to stylize it, to harmonize the imitation, to strike an attitude — and I am referring to attitudes rather than genres. The tragic point of view is just as sweeping an overdramatization as the comic; but in the long run it may be a little wiser, in the sense that prudence risks less by fearing the worst than by hoping for the best, and that the better part of wisdom is to face — rather than to escape from — possible disappointments. "Call no man happy until he is dead," the tragic axiom, is not truer nor more false than the comic generalization, "All's well that ends well." The optimism that would interpret existence as a design for man's personal well-being, in which every wrong is ultimately righted, if need be through the melodramatic intervention of some god in some machine, is neither more nor less plausible than the pessimism that would attribute all unhappy accidents to the operation of nemesis, the devil, or some abstracted principle of evil.

But to exist is to weather adversity. Most human beings, during the course of their lives, are called upon to endure a

certain amount of grief, and all of them are destined to undergo
the private catastrophe of death. Tragedy is a ritual, as it were,
which initiates the individual into some foreknowledge of those
impending mysteries. There have been many attempts to explain its method of exercising the emotions — most notably the
Aristotelian doctrine of catharsis, the purgation of the mind
through pity and terror. More up-to-date and no less open to
argument is the Freudian theory of sublimation, the satisfaction of repressed impulses on a vicarious plane. These expla-
nations, coming from such different quarters, run sufficiently
parallel to lend each other support; they account for what happens when art successfully manages to exert a control over
life, as when Goethe mastered a suicidal urge by making that
the theme of *The Sorrows of Werther*. But the effect is not
always so therapeutic; sometimes it is held to be contagious, as
when art furthers propagandistic or pornographic intentions;
as it turned out, the success of *Werther* was marked by a wave
of suicides. Variable though such influence may be, one necessary condition seems to persist through the innumerable
variations. This is not entirely clarified when, in the parlance
of esthetics, it is named empathy; yet the concept will serve
to sum up that projection of feeling which enables the artist
to engage the spectator's concern and permits the spectator
to participate in the artistic situation.

The engagement centers upon those elements in the situation which are both artistic and human, the dramatis personae,
as well as upon the spectator's willingness to identify himself
with them. Through this identification he is released from the
limits of his own personality, and prompted to share the adventures of those imaginary personages to whom his sympathies
happen to be linked. They happen to be his heroes and heroines because, in some guise or other, they incarnate his values;
hence they not only broaden his orientation, they encourage
his emulation. The cult of Aeneas or Roland involved not only
hero-worship but the observance of a civic or a courtly ethos.
The same underlying pattern finds religious sanction in the
imitation of Christ, and in the Christian emphasis on communion and sacrifice. So the tragic spectator communes with

the victimized protagonist and feels, in some measure, redeemed by another's sufferings. In a more worldly sense, as La Rochefoucauld dared to say, we are not entirely displeased at seeing others in pain. This is not as sadistic as it sounds; nor is it simply a matter of saying, "There but for the grace of God go I." It may well be a perfectly normal reaction to enjoy the sensation of anguish when we are securely absolved from its painful consequences. It is pleasant to witness a shipwreck or a battle from a lofty distance, Lucretius has affirmed: to set the contentions and grievances of men against the larger perspectives of understanding.

The consummation is the disengagement, the return from the esthetic to the actual. But we cannot distinguish too categorically between these states without questionably implying that art is a retreat from, rather than an approach to, life. Old-fashioned systems of ethics used to assume a kind of polarity, in which the automatic pursuit of pleasures and avoidance of pains was mitigated solely by occasional foresight or enlightened self-interest. We, having seen men attracted to the painful or repelled by the pleasant, cannot be sure that such motives are mutually exclusive or that such emotions are unmixed. When Melville spoke of discovering in Shakespeare "that which we seek and shun," he voiced this ambiguity between the tempting curiosity and the guilty retribution. We seek to fulfill our wishes, to satisfy our desires, yes, in revery if not in reality. We shun our fears, but they hound us like furies; anxiety, when dispelled from our daily lives, turns up in our imaginative efforts. These are daydreams sometimes, but at other times they are nightmares; fantasy is supremely adept at both. Fact, in the very state of being mentally reflected, gets refracted — modified for the better or distorted for the worse, according to whether or not it is welcome news. The ancients expressed this antithesis by their parable of the gates of dreams, gates of ivory and horn, whereby appealing fictions and bitter truths made their respective entrances into the minds of men.

Artists like to imagine themselves as demiurges, minor deities who create out of chaos by imitating a preëxistent cosmos, adapting it to the scale of their medium and the scope of their talent. Such creations are heterocosms, artificial worlds whose likeness to their living model is conditioned by the sensibilities through which they are filtered. Some degree of refraction is thus unavoidable; but the angle can probably be determined in any specific instance; it is a question of how the work is slanted in relation to its subject; and though the artist has many choices, he can scarcely be neutral. Relaying emotions, he himself is ultimately motivated by one of two forces, attraction or repulsion. Therefore the resulting configuration will prove to be either an embellishment or a caricature. It must, to borrow Schiller's categories, be elegiac or satirical: it must either idealize the picture or present a criticism of reality. And these considerations might be extended into the wider realm of the social imagination, where — as Karl Mannheim has shown — the differing classes tend either to project utopian schemes or to expose each other's ideologies. Or again, the idea might be scaled down to its most naïve application in magic: the dualistic belief that sympathetic charms can make wishes come true and that dangers can be warded off by baneful exorcisms.

I have emphasized the illusory character of the imagination because I would not minimize its way of evading scientific inquiry. We must be wary, if we would disentangle its contributions to knowledge from its deceptions. What is it, after all, but man's capacity for seeing things otherwise than as they are? It is a perverse gift, that continuous awareness of alternatives which are likely to be illusions, but which may also be possibilities of the sort that have differentiated the human race from all the other species. In these extremely general terms, but more positively, it might be said that art practices a deliberate undeception, gaining our confidence in order to disabuse us, and educating us through the disillusionment. The ego, through its fabulous involvements, achieves some point of detachment from itself. When it no longer considers itself the center of the universe, it begins to comprehend the contingencies that frame its own existence. Here is where science surpasses imagination, in the sense that it opens up vistas of knowledge which stretch to the very horizons of comprehen-

sion. But, in the sense that life stretches far beyond those horizons, imagination is given a second chance. Socratically, it
knows what it does not know, and is never ill at ease amid the
unknowable. Perhaps its wisest insight is cosmic irony, the
perception of the unexpected difference between man's aspira-
tions and the nature of things.

3. Objectifying the Subjective

The train of thought set into motion by Bacon, when he
called for a science of the imagination, might have been greatly
advanced by Coleridge; but when the latter came to set down
his theories, he substituted dogmatism for logic; and the subsequent trend of literary criticism, on the whole, has taken this
strategic and difficult subject for granted. Happily, as I have
tried to suggest, several other disciplines have been converging
upon it, so that today there may be hope for another instauration. There is also good reason to be reminded that its presence or absence is by no means the peculiar attribute of any
single field. *"L'imagination dispose de tout."* Because it operates so pervasively, and so elusively, I am constrained to draw
my examples from a department of knowledge where it is my
business to be at home. But I trust that some of them may
have a broader application; and I should undoubtedly have
to admit, if pressed, that there seem to be more signs of imagination at work in experimental physics than in contemporary
poetry. One sign of the times is our habit of specializing what
used to be a universal idea. We may wonder, for example, how
"the religious imagination" of which Mr. Eliot speaks is connected with "the liberal imagination" whose spokesman is Mr.
Trilling. Each critic, as I understand him, has voiced a significant concern over the imaginative decline of the sphere he has
delimited.

We already have the study of esthetics, which purports to
be — quite literally — a science of the feelings. Perhaps that is
why, in the two hundred years we have had it, it has been
productive of little else except rival terminologies. During that
period, usage has more and more tended to refer to the diverse
arts as if they all represented essentially the same type of

activity. Previously, artists were equated with artisans or, at best, technicians; gradually their status benefited from the widening division between the practical and the so-called fine arts. Though the ancient rhetoricians drew parallels between poetry and painting, like Lessing they were more acutely conscious of the distinctions. Though the Muses were fabled to be sisters, they were chiefly remarkable for their individuality. The arts of the Middle Ages were the liberal methods of knowledge, the seven branches of the scholastic curriculum. It was not until a century ago, with the appearance of Théophile Gautier's magazine, *L'Artiste,* that men of letters consented to share a professional name they had borrowed from painters and sculptors. This comradeship, which has proved mutually rewarding, has been reinforced by a mutual uneasiness before a middle-class public. Concomitantly, there has been an intensive revival of the poet's traditional sense of vocation, together with an increasingly self-conscious attitude toward artistry both as a craft and a way of life. Something of this can be seen in Croce's generalized notions of art as an emanation of personality, albeit Croce was no more concerned with the details of biography than with the minutiae of craftsmanship.

My present assignment gives me a good deal of sympathy with anyone who faces the problem of talking meaningfully about some generic practitioner of the arts, some artist who is not necessarily a poet nor a painter nor a musician, but might hypothetically be any of these. Clearly, no such prodigy exists outside the discourse of estheticians; hence the pertinence of my own generalizations may well be limited to literature, which is highly atypical. Since each of the arts is quite unique, it is idle to arrange them in any hierarchy. Yet we can distinguish literature from the others by the amplitude of its resources, the extent to which the words of the language exceed the colors of the palette or the notes of the scale. We can recognize its heterogeneity, its capacity for absorbing elements extrinsic to itself, esthetic impurities which are likewise sources of human interest, much as they may complicate the problem of methodology. We cannot afford to assume that literature is wholly or even mainly a fine art: it has its pedestrian functions, although it is not so practically functional as architecture. Moreover, although it has its technical forms, it is not so abstractly formal as music. Like painting but more comprehensively, it is representational; but, except for the drama, its modes of representation are neither audible nor tangible, and neither self-contained nor self-evident. A book does not need to be an esthetic object, a thing in itself. Its expressiveness is based on the presuppositions of language, the context of associations, the writer's cross-references and the reader's responses.

This last stage is the crucial one for the majority, since they are rather consumers than producers. For readers it may be more intimate than for members of a public audience, but every artistic form invites its characteristic response. Esthetics consequently shifts its attention from the expression to the impression, from the inception to the reception of art, from the artist's mind to the eye of the beholder. There it seeks a common denominator in the spectatorial reaction. But if feelings of pleasure are elicited by a painting or a string quartet, they are no less excited by nonartistic phenomena: a mountain view, a pretty girl, a vintage wine. And if there is such a thing as a sense of beauty, it is no less protean in its preferences than in its manifestations. In its famous triad with the true and the good, the beautiful loses most by standing apart, since it is regulated by nothing comparable to scientific criteria or social codes. The notion of *belles lettres*, like that of *beaux arts*, is premised upon a frivolous distinction between the useful and the ornamental. As vehicles of man's most serious interests, letters and arts have usually combined incidental beauty with fundamental usefulness. Art-for-art's-sake has been preached more often than it has been practiced, and attacked more often than defended; it is best explained as art's fitful revolt against too many extraneous demands. *Esthete* has now become a pejorative because it implies a certain lack of balance, an airy egocentricity. What of *esthetics?*

It finds more promising ground for speculation when, avoiding the pitfalls of subjectivity, it contemplates a relevant series of objects. Sometimes its findings are almost too palpable, as when Hogarth displayed a "line of beauty" to which he attributed the effectiveness of all pictorial composition. But within the more concrete media, some principles of order are discernible, harmonic and rhythmic relations which can be stated, sometimes with mathematical exactitude. How much of a transference can take place between one medium and another seems more doubtful. A formalistic approach, despite its synesthetic vocabulary, would seem to stress the variability of textures and surfaces. If music is an acoustic and temporal structure, and sculpture is a plastic and spatial structure, then what is structure? A catchword of recent discussion has been *baroque*: after hearing it applied to mystical ecstasy and classical symmetry, Jesuit churches and Lutheran chorales, the Royal Society and the *commedia dell' arte*, Racine and Shakespeare, we may ask whether any shred of connotation is left beyond the mere accident of chronological proximity. Such skepticism is prompted more by respect for the richness of the material than by scorn for the inadequacy of the formulation. Nonetheless we are left with so many disparities, both in means and in ends, that we cannot envisage systems of correspondence between the arts — unless it be on a plane of generality so high as to be virtually inaccessible.

This is not to deny the major classification that we have accepted in juxtaposing the arts and the sciences. Nor is it to overlook specific connections, which on occasion may fit together as closely as a lyric and its melody. Nor is it to abandon the prospect of drawing fruitful conclusions on the basis of adequate evidence. It is only to insist upon the complexity of the imaginative process and the autonomy of the various forms it adopts. No philosophy, imposed from above, is equipped to deal with that set of circumstances. Too much is required in the way of techniques, the innate skills and precise instruments of artistic knowledge. Yet we possess authorities on such matters: first-hand documentation from practiced masters, such as the notebooks of Leonardo. And we as students are increasingly curious to observe, to experience, and to experiment with the formal properties of art. Some of our recent investigators have been analyzing its elaborate compounds by reducing them to their basic physical components: studying, for example, the interrelationship between sound and meaning in poetry. On the other side, the spectator's side, our epoch has shown particular alertness and a special aptitude. The arts have been reproduced and circulated, to an unprecedented degree, by the ingenious devices it has developed; and some of the same ingenuity has gone into the procedures of research and pedagogy. The more we learn about semantics, communication, and public opinion, the better we shall understand the dynamics of artistic appreciation.

Art begins in someone's consciousness and ends in the consciousness of someone else; the trajectory of the imagination must have its goal as well as its point of departure; and though the creative act may be inscrutable, the critical acceptance is most explicit, one way or another. Criticism itself is a genre of literature; it is the literature of art, the corpus of all that is thought and said in response to all that artists produce. But it is also — in spite of itself and inadequately — a branch of science, insofar as it devotes itself to the empirical investigation, the systematic organization, and the objective interpretation of the facts pertaining to its subject-matter. It seems so unscientific because those facts so often present themselves as fantasies; and, instead of pinning them down, we allow them to carry us away. Indeed the archives of literary criticism reveal as much waywardness and diversity of thought as do the annals of literature itself. The controversies start — and they have not stopped — by questioning art's very right to existence, in the name of beauty's alleged unfaithfulness to truth or to goodness. Critics proceeded to build up bodies of law, which conflict with each other just as sharply and widely as do the laws of nations. Rules, originally based on simple induction, became prescriptions for the concoction of masterpieces; conventions, once adapted to local conditions, were decreed to be fixed and eternal. But most of this obsolete legislation has long been discarded.

To criticize means to judge in Greek; but the original verb meant to cut, to distinguish, to analyze. It might be inferred that criticism makes the most progress when it takes an analytical viewpoint, as Aristotle did in his *Poetics*, and that it perplexes itself with cross-purposes when it assumes a judicial role, as did so many of the critics that followed him. While claiming that they judged according to his criteria, they frequently disagreed among themselves. Such disagreement was multiplied immeasurably, when official standards no longer prevailed, and individuals were forced to fall back on their private judgments. A Pandora's box was thereby opened up, whence every opinion has sooner or later run counter to its opposite; and every great artist at some time or other has been the victim of some hostile critic. The maxim with which we arm ourselves against this anarchy, *De gustibus non disputandum*, is somewhat ambiguous. It means, of course, that there is no point in arguing; but it might be taken alternatively to mean that there were no grounds for argument. It was still possible for Burke to speak of "the Taste," using the definite article and the capital letter because he assumed that all properly educated gentlemen would profess identical tastes. Yet even then, in the middle of the eighteenth century, the new expression *Aesthetica* was being introduced to subsume the diverging areas of dispute.

These vicissitudes should prove discouraging only to those who prematurely expect to arrive at some ultimate and monistic solution. Those who accept the pluralism of the universe are aware that fellow men, differing in their backgrounds, endowments, and commitments, are bound to differ in their reactions. When they react so emphatically and so emotionally, it speaks well for the vitality of the stimulus — and in this case, as I have ventured to argue, the response is a vital part of the process. Though we cannot take these engaged opinions at face value, we need not ignore the purport of value judgments. They are by no means certainties; but they may be considered as data, which register the effect of a work of art and fall into place in our total conception of it. It does not follow that every reaction is equally important; importance is largely a matter of relevance, which is largely a matter of history. So long as we exist in history, we are bound to see ourselves and everything else in relation to it — relatively, rather than under the aspect of eternity. Marxism and Neo-

Scholasticism may profess their conflicting absolutes; but their very coexistence is simply another argument for relativism. While the historical method has sharpened our sense of direction, the comparative method has heightened our sense of relationship, so that André Malraux discusses art — as Arnold Toynbee discusses civilization — in the light of its totality. Even the layman, through museums and libraries and other modern facilities, has easier access to more varieties of culture than ever before.

Such a situation tends to encourage eclecticism and catholicity, rather than traditionalism and dogma. The main duty of the critic, as Taine held, is neither to praise nor to pardon but to understand; or to consider matters, in the Johnsonian phrase, "not dogmatically but deliberatively." Judgment eventually submits itself to analysis, and the subjective elements in criticism can be objectified by being related to their objects and viewed in a larger perspective. Our conclusion may extend no farther than that noncommittal comment of Abraham Lincoln's which so aptly fits any book: "People who like this sort of thing will find this the sort of thing they like." This, at first sight, seems just as wearily fatalistic as *De gustibus* and rather more circular in its reasoning. However, it teems with pertinent questions: who are those people? what sort of thing? and why do they like it? When these blanks have been filled in with exact information, we may see our way out of the circle. What confuses us meanwhile is that people seldom tell us flatly whether they like a thing or not. They prefer to pronounce it good or bad. When such pronouncements conflict with each other, as they so often do, we have no way of reconciling them or of pronouncing any of the respondents right or wrong. The best we can do is to ask "Who?" and "Why?", our sociological and psychological interrogatives, hoping that the answers may cast some light back upon our substantive question, "What?" Once we have reckoned the values held by our critics, their conflicts do not seem irreconcilable; their likes and dislikes seem to fit consistently into the pattern established by the interplay between their respective positions and the work at hand.

Every single response to the work is a critique, though the

common reader speaks for himself alone. The reviewer speaks to — if not for — his readers, whom he is expected to influence. The criteria he observes are among the unspoken assumptions that draw them to his periodical. The range of our innumerable periodicals, from the daily newspaper to the academic quarterly, is an index to the divergent levels on which reviewers must operate. Thus it is hardly surprising when several books, as reviewed by the same critic, sound more alike than reviews of the same book by several critics. The book review, at its commonest level today, is little more than an advertisement; at its most serious, it is a prediction; but that depends, to some degree, on the seriousness of the book, as well as on the reviewer's willingness to look beyond the moment. To look very far ahead is to admit that contemporaries are short-sighted judges, and to appeal over their heads to posterity. Statistics have less and less to do with significance, as a glance at any best-seller list will indicate. Survival is a better test precisely because it overlooks those extrinsic features which make for contemporaneous popularity. But even the long run varies; posterity turns out to be just as changeable as contemporaneity; and evaluation, short of doomsday, is never final. It is simply a consensus of all the responses that a work has gathered to itself, with due regard for what they may individually and collectively signify.

There can be no infallible touchstone for determining what we call a classic, not merely because the canon is always changing, discovering new classics and forgetting old ones, but because variety is a factor in the selection, and the rough agreement reached on what works are most valuable reflects a diversified combination of qualities and concerns. The concept of artistic immortality, which has so often animated poets, is altogether as conditional as those monuments which they boast of outlasting. Their existence and ours, however, is framed by just such conditions; and man as a creator is definitively limited by them; it is still a proud boast if, by means of his creations, he succeeds in transcending the immediate limits of time and place and personality. He does not escape them himself; he rather transmits his awareness of them to other times and places and personalities, that they in turn may be stimulated to further transmission. It is not a question of living for ever, but of putting some of his life into something which may outlive him, and which above all embodies what he has learned and what later generations might well be taught. And though he himself is predestined to fall by the wayside, his fragmentary records and ruined constructions will remind them that civilization has a history, and that nothingness has here and there yielded to consciousness.

Contexts of the Classical

The American Philological Association, having set "The Nature of the Classical" as the general topic of its joint meeting with the Archaeological Institute of America at Philadelphia on December 29, 1956, graciously invited an outsider to attend and participate. This response has not been printed before.

▼▼▼

1. Traditional

One cannot begin to speak of the classical without becoming categorical. Presumably that is why Benedetto Croce, a rigorous critic of all critical categories except his own, roundly declared that the word was meaningless. Strictly speaking, it denotes relation rather than quality, inclusion and — by implication — exclusion. Since it distinguishes one class of objects from all the others for some unspecified reason, its specific meaning derives from and varies with its context. The original context, our *locus classicus* in the fullest sense, is frequently quoted from Aulus Gellius, although it is usually forgotten that Gellius himself was quoting Fronto. The orator was advising the antiquarian, with regard to certain indecisions of Latin grammar, to look for authoritative precedents in some first-class and substantial author, not a proletarian: *"classicus adsiduusque scriptor, non proletarius."* The figure of speech for literary status, borrowed from the Roman classification of taxpayers, is frankly social and snobbishly economic enough to gratify the worst suspicions of Marxist historians. This particular use of the adjective *classicus*, which seems to have no other ancient or medieval example, would not become a catchword until the humanistic revival of the classics. Then, as Pauly-Wissowa indicates, Melanchthon could use it in recommending Plutarch; and thence it was but a short step to the vernaculars, with programs of education based — like Milton's — on "works of classical authority."

Commenting upon the peculiar contingencies that have shaped our terminology, Ernst Robert Curtius has asked: "What would modern esthetics have done for a single general concept that should embrace Raphael, Racine, Mozart, and Goethe, if Gellius had never lived?" The question, if it is not to be left a negation, stimulates two conflicting trains of response. The first is that, given the importance of the concept as well as the waywardness of the term, doubtless some other and possibly better term would have emerged to fill the gap. The second is that, given a group of figures so heterogeneous in time and place and medium and style, whatever they have in common may also prove to be a matter of accident rather than substance. Professor Curtius obviously did not think so; he conceived the classical as an absolute which transcended such differences; and thus he stands at the other pole from Croce, for whom the difference comprised the essence. Our subject abounds in such polarities. More often than not, as on its first appearance, it presents itself in the form of an antithesis. Originally it benefited from an implicit comparison with the nonclassical; but in later years the odium has fallen more and more upon the classical side. Consider, in up-to-date musical parlance, the overtones of *classical* as against *popular*.

Now the opposite number with which *classical* finds itself most often yoked is *romantic*; and *romantic* enjoys the historical advantage of having, as an innovation, challenged the *status quo* described by *classical*. Hence romanticism has defined itself, through a sequence of polemical manifestoes, as practically everything that classicism was not. When the self-proclaiming romanticists set forth their diverging aims, they made a virtue of the undefined, the ineffable, the infinite; while their emphasis on individuality reflected back a sense of limitation upon whatever they were reacting against. The very habit of definition came to be regarded as an exaction of the classicists, who allowed their position to be circumscribed by the fixity and the rigidity of their own increasingly narrow formulas. Romanticism, though it was so expressly a manifestation of its epoch, claimed to be an inherent force of human nature; furthermore, it dramatized its antithetical attitude toward a late and debilitated classicism as if it were a renewed campaign in the perennial warfare between the spirit and the letter. But as the observer who signed himself Stendhal clearly noted, perhaps because he was not an engaged romanticist, the romantic simply happened to be the contemporary at a moment when the classical was the traditional: what had appealed to the readers of his great-grandfathers' day.

Stendhal's manifesto, *Racine et Shakespeare*, had little to say about either dramatist; they were no more than tutelary spirits, presiding over a dialectic which German romanticism had learned from Lessing. The immediate argument, for Stendhal, was a discussion by the Académie Française as to whether *romantique* should be admitted into its official dictionary of the French language. *Classique* was already there, of course, but somewhat confused by mistaken etymology: *"qui est en usage dans les classes."* Though *le romantisme* has found its way into succeeding editions, curiously enough *le classicisme* has never done so; and though both words are currently listed in the more broad-minded lexicon of Littré, it is *le classicisme* which is stigmatized as a neologism. This would seem to suggest that, so long as the concept prevailed, the term was hardly necessary; only when confronted by a dialectical alternative could the classical be seen as a rival movement, and not an eternal order. The suggestion is supported by the fact that *classicism* was introduced into English, along with a number of other words in *-ism*, by the arch-romantic and philo-Germanic Carlyle in 1837. German literary history, in referring to its eighteenth century as *Klassizismus* and to its post-romantic period as *Klassik,* reminds us that classicism need not always be classical.

This distinction seems to follow Goethe's unique career through youthful *Sturm und Drang* to Olympian — or, at all events, Biedermeier — maturity. Faust's abandonment of Gretchen may seem to us more authentic than his possession of Helen of Troy; what would be most significant for later poets was the possibility of an eclectic choice, the progression from the Harz Mountains toward the Pharsalian Plain. It is hard to specify any intrinsic attribute which the *Klassische Walpurgisnacht* shares with the *Parnasse contemporain* of French poetry, or with the Anglo-American resurrection prophesied by T. E. Hulme and incarnated in T. S. Eliot, except for a general reaction against romanticism. But if recent movements have not altogether succeeded in reëstablishing the classical, they have rescued it from the role of whipping-boy. It looked old-fashioned from the timely viewpoint of the romanticists: from Stendhal's observation which Walter Pater broadened into the generalization that "all good art was romantic in its day." The corollary, retroactively balancing the claims of endurance against the charms of novelty, would recognize all good art that survives its day as classical. So Goethe recognized Shakespeare as a classic in spite of himself. The whole idea, in spite of itself, is relative. Therefore we can best understand it by relating it to other ideas and to changing circumstances.

2. *Cultural*

How the classical came to smell of the classroom is a cognate point which need hardly be labored here. The shift from the original distinction — *"les auteurs du premier ordre"* — to the pedagogical category is made explicit by a sentence which I translate from a stock definition in Diderot's *Encyclopédie*: "This word applies only to authors studied in schools; their language and phraseology serve as models for young people." Given the staple curriculum of Western education, it is not surprising that the word was then applied collectively to the civilizations of Greece and Rome; what may surprise us is that this application was not current before the nineteenth century. The usage is concrete, if comprehensive, resembling that prospectus for Dotheboys Hall which promised instruction "in all languages living and dead, mathematics, orthography, geometry, astronomy, trigonometry, the use of the globes, algebra, single stick (if required), writing, arithmetic, fortification, and every other branch of classical literature." Dickens' account of *litterae humaniores* in Yorkshire is no more sardonic than

Gibbon's autobiographical diatribe against the "primitive discipline" of Oxford. Yet when the historian characterizes the Arabs in his *Decline and Fall of the Roman Empire*, he cannot help wishing that they too had availed themselves of the classics and formed their minds on Greek and Roman ideals.

Gibbon had practiced what he preached so consummately that an anthropologist might call him culture-bound. We may well agree with his value judgment; most of us still feel somewhat closer to the isles of Greece than to the Trobriand Islands, and prefer to believe that fifty years of Europe are better than a cycle of Cathay. We admire the majestic view of Werner Jaeger, for whom all other cultures are subordinate to one central cultural tradition, *paideia*. But the world, at the present stage of its history, is not quite so Hellenocentric as it must happily seem to its most eminent Hellenist. Hellenism has indeed been a crucial factor in the development of Christianity; so has Latinism in the West. But Hebraism, as Matthew Arnold regretted, had its outcroppings in Anglo-American culture; the various strains were so intermingled by the Renaissance that Milton could end his principal Latin poem with an allusion to "the thyrsus of Zion." The revivers of learning, in founding the Collège de France, Louvain, Alcalá, Corpus Christi, and other trilingual colleges, prided themselves on augmenting the Latinity of the schoolmen with Hebrew as well as Greek. No other collection of classics was ever so ecumenically distributed as the Old Testament in its Reformation versions — the New Testament being a compilation of a wholly different character.

The treatise *On the Sublime* could take the synoptic overview of comparative literature by discussing Greek style with cross-reference both to Cicero and to the book of Genesis. But classicism itself remains the offspring of the Greco-Roman interrelationship. The status of classic must be conferred by others; it is not attained by deliberate striving; this is perhaps the difference between being classical and being a classicist. Among themselves, the Greeks were conscious of certain internal discriminations: notably, the Periclean conception of Athens as the school of Hellas, or the rhetoricians' unfavorable contrast between the Attic and the Asiatic. However, it was Alexandrian retrospect that organized Greek literature into a corpus; it was Roman adaptation that abstracted and perpetuated its forms; and it was, significantly, a conversation between two Philhellenic Romans of the Antonine epoch that gave us our term. When we turn to the formative epoch of modern Europe, it seems only natural that Italy should envision itself as Rome restored. Yet Arnold Toynbee, in the ninth volume of his *Study of History*, waxes unwontedly skeptical over "contacts between civilizations in time." He even avoids the metaphor of renascence by a studied insistence on *revenant*, which in effect reduces the contribution of humanism from a rebirth of classical antiquity to a ghostly illusion.

It is true, and poignantly attested by the epitaph of Leonardo da Vinci, that the Cinquecento did not fully recapture the antique symmetry: *"Defuit una mihi symmetria prisca."* But history never repeats itself in the same way; and though the restoration was imperfect, it was the herald of a new instauration. In his well-meaning efforts to do justice to other civilizations than our own, Mr. Toynbee underestimates the forces of continuity and cross-fertilization. It is we who are pedantic, not the humanists, if we do not appreciate the zeal they devoted to the recovery of texts. The vernacular gropings that followed, under the aegis of translation and imitation, were naïvely literal if not unnatural. Nonetheless fresh excitement was in the air when fellow poets vied with one another to Pindarize in French for the first time, or boasted of pillaging stones from the sack of Rome to lay the foundations of a native poetic. With touching eagerness, critics like Francis Meres looked for Elizabethan counterparts of the established masters: "As Euripides is the most sententious among the Greeks, so is Warner among our English poets." Alas, poor William Warner! His *Albion's England* has scarcely survived that quasi-Aristophanic competition. But Meres survives as an important witness for the young English competitor of Ovid, Plautus, and Seneca who bore the rather barbaric name of Shakespeare.

The moderns, as their works and ambitions accumulated, were spurred on to brave a comparison with the ancients. This

historic battle of the books was essentially a reënactment of
the unending rivalry between vested elders and a generation
which is coming of age. Though one side saw decadence where
the other saw progress, both appealed to the same standards
of correctness. Some of the modernists tried to be more classical
than the classics, and Chesterfieldian refinement denounced
Homer's heroes for displaying the low manners of porters. The
notion of what is fitting and proper, decorum, could not be settled except by higher authority. Private academies could influence public judgment; with the power of Cardinal Richelieu
behind it, the French Academy constituted a state tribunal for
controlling language, consolidating the arts, and systematizing
a culture. The text case was *Le Cid*, Corneille's immensely
popular tragicomedy, inspired by the free-flowing Spanish
drama and condemned by the stiffening doctrines of the aca-
demicians. During the three-hundred-and-twenty years since
that quarrel, *academic* has become all but synonymous with
orthodox and often with *mediocre*, while *classical* has been
more and more closely identified with *French*. It seems quite
appropriate that Henri Peyre's compact study, *Le Classicisme
français*, should be an enlarged and revised edition of an earlier
volume entitled *Qu'est-ce que le classicisme?*

3. Formal

The contrast with England is striking in this regard. There
too, during the seventeenth century, a national academy of
letters was projected; but the elaborately detailed plan drawn
up by the historiographer, Edmund Bolton, hinged upon the
transitory patronage of the Stuarts; and today it may appropriately be consulted in the library of the Society of Anti-
quaries. Although the idea was revived from time to time,
even Dr. Johnson rejected it. "The present manners of our nation would deride authority," he explained. Those individualistic and experimental habits of the English mind found fulfillment in a more characteristic institution, the preponder-
antly scientific Royal Society; and neoclassicism, as we are careful to call it, has never been more than a recessive trait in
English literature. The consequence, as pointed by Matthew

Arnold in his essay on "The Literary Influence of Academies," may be "a note of provinciality," a centrifugal — not to say eccentric — tendency, as contrasted with the highly centralized culture of France. Classicism, as France has represented it, may have been less the product of Greece and Rome than of Bourbon courtliness and Cartesian rationalism. Yet assimilation has been so complete that extreme modernists, like André Gide and Jean Cocteau, have not only sustained a manner of elegance and clarity but have often reverted to classical subject-matter.

A classical art, as Paul Valéry could authoritatively state, "is inseparable from the notion of precepts, rules, and models." The judicial and legislative processes of criticism derive their sanction from a limited number of received masterpieces. The ground was prepared for classicism when Aristotle canvassed existing tragedies and epics with the same analytic scrutiny he applied to the works of society and nature. What was descriptive method in his hands became prescriptive dogma for generations of followers. That the *Poetics* should have been canonized at a time when Aristotelian philosophy was being discredited is one of the ironies in the history of ideas. The neo-Aristotelians, to be sure, had other axes to grind. Castelvetro's doctrine of the dramatic unities may not have been solidly founded on Attic scripture, but it was well adapted to a theater which had just begun to use a proscenium stage and perspective scenery. Peri's *Dafne* was not what its sponsors had hoped for, a replica of Greek tragedy; it was something new, an Italian opera. Generally speaking, despite the prestige of the *exemplaria Graeca*, the Latin models were more accessible and easier to emulate. For all the lip-service paid to Aeschylus, Sophocles, and Euripides, it was the dead hand of Seneca that exercised a determining influence over Elizabethan drama.

Formalism was pressed by Roger Ascham to the point of withholding the label of tragedy from one academic play because it employed trochaic *octonarii* in the *protasis* instead of the *epitasis*. When there can be no swerving from such rules, no attempting what has not been accomplished, it is critical precept which regulates artistic example. Thus the academician Georges de Scudéry, in publishing his poem, *Alaric, ou Rome vaincu*, sought to forestall the censure he himself had brought down upon Corneille by a prefatory acknowledgment that his practices conformed to the theories of Aristotle, Horace, Macrobius, Scaliger, Tasso, Castelvetro, Piccolomini, Vida, Vossius, Pazzi, Riccoboni, Robortello, Paolo Beni, Père Mambrun, "and several others." The name of a genuine poet, Tasso, seems out of place in this roster of critics, commentators, and translators, unless we assume that Scudéry was alluding not to the *Gerusalemme liberata* but to Tasso's apologetics for heroic poetry. Small wonder that Renaissance poetic, with a few problematic exceptions, fostered a series of failures in its most ambitious mode, the epic. There is some pith in Horace Walpole's query: "Why has everybody failed in this but the inventor, Homer?" And there is cogency, as well as complacency, in Walpole's conclusion: that the Homeric poems were the creation of a more primitive world, and that the form "is not suited to an improved and polished state of things."

We may agree to the extent of recognizing that different genres flourish under different circumstances. Such unproductive issues as the quarrel between the ancients and moderns arise when the arts are considered out of historical context. A relativistic solution to that controversy was shrewdly foreseen by Saint-Evremond, from the vantage point of a French critic residing in England. One of the earliest American critics, Timothy Dwight, would go characteristically farther: "Aristotle's ideas of criticism were taken from a few performances; and had he lived in the present age, with the same independence of mind, he would have altered many of them for the better." Certainly the style of life then being cultivated at Monticello was as classical as anything in Europe. It remained for a twentieth-century English novelist to focus, upon our nineteenth-century writers, *Studies in Classic American Literature*. But although political revolutions were attended by certain Plutarchan flourishes, the literary direction was unreservedly anticlassical. Keats was just in singling out "one Boileau" as the neoclassicist par excellence and consequently the archenemy for the romanticists. But Blake was all-embracing in his repudiation. "The Greek and Roman classics is the Antichrist," he wrote, adding grammatical insult to cultural injury. "I say *is* and not *are* as most expressive and correct too." The singular, however, is inappropriate; for the rise of archeological science coincided with the decline of classical art; and the totality of Greece and Rome could no longer be regarded as a single undifferentiated continuum. It was Winckelmann's premise that all good taste originated in Greece, and had degenerated in moving westward. A rediscovered Hellas, disencumbered of Latin associations, became so cherished a goal of German romanticism that an unsympathetic scholar has termed this conjunction *The Tyranny of Greece over Germany*. Schiller, who lamented the Hellenic *Götterdämmerung* in a nostalgic elegy, propounded his sweeping dichotomy between naïve and sentimental poetry in order to justify his own subjective approach — or so the more objective Goethe claimed. Schiller's interpretation of the Greeks was much too naïve for Nietzsche, who had been trained as a Hellenist, albeit his researches proved more acceptable to Wagner than to Wilamowitz-Moellendorf. By differentiating the Dionysiac from the Apollonian point of view, much as Lessing had differentiated the temporal from the spatial arts, Nietzsche adduced that Greek culture had its proto-romantic intensities along with its more conventional aspects. But this distinction has been blurred by Oswald Spengler, who substitutes the Faustian for the Dionysiac, opposes a dynamic modernism to a static antiquity, and arrives at the platitudinous equation: whereas moderns tend to be romantic, the ancients were classical.

4. Archetypal

Can the classical be the special perquisite of any given period or country as a whole? The opinions we have been entertaining are miscellaneous and contradictory enough to warrant our doubts. Is it not rather a retrospective designation, a sort of hallmark superimposed by the values it helps to promote? As such, it has provided a pedagogical basis for the ascendancy of one culture over another, over a succession of others; it has opened up fruitful renascences, has been fossilized into the closed systems of neoclassicism, and has provoked romanticism by way of opposition. Goethe's double-barreled formulation may have been loaded against the romantic, which he finally identified with disease; yet, in identifying health with the classical, he was seeking to reaffirm its normative function. Subsequent writers have shown themselves preoccupied, sometimes to a morbid degree, with the abnormal phases of experience. Pathology is the most powerful source of insight, Thomas Mann argued, though his own developing concern led him away from the exceptional case-history and back toward the recurrently typical myth. Thus the ancient-modern quarrel has been resumed; and the debate continues that Swift personified in his parable of the bee, the classic producer of sweetness and light, and the spider, whose bitter and irrational art is woven out of its entrails.

The legislators of Parnassus have always taken probability as their basic criterion, and have been quick to outlaw manifestations of wonder or strangeness as monstrosities. Serious critics have also realized that certain effects, perhaps the most moving, could not be obtained by mere prescription or calculation. This realization has its undefinable embodiment in the concept of the sublime: that *je-ne-sais-quoi*, that "grace beyond the reach of art," which supplements the all-too-definable position of the beautiful in neoclassical esthetics. But to formulate sublimity is to formalize it; by the time it reached the romanticists, it was almost indistinguishable from beauty; and its former connotations of mystery had to be supplied by the Gothic adjective, *grotesque*. The ideal of perfect beauty, *le beau idéal*, left out too much; the classical was, by definition, exclusive; in its very wholeness, it ignored the unknown. Such was the reasoning of Ernest Renan, as addressed to the goddess of reason herself, in his grandiloquent prayer on the Acropolis. The ex-priest, through his oriental studies, had become aware of stranger gods than were included in Athena's philosophy. His ever curious mind, he confessed, would be bored by constant perfection; and, in a final apostasy, he preferred the abyss of unfathomed knowledge. *"O abîme, tu es le dieu unique."*

A few years previously, just a hundred years ago, another pilgrim — as unlike Renan as possible in every other respect — had made his invocation at the same shrine. Herman Melville had not had much formal education in the classics; he had spent the best part of his youth roaming on desperate seas and living among the cannibals. During the next decade, in ten volumes of imaginative prose, he had first charmed readers with his adventures and then bewildered them with his reflections. Now at last, his travels had brought him to Greece, and he expressed his reactions by turning to verse. Under the heading, "Greek Architecture," he wrote these inscriptive lines:

> Not magnitude, not lavishness,
> But Form — the Site;
> Not innovating wilfulness,
> But reverence for the Archetype.

This homage to the goddess is not less impressive because it was offered by one who had explored the abyss, one who perceived the giant Enceladus struggling under Mount Greylock, even as universals struggle under the mounting burden of particulars. Were it not for such perceptions, the accumulating complexity of existence would make it seem formless. Form is envisaged in this connection, not as a series of technicalities, but as a definitive simplification: the primordial and ultimate pattern of behavior, which lends its outlines to the situation at hand. The latter may be too easily obscured by ephemera; hence the felt need for returning to the Greeks; as Virginia Woolf has attested, "the stable, the permanent, the original human being is to be found there."

This would seem to take us back where we started. Just so; for Greece is inevitably the starting point of Western tradition, having felt so little indebted to what went before and having put what came afterward so much in its debt; having, in Jefferson's testimonial phrase, "the first of civilized nations, presented examples of what man should be." If it had never existed, of course, we should have had to invent it; therefore our gratitude has been mingled with resentment at having been deprived of so glorious an opportunity for invention; and we join in the ambivalent curse of Donatus against those who anticipated our grandest utterances: *"Pereant qui ante nos nostra dixerunt!"* The classical, whatever else it may or may not be, remains the archetypal. As with the classical cases of medicine, where major problems are examined through salient instances, so literature still renders its diagnoses by citing the cases of Oedipus, Prometheus, and Odysseus-Ulysses. Greek mythology established a repertory of themes, upon which Roman metamorphosis did not exhaust the conceivable variations. The dominant role that the gods of Olympus have played in the lore and imagery of Christian Europe is a paradox we are not likely to overlook, especially when guided through English poetry by Douglas Bush or through the plastic arts by Jean Seznec.

With the crystallization of neoclassicism, archetypes turned into stereotypes, which were too opaque to be suggestive. "Harp? lyre?" said Coleridge's schoolmaster. "Pen and ink, boy, you mean." But though the romantic poets repudiated the pantheon and all its machinery, they could not help mourning the dream that had peopled the woods with nymphs, and they longed to see old Triton rise again from the waves. Walt Whitman called upon the Muse to migrate from Ionia to Philadelphia. Her equivocal response to his invitation might be inferred from the poem of his twentieth-century disciple, Hart Crane, where the poet echoes the epithet *Panis angelicus* under the unfortunate impression that he is invoking the great god Pan. Great Pan is irremediably dead at this juncture, and pagan names have been losing their natural magic. Yet, under other names, the types persist: there have been strong men since Agamemnon, and their prowess has not gone uncelebrated. "Think of the great DiMaggio," says the protagonist of Ernest Hemingway's latest tale, *The Old Man and the Sea*. That Cuban fisherman has never heard of Achilles, swift of foot; he can barely read the baseball scores; but it is his hero-worship that prompts him to heroism; and Mr. Hemingway does not let us forget that the heroic Joe DiMaggio, like the son of Thetis, has a vulnerable heel.

5. Canonical

Modernity has not succeeded in abolishing the necessity for myth, according to the Roumanian folklorist, Mircea Eliade. "Man's desire for a model, an example to imitate in his life, is not always satisfied by religion or history; a rather large part is taken by literature, which can transform individuals into archetypes and historical events into patterns of behavior, just as oral literatures regularly did." This is one of the opening remarks in the new three-volume *Histoire des littératures* — notice the plural — currently appearing under the imprint of the Bibliothèque de la Pléiade. It is salutary, if somewhat breathtaking, to observe that the first volume treats more than fifty literatures, "ancient, oriental, and oral," and that the writings of classical antiquity occupy one out of its eleven sections — the longest, if that is any salve for our vanity. Here, then, we are given intriguing glimpses of what may lie beyond the widest orbit of Greco-Roman cultural diffusion; and we are stimulated to wonder whether, under conditions of spontaneous growth, what we know as the classical may have developed elsewhere. For the purpose let us briefly glance toward Japan, that highly civilized country which has had no contact with the West until the past century, and which has seemed so quaintly exotic when judged by the norms of our culture.

A sharper glance would dwell upon the ideas of order that underlie Japanese society and permeate the arts. Most relevant for us would be cult of dramaturgy that still thrives in the Noh. Its plots should not seem unduly far-fetched to students of classical drama; they deal with such subjects as the relations of gods and men, the conflicts of communities and dynasties, rejected love, demonic possession, revenge, expiation. Above all, we may be struck by the similarities between its conventions and those of the Attic theater: the chorus, the masks, the intoned cadences, the dancing and singing, the interplay between the *shite* or protagonist and the *waki* or deuteragonist. Stylized representation, economy of theatrical means, the gift for making much out of little — or, as Racine austerely phrases it, *"faire quelque chose de rien"* — are nowhere more effectively utilized. Nothing could more conclusively demonstrate the provinciality of the assumption that tragedy is uniquely occidental. And if classicism is defined as a school of taste and restraint, in Ruskin's terms, it may be more consistently exemplified in Japanese painting than in the baroque painters that Ruskin was discussing. We may, at the least, view the Japanese as classicists, modeling their culture on the monuments of China and India as Europe's have been modeled on Greece and Judea. This implies farther horizons for the classical.

Extending beyond the Greek and Roman writers, it does not automatically include them; for if there is any common feature that runs through all the contexts of the classical, it resides in the principle of selection. The first recorded use of the term itself in English, from 1599, paired it with *canonical*. What has been selected is accepted as the best of its kind, what Arnold would approve as "the really excellent." Excellence, invidious though it may be, is the one invariable merit of works that gain acceptance into the canon. So George Chapman could preface his *Iliad* with the declaration: "Of all books extant in all kinds, Homer is the first and best." The Homeric poems had indeed been canonical ever since Solon commanded their public recitation. Yet Dante's tribute, in the absence of Greek, had to be perfunctory; and on the same plane with Homer — *"altissimo canto"* — Dante placed not only himself and Vergil, not only Ovid and Horace the satirist, but also Lucan. Clearly, Dante's canon is not ours; and the divergence might prompt us to question authority further: to speculate whether the seven tragedies we have from Aeschylus or from Sophocles are the ones we should ourselves have chosen, or why the quality of the letters of Phalaris did not fall off until they lost their claim to authenticity.

When T. S. Eliot asked himself *What Is a Classic?* a few years ago, his answer was dictated by the occasion, a meeting of the Vergil Society. Sainte-Beuve, asking *Qu'est-ce qu'un classique?* in 1850, had answered by stressing catholicity. The temple of taste should have niches, he announced, for classicists and romanticists, ancients and moderns, Christians and infidels.

But what should be the grounds for canonization? Huntington Cairns has compiled an anthology consisting entirely of passages which have been recommended by superlatives from one critic or another. Though the result impressively demonstrates the breadth of Mr. Cairns's reading it tends to make facile praise the touchstone of criticism, even as it is upon the jackets of best-sellers. Critical evaluation is a notoriously variable process. The repetition of *great,* together with *greatest* and *greatness,* more than twenty times in two pages of the *Encyclopaedia Britannica,* tells us less about the subject of the article, Victor Hugo, than about the author, A. C. Swinburne. A classic — by which, I take it, we mean neither more nor less than a great book — is such by consensus and not by personal judgment. The Longinian requirement — that it please all and always — is probably too demanding, since books exist within the sphere of time; but if they cannot be timeless, they may become time-hallowed.

Their survival is the testament that enables us to profit from the experience of those whose lives have preceded ours. That act of communication across the centuries is not so one-sided as it might seem; for the past can have no existence in the present, except as it is continually recreated by a joint effort of scholarship and imagination. Our facilities for disseminating the classics are now more extensive than ever, and so are the distractions that contend for the attention of our students. Socrates deplored the introduction of writing, because he foresaw the mechanization of culture; but manuscript preserved the spoken voice and the human dimension, in Greek philosophy and history as in poetry and drama. The invention of printing, which promised to stabilize literary form, accelerated the momentum of change. Another technological revolution confronts us today, no less far-reaching in its cultural impact. With the audio-visual, we face the very inversion of the classical: imprecise medium, ephemeral material, a rating dependent on the size of the audience. Our popular arts deliberately set a collective tone which is undistinguished rather than distinguished — *proletarius, non classicus.* We cannot complain, as Ezra Pound once did:

The thought of what America would be like
If the Classics had a wide circulation
Troubles my sleep.

But if the cultivation of the classical is no longer a universal
ideal, if it has narrowed down into a profession, then — I
would maintain — our obligation to those who profess it is all
the greater, and the link they are holding for us in the chain
of history is all the more strategic.

The Tradition of Tradition

At a meeting of the Modern Language Association of America in New York on December 27, 1950, after a series of papers discussing the role of tradition in the work of several English writers from Dryden to Eliot, these remarks were designed to serve as an epilogue. Since the Hopkins Review *— in which they were published, IV, 3 (Spring, 1951) — has subsequently disappeared, I should like to express my sympathy as well as my gratitude to its former editors. An Italian translation by Luigi Berti was published in* Inventario, *IV, 2 (March–April, 1952); a Dutch translation by Halbo C. Kool in* Amerikaans Cultureel Perspectief *(Utrecht, 1954).*

━━━

I hate *Traditions*:
I do not trust them.

These would be strange words, coming as they do from so thoroughgoing a traditionalist as Ben Jonson, if he had not made a point of placing them in the mouth of a character named Ananias. Clearly we cannot trust Ananias; yet, just as clearly, we can take his warning that our subject is a matter of opinion; a matter in which, as often as not, received opinion has been controverted. One of his contemporaries, whose name is more noteworthy for a disinterested love of truth, explored the murky Cave of Montesinos — so Unamuno tells us — to distinguish between true and false traditions. But that was the most ambiguous of all Don Quixote's adventures, and Cervantes confessed himself unable to verify it. This is precisely our difficulty; for tradition begs the question of origins; hence, in speaking of it, we hardly know where to begin. We personify it and invoke our personification whenever the authorship of a work is lost, or whenever we find ourselves at a loss for more logical arguments. Using the word with increasing frequency, but ignoring the different contexts in which we use it, we come to regard it as a single entity and to introduce it by the definite article. We speak of "the classical tradition," which is almost a tautology; we also refer to romantic, naturalistic, and revolutionary traditions, which are veritable contradictions in terms. Faced with this plurality of conflicting traditions, some critics undertake to single out one particular tradition and dub it "the great." Thereupon they reopen the eternal debate of criticism, and indeed of ethics, over what does and what doesn't constitute greatness.

It might prove salutary to remember — with the help of Du Cange's glossary — that the so-called Great Turk sent a letter of protest to the Archbishop of Pisa, early in the sixteenth century, referring to certain acts of piracy and carnage as *illam magnam traditionem*. Although that great betrayal may sound far-fetched, it is worth recalling if only to remind us that its homonym can also be treacherous. Furthermore, it should jog our awareness that the inert mass of tradition is merely the end-product of a dynamic process: that process of accumulation, assimilation, and dissemination which has been so strategic in the development of civilization itself. Thus the Romans spoke first of *traditio* in a military sense; and since it had the double meaning conveyed by our phrase "handing over," it could literally mean both surrender and treason. On a more figurative plane, it was employed in legal and historical connections; and, closer to our purpose, the Latin rhetoricians made *tradere* a common verb for "teach." As usual they followed Greek example, particularly Plato's *Theaetetus,* which identifies tradition (παράδοσις) with the art of teaching, the oral transmission of knowledge. Here is the basis of the humanistic conception, which was enlarged and reinforced by the very processes that transmitted the classics to the Renaissance. It is with a sense of this continuity that Bacon writes of "tradition or delivery" in his *Advancement of Learning*:

> Since the labor and life of one man cannot attain to perfection of knowledge, the wisdom of the tradition is that which inspireth the felicity of continuance and proceeding.

But the emphasis shifts from the teacher to the pupil, and

from pedagogical pronouncement to scholarly inquiry, as Bacon alerts us against the temptations to fallacy:

For as knowledges are now delivered, there is a kind of contract of error between the deliverer and the receiver: for he that delivereth knowledge desireth to deliver it in such form as may be best believed, and not as may be best examined; and he that receiveth knowledge desireth rather present satisfaction than expectant inquiry, and so rather not to doubt than not to err; glory making the author not to lay open his weakness, and sloth making the disciple not to know his strength.

The youthful giant was to realize his full strength in the light of scientific method and methodological doubt; and history endeavored to overthrow the idols into which tradition had crystallized; but the latter, retreating before the examination of reason, continued in the various realms of faith. Traditionalism has bound the Jews together from the days of Abraham to those of Zionism. It is from the Judaism of the Scribes and Pharisees that Jesus dissents in the Gospels, upholding "the commandment of God" against "the tradition of the elders." Significantly, it seems to have been Paul who brought the traditional note into Christianity, exhorting the Corinthians: ". . . hold fast to the traditions, even as I delivered them to you." Such are the links that bind the Apostles to the Fathers, the original witnesses to their interpreters. Out of that succession and interpretation rises the *catholica traditio,* the rock on which Tertullian places the Church. Conversely Dante, writing *De Monarchia* after the Church has been firmly established for centuries, argues that tradition is derived from it. But Catholic doctrine consistently maintains that the word of God, handed down by word of mouth, is by no means limited to scripture: much of it remains, as Saint Augustine repeatedly asserts, *non scripta sed tradita.* The Protestants, in making the Bible their sole authority, were rejecting tradition. Perhaps its most formidable challenger was Calvin; doubtless its most eloquent defender was Bossuet. Its later apologists felt compelled to recognize the existence of rival traditions: we find even Joseph de Maistre questioning the traditionalistic argument, when a Russian theologian cited it to support the claims of Eastern orthodoxy.

Now with tradition, in its theological aspect, English culture inherits the Protestant quarrel. The oldest usages in the Oxford Dictionary, from Wycliffe late in the fourteenth century, are strongly pejorative. The Thirty-fourth Article of Anglican doctrine stresses the diversity of traditions and ceremonies, which vary with "countries, times, and men's manners," and are "ordained only by man's authority." Richard Hooker deals charily with "uncertain tradition," and Sir Thomas Browne treats it as a source of vulgar errors. For Milton it is at best a "broken reed": traditions are equated with "superstitions" in *Paradise Lost* and with "idolisms" in *Paradise Regained.* This approximates the puritanical view satirized by the erstwhile Catholic, Jonson, in *The Alchemist.* The distance between those extremes had been viewed from the other side, in the Tudor interlude of *Lusty Juventus,* when the Devil complained of the Puritans:

> They will not believe, they plainly say,
> In old traditions and made by men,
> But live as the Scripture teacheth them.

The exception that proves the rule is the Roman convert Dryden, whose Hind confounds his Panther by stating the case for tradition. Pope is conventionally deprecatory in the passage quoted by Dr. Johnson's dictionary, which likewise reflects the antitraditional tendency. Less conservative authors are *a fortiori* more distrustful: Mr. Tradition, in Bunyan's *Holy War,* fights briefly for Mansoul but goes over to the enemy, Diabolus. The will in Swift's *Tale of a Tub,* the role of Polonius in Shakespeare's *Hamlet,* are caricatures of tradition — or so, at any rate, commentators have said. If the break with older religion was completed by the Civil Wars, the rift in classical humanism can be traced to the battle between the Ancients and the Moderns. Philological scholarship, largely continental, had for some time been scrutinizing decretals and raising questions of authenticity. With Gibbon, as with Voltaire, historical method set out to undermine traditional belief.

Believers in the idea of progress could affirm, as George Eliot did in *The Spanish Gypsy*:

> We had not walked
> But for Tradition; we walk evermore
> To higher paths by brightening Reason's lamp.

Following that gleam of enlightenment, Friedrich Engels defined tradition as "the *vis inertiae* of history." Marx, though he considered it an incubus, nonetheless acknowledged the force of the *argumentum ad verecundiam*, that appeal to authority which even the French revolutionists made when they justified their actions by classical precedents. But the Revolution, like the Reformation, was fundamentally hostile toward tradition; and it was the counterrevolutionary reaction that began to rehabilitate the idea. It was the Vicomte de Bonald who propounded a philosophical and political system which he explicitly labeled "traditionalism," and who founded a line of reactionary thought which extends from Balzac through the Action Française and beyond. In England there were implicit parallels: Coleridge's spectacular failure of nerve, Carlyle's invidious comparison between *Past and Present*, the medieval resurrections of Scott and Ruskin. The name of tradition, however, is scarcely mentioned — least of all by the foremost British traditionalist, Edmund Burke. Its connotations were still primarily religious; yet now it carried sympathetic overtones; and for this our principal witness is Cardinal Newman's *Apologia pro Vita Sua*. John Keble's sermon of 1836, "Primitive Tradition Recognized in Holy Scripture," signalizes the attempt to revive tradition within the Church of England. With the Oxford Movement, then, our wheel comes full circle; thereafter Matthew Arnold can apply the noun more generally and favorably; yet, quite specifically and revealingly, he associates it with his university. And when Yeats discusses "Poetry and Tradition" in 1907, he still seems to be discussing two unrelated categories, forced to cohabit by the exigencies of Irish politics.

Meanwhile our term had been introduced into the critical vocabulary, very appropriately by Sainte-Beuve in 1858. During the previous year *Madame Bovary* had made its devastating comment upon its century, and Flaubert had now gone to ancient Carthage in search of more congenial material. As a young poet and novelist, Sainte-Beuve had joined in the manifestoes of *La Jeune France;* he had been both a socialist and a romanticist, and had characterized romanticism as royalism in politics, Catholicism in religion, and Platonism in love — a credo which T. S. Eliot was slightly to modify. Now for some years a member of the Académie Française, asked to deliver a series of lectures at the Ecole Normale, Sainte-Beuve chose for his inaugural topic: *De la tradition en littérature, et dans quel sens il la faut entendre.* Addressing himself rather consciously to the occasion, he discriminated the roles of the critic and the professor; he apprised his students of their responsibilities in maintaining a vital relation between past and present; above all, he advised them against conceiving tradition too narrowly or too rigidly. His most suggestive point was his concept of tradition as one comprehensive whole: by belated inclination a classicist, he included Shakespeare and Goethe among his classics, and had provided room for every kind of literary merit in the eclectic temple of taste that he described in *Qu'est-ce qu'un classique?* To wander through it, to adventure among masterpieces, to enjoy one's patrimony as heir of the ages, presupposes more leisure and disinterestedness than *homo europaeus* has latterly known. Proust, the connoisseur of Gothic architecture and French cookery, discerned the same traditions at work in both, and did not value them less because they were dead or dying.

To turn to *homo americanus* is, tradition-wise, to confront an antipodal species. For our oldest tradition is that we have no traditions: "history is bunk," "the past is a bucket of ashes." Therefore the problem is not historical but geographical, involving the cultural relations of old world and new. The antitraditionalism of the mother country is amplified in this breezy mental climate: we are pragmatic rather than empirical, inconoclastic rather than skeptical — but one cannot vie with Walt Whitman in sounding our virtues. Emerson's advice to ministers was "Beware of Tradition." Howells'

watchword for novelists was "escape from the paralysis of tradition." Stephen Crane gave a twist of transatlantic bravado
to the sentiment we have heard from George Eliot:

> Tradition, thou art for suckling children,
> Thou art the enlivening milk for babes,
> But no meat for men is in thee.

Enlightened Europeans, looking westward, glimpsed the democratic future unobstructed by the dead hand of custom. Goethe
congratulated the United States for having no ruined castles
and — halcyon era! — no useless memories nor fruitless strug-
gles. For pretending to build such castles the South, always
our most traditional region, drew upon itself the ridicule that
Mark Twain more habitually leveled at Europe. Yet Henry
James, echoing a strain from Hawthorne, declared that the
absence of feudal landmarks made conditions especially difficult for the American artist. And in an Oxford garden, a
virtual "chorus of tradition," his *Passionate Pilgrim* came
to this dying realization:

My diminished dignity reverts . . . to the naked background of our
own education, the deadly dry air in which we gasp for impressions
and comparisons. There's a certain grandeur in the lack of decorations, a certain heroic strain in that young imagination of ours which
finds nothing made to its hands, which has to invent its own traditions and raise high into our morning air, with a ringing hammer
and nails, the castles in which we dwell.

This, of course, is a counterstatement more typical of American
than of James. The subsequent trend of our academic architecture, along with the currents of academic thought, has
managed to outdate it by moving backwards. The nostalgic
medievalism of Henry Adams, the "new humanism" of Irving
Babbitt and others, Barrett Wendell's course in "The Traditions of European Literature," the "genteel tradition" that
George Santayana criticizes and sentimentalizes — these are the
stations of the pilgrimage from Henry James to T. S. Eliot.

This rough and rapid conspectus should, for better or worse,
make clear that Mr. Eliot was not exaggerating in 1917, when
he opened his essay, "Tradition and the Individual Talent":

"In English writing we seldom speak of tradition. . ." Since then we have spoken of it so much that we forget how novel the term was to critical discourse, and how antipathetic the concept has been to many of the characteristic spokesmen for Anglo-American culture — if not for the more highly academized French. Brilliantly formulating the interdependence of the contemporary and the classical, Mr. Eliot extended Sainte-Beuve's continuum; by means of a striking and doubtful scientific metaphor, he sketched a more impersonal theory of poetry than any poet's practice has yet fulfilled; and he candidly stated that poets are not born to, but must work for, tradition. Sixteen years later, in *After Strange Gods* — a title loaded with implications for the student of comparative tradition — he went on to elaborate his definition and to supplement it with the concept of orthodoxy, which is professedly rational where tradition is admittedly intuitive, and functions mainly as a base of operations from which to fling the charge of heresy. G. K. Chesterton had played with such words a generation before, in an ingenious effort to keep up with the fast company of Bernard Shaw; but in the moral atmosphere of the nineteen-thirties, the gaiety of paradox was overcast by the grimness of dogma. Mr. Eliot has censured Arnold for confounding esthetic with religious values; yet he himself has made happier contributions to literary discussions than he did when he imported into them the language of the Inquisition.

At the end of the nineteen-twenties, in a volume entitled *Tradition and Experiment in Present Day Literature*, Mr. Eliot defended "Experiment in Criticism." Several of his collaborators emphasized the untraditional bias of English writing, and Ashley Dukes went so far as to observe: "Tradition is successful experiment." Granted the necessity for both, as well as the prevailing experimentation of that decade, have we not for the last two decades been swinging in the opposite direction? Have the experimentalists of our century succeeded so well that we stand at this moment in the shadow of their tradition?

> . . . To forge in Ireland a new sword on our old
> traditional anvil

as Yeats did,

> . . . to forge in the smithy of my soul the uncreated
> conscience of my race

as Joyce did with a difference,

> To have gathered from the air a live tradition
> or from a fine old eye the unconquered flame

as Ezra Pound tried so desperately to do —

> This is not vanity.

Literary history understandably dwells on innovation and originality, though the wholly original and traditionless poet — *überlieferunglos,* as Goethe once imagined him — would ultimately become a tradition in himself. Novelty emerges, as the other papers on this program have so well demonstrated, through the talented use of sources and conventions. Whether a tradition is dead or alive depends upon the living, and whether they passively accept it or actively control it, selecting exemplars as Baudelaire did with Poe or Eliot with Donne. The displacements and realignments, which make tradition one thing for Arnold's generation and another for Eliot's, can be gauged by comparing Ward's *English Poets* (1880) with Auden and Pearson's *Poets of the English Language* (1950). Cleanth Brooks's *Modern Poetry and the Tradition,* as the arbitrary particle suggests, has been effective propaganda for this shift of taste. Yvor Winters' various polemics, so fiercely recommending the tamest writers, have carried neo-traditionalism to its occidental extreme. The antiromantic Pound, extolling "the tradition" in the newly established *Poetry* magazine while his fellow contributors were campaigning for free verse, had inaugurated a counterrevolution.

A recent English book by F. R. Leavis, more recently reprinted in this country, is flatly called *The Great Tradition.* It might have been called, more acurately, *Novels I've Liked* — or more pointedly, *Novels Lord David Cecil Doesn't Appreciate.* Its opening statement — "The great English novelists are Jane Austen, Henry James, George Eliot, and Joseph

Conrad" — is repeated throughout an introductory chapter, varied by occasional reflections against other novelists and critics, and terminating with italicized shrillness: "The Great Tradition of the English novel is *there.*" The chapters that follow make up in emphatic assertion for what they lack in humane learning or penetrating analysis. Since *Hard Times* is the only novel of Dickens that Mr. Leavis admits into his canon, we might infer that his undefined criterion is somewhat akin to Arnold's "high seriousness." Mr. Leavis' other writings reveal him to be the Arnold *de nos jours.* Unhappily, our day seems rather too late for an Arnold; it was already somewhat late for an Arnold in the nineteenth century. American readers will be further confused, remembering a book called *The Great Tradition* published by Granville Hicks in 1933. Mr. Hicks's tradition, though it may have owed something to Waldo Frank's *Rediscovery of America* (1928), coincided in no respect whatsoever with Mr. Leavis'; indeed it had all it could do to indicate some degree of coincidence between the main line of American literature and the current line of the Communist Party; and afterward, when the party line changed, the book was revised. Its coincidental resemblance to *The Great Tradition,* a tale of elegant society published by Katherine Fullerton Gerould in 1915, must have occasioned mutual embarrassment. It is only fair to add that Mr. Hicks has since repudiated his Marxism. Who knows what position Mr. Leavis will be taking in mellower years?

Eriger en lois ses impressions personnelles — every critic experiences the temptation, which Remy de Gourmont has so expressed, to claim dogmatic sanction for his personal impressions, to canonize his likes and anathematize his dislikes. But criticism is, or has been, an intellectual pursuit; and if intelligence itself is to survive, through an epoch of witch-hunting and book-burning, it needs more rational and sensitive instruments than bell, book, and candle. Pope Pius IX could authoritatively declare: *"La tradizione son' io."* But our neo-traditionalistic critics have no authority beyond their authoritarian metaphors; on the other hand, they have the privilege of being fallible, even when they speak *ex cathedra.*

They are free to disagree among themselves — and may no directive from any Politburo convert their orthodoxies into heresies, thereby compelling them to recant overnight! May they go on writing their own revisions of history, and making words mean what they want them to mean! Yet why should we, abhorring thought-control, be hankering so much after mental conformity today? Why should our colleges be fabricating, not merely campus traditions, but reactionary curricula? Our younger voices, which ought in the course of nature to be radical, exhort us to revisit conservatism, to vitalize the center, to do penance for the sins of the liberal imagination. Our publishers shower us with reprints, revivals, anthologies; our novelists display the smooth, derivative, gracile talents; our poets are professors; our artists are retrospective. Our techniques are geared to reproduce the best that has been thought and said, but rarely to create; our culture, diffused over wider areas than ever before, is more thinly diluted. Have we, as Alan Pryce-Jones suggested in *The New York Times Book Review* a few weeks ago, reached the tired middle age of the twentieth century?

If we admit the impeachment, we can plead extenuating circumstances: pressures that make it expedient to rest on the laurels of others, and more and more inviting to live in the past. But traditionally, when we reckon up our own traditions, we find ourselves committed to experiment, exploration, examination, progression, and from time to time subversion. "*Le monde moderne avilit . . .*" and it gets harder and harder to challenge that observation of Charles Péguy. The very adjective *modern* has been renounced by ultra-respectable museums, and the period of modernism in the arts seems to have terminated somewhere in the last decade. In the twentieth-century battle of the books, the odds favor the ancients — or, at all events, the *laudatores temporis acti*. Yet the modern world — "post-modern" Toynbee would say — has one unique advantage for us: uncertain though it is, it is the only one of which we can be certain. "*On peut regretter les meilleurs temps,*" sighed Montaigne, "*mais non pas fuir au présent.*" We cannot escape from the present, to which the past belongs;

so far as it continues to exist, it lives in us — and not in parchment, as Faust admonished Wagner. Our *Zeitgeist*, and not the spirit of other times, is reflected from our studies:

> Was ihr den Geist der Zeiten heisst,
> Das ist im Grund der Herren eignen Geist,
> In dem die Zeiten sich bespiegeln.

If this conclusion is inescapable, so is our responsibility. Scholars may have a vested interest in tradition, but they have a heavier stake in truth. Not that the two must inevitably conflict, yet sometimes truth has less to fear from overt attack than from inner stagnation:

Truth is compared in Scripture to a streaming fountain; if his waters flow not in perpetual progression, they sicken into a muddy pool of conformity and tradition.

It is not surprising that Milton, who uttered this precept in his *Areopagitica*, should be denigrated by our heresy-hunting critical tradition-mongers; and even his admirers could wish him an easier resurgence than to be living at this hour. But it would be healthy if, reversing the process of tradition, we could be judged by his standards rather than he by ours. When we think of great writers, according to Sainte-Beuve, we should ask ourselves what they would think of us. One quails before the notion of such a counter-scrutiny; and yet, however justly severe it might be, it would be tempered with qualities all too rare in our criticism: tolerance, independence, magnanimity.

What is Realism?

This statement condenses a point of view arrived at through a continuing series of studies in the French novel. Under the title, "The Definition of Realism," it was read on December 30, 1948, to a section of the Modern Language Association concerned with comparative literature and, more particularly, with prose fiction. Under the present title it served as the introduction to an issue of Comparative Literature, III, 3 *(Spring, 1951), which was devoted to problems of realism. It is with the kind assent of my fellow editors that I reproduce it now. From an appended paragraph, here omitted, the following sentences may be relevant: "In reducing our theme to a handful of historical and critical generalizations, I am aware that these preliminary comments do much less than justice to its large diversity and striking particularity; and, for this reason and others, I have greater confidence in the major part of our collective undertaking, which is embodied in the five essays that follow. . . . Our task . . . is not conclusive but introductory; we merely wish to open a discussion which, we sincerely hope, others will broaden and deepen." An Italian translation by Anna Lambertini had meanwhile appeared in* Inventario, II, 3 *(Autumn, 1949); and an unauthorized Chinese version has since come out in* Wên I Yüeh Pao *(Literary Monthly, Taipei).*

▲▲▲

In stating an issue which others will be called upon to face, propounding very sketchily the terms to which example must lend concrete significance, perhaps I should invoke the special protection of jesting Pilate — that patron saint of profound inquiries superficially pursued. For the problem that I have undertaken to pose brings up a number of incidental and ultimate questions which we could not stop for, even if we knew the answers, here. The most we can hope for is to focus, upon the main tendency of modern literature, the same sort of analytic and evaluative discussion that has already been concentrated upon the topic of romanticism. At the outset we can answer Pilate's question, positivistically and tautologically, by defining truth as the accurate correspondence between reality itself and a given account of reality. We are thereupon confronted by the question, "What is reality?" Since it cannot bear precisely the same significance for any two human beings, Carlyle declared that "reality escapes us." Let us concede the point; let it stand as *x*, the unknown element in whatever formulation we may reach. We come closer by approaching the problem from the other side — by sorting out the testimony that various witnesses have deposed, charting the general direction they seem to indicate, and tentatively calling this process of approximation *realism*.

But here another difficulty arises, insofar as some of them lead in opposite directions. For instance, the trend of modern thought toward empiricism, materialism, pragmatism, naturalism came to a head a generation ago when two schools of philosophers all but agreed: the so-called "New Realists" and the so-called "Critical Realists." V. L. Parrington broadened the area of agreement by applying the term "critical realism" to the recent period in American literature. More recently, however, there have been accumulating signs of reversion to an older kind of realism, the scholastic kind that proceeded from the doctrine of *universalia ante rem*. Shunted between two extreme positions which claim the same title, we may turn from epistemology to etymology, and take the Latin root word *res* as our starting point. It is well to remember that the word contains, as it were, the thing. It is not altogether far-fetched to observe that, semantically speaking, *realism* is distantly connected with *real estate*. That quasi-legal connection is tangibly supported by the bonds of interest that tie so many novelists to the realistic tradition: by Balzac's sense of property, Dickens' inventories and Tolstoy's estates, Henry James's preoccupation with "things."

We lose little by confining our attention to that terrain of experience which philosophical sophistication would label "naïve realism." Its classic gesture occurred when Dr. Johnson kicked the stone. Characteristically it manifests itself by repudiating some manifestation of idealism. When publicists tell us to look at a situation realistically, we can be fairly certain that we are about to be asked to condone some piece of moral skulduggery. Instead of an appeal to principle, we are presented with a repudiation of principle. Thus the realistic attitude derives its meaning from the conditions of its application. Like the concept of liberty, it cannot exist in a vacuum; in the abstract it means virtually nothing. History defines our liberties in terms of the specific constraints they sought to overcome; free speech and free trade presuppose unjust imprisonment and arbitrary taxation, the *lettre de cachet* and the *gabelle*. The purport of President Roosevelt's Four Freedoms lay in their counterattack against four tyrannies. In this respect as in others, realism closely parallels the development of liberalism — another protean phenomenon which can only be pinned down by firmly grasping its varied responses to particular issues.

So much is clear, as Karl Mannheim has said: "Realism means different things in different contexts." Its would-be historians may well be deterred by the object-lesson of Lord Acton's uncompleted *History of Liberty*. But students of literature have the measurable advantage of working from texts as well as contexts, and Erich Auerbach's *Mimesis* has lately shown what stylistic analysis can do, when trained upon the descriptive techniques of selected authors from Homer to Virginia Woolf. When Professor Auerbach finds no formula for the presentation of actuality (*dargestellte Wirklichkeit*) in different languages at different epochs, he impressively documents our need for assuming a relativistic point of view. Possibly an absolute standard could be set up in the plastic arts, where the actual object can be directly compared with its artistic treatment. Yet even there the realism seems to be a matter of degree, varying with choice of subject and emphasis on detail. Even when we speak of "photographic reproduction," we cannot take for granted its objectivity. The very phrase *trompe-l'oeil* gives it away. The camera's eye is relatively less subjective than the eye of the beholder; yet it was photography which opened the way for impressionistic painting, which in turn has angled and composed and highlighted the art of the photographer.

Perhaps, like students of the diverging "romanticisms," we should pluralize our subject; but we should not, like some of them, allow divergences to obscure a fundamental impetus. Art has continually adapted itself to man's changing conceptions of reality — that is to say, his successive adjustments to society and nature. In a static culture, where his position is fixed and his worldview unchanging, expression is likely to be conventionalized. But occidental culture has been dynamic, and its arts have endeavored to keep pace with its accelerating changes. This distinction, which is broadly exemplified in the contrast between East and West, sharply emerged from the Iconoclastic Controversy, when Eastern orthodoxy prescribed a rigid convention while Western artists were free to move toward secularization, individuality, realism — from the symbolic, in short, to the representational. Now if, as Aristotle maintains, art springs from the interplay of two complementary instincts, μίμησις and ἁρμονία, there are times when the imitation of nature predominates and other times when it is subordinated to the imposition of a pattern. When Plato condemned poetry for its unreality, in the most idealistic and paradoxical sense of that term, Aristotle proposed a compromise in the name of poetic truth and higher reality, and thence handed on the doctrine of verisimilitude to the neoclassical critics.

Meanwhile the sphere of the probable expanded, while much that the ancients regarded as universal was seen by the moderns to be more limited. Against such limitations romanticism protested, when Wordsworth and Coleridge set out to write about lower ranks of society and stranger wonders of nature than classicism seemed willing to recognize. Not that the classicists excluded realism, but they relegated it to the comic stage; comedy was the *imago veritatis,* and the common man was no hero but a figure of fun. The medium that most completely mirrors the increasing stature of the middle class has been, of course, the major vehicle of literary realism, the novel. The novel originated, with a characteristic gesture, by repudiating its medieval predecessor; the picaresque tale overtook the knightly romance; and Cervantes, by pitting the daily realities of the developing city against the chivalric ideals of the declining castle, provided an archetype for all novelists and future realists. *"La rivalité du monde réel et de la représentation que nous nous en faisons"* — this might be a French critic's description of *Don Quixote.* It happens to be André Gide's description of what his novelist is attempting in *Les Faux-monnayeurs.*

Conversely, looking backward from Gide, we can see how every great novel has attempted — *mutatis mutandis* — to distinguish what is real from what is counterfeit. Defoe's narrations, he invariably assured his readers, are not fiction but fact; and Diderot pointedly entitled one of his stories *Ceci n'est pas un conte.* To convince us of his essential veracity, the novelist must always be disclaiming the fictitious and breaking through the encrustations of the literary. *"La vraie éloquence se moque de l'éloquence."* It is no coincidence that, from Rabelais to Jane Austen, so many realists have begun as parodists; it has even been argued, by Viktor Shklovsky, that parody is the basis of the novelistic form. We must not assume that, because it is polymorphous, the novel is formless; nor that writers very easily or spontaneously express themselves in a realistic mode. "No more literary school than the realists has ever existed," as George Moore, their leading British apologist, allowed. But we must first go — as Moore did — to France, where most of the problems of modern literature have been formulated, if we would track the critical usage down to its historical context. If we would trace it to its metaphysical chrysalis, we should have to look even farther back to Germany, to Schiller's *Über naive und sentimentalische Dichtung,* where antique *Realismus* is contrasted with the idealistic outlook of the romantics.

The earliest applications of the term that we encounter in the *New English Dictionary* are cited from Emerson in 1856 and Ruskin in 1857: the first is roughly synonymous with "materialism," the second with "grotesquerie," and both are decidedly pejorative. In France, on the other hand, the latter year marks the trial and vindication of *Madame Bovary* — a date as important for realism as the *première* of *Hernani* is for romanticism. The relationship between the two movements, as we acknowledge more and more, is continuous rather than antithetical. The realism of the romanticists has its dialectical counterpart in the romanticism of the realists, and it would be hard to say under which category we should classify *La Chartreuse de Parme* or *Les Misérables.* As early as 1826, investigation has shown, *le romantisme* and *le réalisme* echoed interchangeably through contemporary periodicals. But in the phrase of its journalistic fugleman, Champfleury, realism was one of "those religions in -*ism*" which came into the world in 1848. Its preparation had been technical as well as ideological; it profited from Daguerre's epoch-making invention, which entered the public domain in 1839, as well as from Houssaye's history of Flemish painting published in 1846. It reached its artistic climax when Courbet, whose paintings were rejected by the Salon of 1855, set up his own exhibition of these solidly executed studies in humble life, which he called his *Pavillon du Réalisme.*

The critic Duranty summed up objectives when he called for "the exact, complete, and sincere reproduction of the social milieu in which we live." His little magazine, *Réalisme,* coincided with a collection of essays under the same title, brought out by Champfleury in 1857. By then the catchword was becoming popular; even M. Prudhomme, the bourgeois incarnate, could sign his letters with assurances of his "distinguished consideration and realism." However, Duranty believed that the realists were too individualistic to establish a school, while Champfleury considered them transitional and expected them to give way before another movement in thirty years. Within half that time, in the eighteen-seventies, Zola was putting out manifestoes for naturalism. Where the older group had posthumously venerated Balzac, the naturalists paid homage to Flaubert; but he remained indifferent to schools and slogans. When Zola amiably admitted that these were devices to gain publicity for younger writers, he scarcely did justice to the grimmer implications of the newer term — the boundless distance between Robinson Crusoe's easy control over his environment and the crushed victims of Hardy's cosmic irony or Dreiser's chemical determinism.

Naturalism found its inspiration in science rather than art, its exemplar in Darwin rather than Courbet. In contrast to the accumulation of things, the jumbled catalogues of realism, its objects were meticulously selected and related through the chain of cause and effect. Seeking to complete the process of identification between literature and life, it conceived a book as a *document humain* and a play as a *tranche de vie*. But Zola's novels were experimental in quite a different sense from the physiological experimentation of Claude Bernard. Their twofold aim is reflected in their subtitle: *Histoire naturelle et sociale d'une famille sous le Second Empire.* As natural history, they demonstrate nothing; they simply illustrate the obsolescent theories of Zola's scientific contemporaries. Their social story is something else again, combining the exposure of bureaucracy with a plea for the underdog, each volume covering another field of documentation. Zola, writing in retrospect, gave voice to the political opposition that the Second Empire had tried to silence. Similarly in Russia, under the czars, in spite of censorship, suppression, and regimentation, writers were able to lodge their protest against an even more autocratic regime. Perhaps because Russians had to live a lie, as Turgenev suggested, their novels were so intensely devoted to truth.

Into the second half of the nineteenth century, realists and naturalists carried augmenting burdens of social criticism and humanitarian sympathy. The brothers Goncourt, for all their aristocratic tastes, furthered the advance of proletarian fiction; they urged, in the preface to *Germinie Lacerteux,* the right of the lower class to a novel of its own. The spread of democracy, the rise in the standard of living, the exploitation of typography and literacy brought pressure for further extensions of the literary franchise. Hence Harriet Beecher Stowe announced that *Uncle Tom's Cabin (or Life among the Lowly)* would treat a theme "hitherto ignored by the associations of polite and refined society." Politeness and refinement inevitably hold a vested interest in the *status quo*, which is loudly outraged by the depiction of uncomfortable facts and ignoble existences, and would outlaw them by invoking the ambiguous sanction of universality. Official and academic sponsorship, reducing the dynamic to the static, produce what William Dean Howells termed "a petrification of taste." Resistance is no less inevitable than movement, and repeats itself over the years. Just as Brunetière deprecated the naturalistic school, just as the disillusioned novels of the First World War were attacked by propagandists for the Second, so the hired moralists of *Life* magazine have latterly been editorializing against *From Here to Eternity* and *The Naked and the Dead*.

Nonetheless realism, heralded by romanticism and continued by naturalism, has been the animating current of nineteenth-century literature. Today it no longer operates as an *avant-garde*; it has acquired tradition and even academies. Watchwords continue to become outmoded, and novelties must be rediscovered again and again; the naturists supersede the naturalists and the verists yield to self-proclaimed veritists; and yet the real thing seems even more remote than before. Can it be that this progression, which has moved on so rapidly from generation to generation, is slowing down to an impasse? The next step, to judge from *surréalisme* (or super-realism), seems to be less a new projection of the old realism than a sharp reaction against it — against representation in favor of symbolism. Such landmarks as Joyce's *Ulysses*, pointing in two directions, lead forward — or is it backward? — via psychology toward fantasy and myth. The technological obsolescence of the novel itself is predictable in an era when fiction can hardly keep up with fact, when the reporter turns novelist and the novelist turns reporter, when the instinct for imitation is more efficiently satisfied by journalism, radio, film, and above all television. Within the abstracted realm now left to the purer arts, it may be that the instinct for harmony — for order, degree, and arrangement — will again prevail.

Whatever happens is bound to register the adaptation to change, but the quality of change may prove so far-reaching as to undermine the tendencies upon which realism has been grounded: a democratic attitude toward society, an experimental attitude toward nature. The forces that work against social mobility and scientific inquiry are those that steer writers back into the province of convention. Much of the writing that confronts us, at this midpoint of the twentieth century, seems transitional in character: conventional in pattern, realistic in detail. Yet an art which must submit itself, either to production codes or party lines, is basically unrealistic. Witness, on the one hand, the Hollywood cinema. And, on the other, the neo-Marxist slogan of "socialist realism" is, in the light of historical definition, a contradiction in terms. The role of the great realists — as who but Gorky pointed out? — has been to transcend their own class, to criticize the bourgeoisie. It does not necessarily follow that their successors ought to panegyrize the proletariat. Middle-class culture, with all its faults, has had its virtue — the redeeming virtue of self-criticism. "*Kunst wird Kritik,*" Thomas Mann has lately remarked, and the bourgeois novel is nothing if not critical. It may have told the whole truth very rarely, and included many other things than the truth; but it has kept open the question "What is truth?" in the teeth of dogmas and systems that strive to close it.

NOTATIONS ON NOVELISTS

The Example of Cervantes

This was the opening paper in a conference on "Imitation and Parody" at Columbia University on September 6, 1955, under the auspices of the English Institute. It has been included in the Institute's annual for 1956, Society and Self in the Novel, *edited by Mark Schorer and published by the Columbia University Press. It also appears concurrently in* Perspectives USA, *XVI (Fall, 1956), with translated versions in the German and Italian editions of that intercultural periodical.*

◂▴▴▸

I

To crown him with an adjective of his own choosing, Cervantes continues to be the exemplary novelist. It is a truism, of course, that he set the example for all other novelists to follow. The paradox is that, by exemplifying the effects of fantasy on the mind, he pointed the one way for fiction to attain the effect of truth. We state his achievement somewhat more concretely when we say that he created a new form by criticizing the old forms. *Don Quixote,* in terms of its intention and impact, constituted an overt act of criticism. Through its many varieties of two-sided observation, there runs a single pattern: the pattern of art embarrassed by confrontation with nature. This is the substance of the critical comment that every chapter makes in a differing context. We can test it by considering the implications of two such passages, taken from familiar and typical episodes, widely separated yet closely related. (With some cross-reference to the original Spanish in the interests of semantics, and a good deal of paraphrase in the interests of condensation, I shall be quoting Cervantes from the contemporaneous English translation of Thomas Shelton. Spelling will be modernized, and parenthetical numbers will refer to any standard text.)

Our first passage occurs in Chapter XXII of the First Part, which is entitled "Of the liberty Don Quixote gave to many wretches, who were a-carrying perforce to a place they desired not." Let us pause for a moment over this heading. It turns into a characteristically dry understatement as soon as we realize that "the place they desired not" was the galleys. But the emphasis falls on the two common nouns in the main clause, "liberty" and "wretches." *Libertad!* The very word, which was to reverberate with such easy sonority for Walt Whitman, carried a poignant overtone for Cervantes. After the famous battle of Lepanto in which he lost the use of his hand, as he never tires of retelling, he had been captured by pirates and sold as a slave, and had perforce spent five long years in Algerian captivity. That enslavement, in a place Cervantes desired not, must have lent special meaning to Don Quixote's gesture of liberation. The tale later told by the Captive — the Spanish Captain enslaved at Algiers who recovers his greatest joy, lost liberty — is highly romanticized; but it hints that the actual truth was stranger than the incidental fiction when it mentions a certain Cervantes (*"tal de Saavedra"*) and the deeds he did — and all to achieve liberty (*"y todas por alcanzar libertad,"* I, xl).

Hence the wretches are more to be pitied than scorned; and here the key word, *desdichados*, is not so much a term of contempt as an ironic expression of fellow feeling. It may not be irrelevant to recall that *El Desdichado* is also the title Gérard de Nerval gives to his melancholy sonnet on the romantic hero. A similar ambiguity characterizes the French *les misérables* or the Russian *neshchastnenki*. The undertones of humanitarian sympathy, implied when Don Quixote liberates the convicts, come to the surface when he finally reaches Barcelona, and we are brought face to face with galley slaves. Again we cannot help thinking of the author — not because his book is, in any sense, autobiographical; but because it is, like most great books, the unique distillation of mature experience. Behind the book stands a soldier of misfortune who had encountered many setbacks on his personal journey to Parnassus. Having tried his one good hand at virtually all the flowery forms of the artificial literature of that baroque period, he had addressed himself to the hazards of the road in the uncongenial guise of tax collector. And again it is of himself that he speaks with rueful humor, when the Priest and the Barber hold their inquisition over the books in Don Quixote's library. Among those which are set aside from the burning is the pastoral romance of *Galatea* by Miguel de Cervantes Saavedra. The Priest mitigates his criticism with a pun: this author is *"más versado en desdichas que en versos"* — better versed in misfortunes than in verses (I, vi).

Don Quixote's ideal of humanistic perfection is to be equally well versed in arms and letters. It might be opined that he fails because his military training has lagged so far behind his literary preparation. Something like the contrary might be maintained about his creator. At all events, after all he had been through, Cervantes would have been the very last man to cherish romantic illusions on the subject of adventure. He was therefore just the man to dramatize a distinction which has since become an axiom, which has indeed become so axiomatic that it might well be called Cervantes' formula. This is nothing more nor less than a recognition of the difference between verses and reverses, between words and deeds, *palabras* and *hechos* — in short, between literary artifice and that real thing which is life itself. But literary artifice is the only means that a writer has at his disposal. How else can he convey his impression of life? Precisely by discrediting those means, by repudiating that air of bookishness in which any book is inevitably wrapped. When Pascal observed that true eloquence makes fun of eloquence, he succinctly formulated the principle that could look to Cervantes as its recent and striking exemplar. It remained for La Rochefoucauld to restate the other side of the paradox: some people would never have loved if they had not heard of love.

The chapter that sees the convicts liberated is rather exceptional in its direct approach to reality. The preceding chapter has been a more devious and characteristic excursion into the domain of romance. Its theme, which has come to be a byword for the transmuting power of imagination, as well as for Don

Quixote's peculiar habit of imposing his obsession upon the world, is the barber's basin he takes for the fabulous helmet of Mambrino, stolen from Rinaldo by Sacripante in the *Orlando Furioso*. If the recovery of this knightly symbol is effected without undue incident, it is because the barber has no wish to fight; subsequently, when he returns to claim his property, he allows himself to be persuaded that it is really a helmet which has been enchanted to look like a basin. Such is the enchantment Don Quixote invokes to rationalize his defeats and embarrassments. Delusions of grandeur, conveniently enough, are sustained by phobias of persecution; somehow hostile enchanters always manage to get between him and the fulfillment of his ideals. Cervantes borrowed his plot from an interlude about a peasant bemused by popular ballads; and though that *donnée* is elaborated through an infinite series of variations, it remains almost repetitiously simple. Each episode is a kind of skit in which the protagonist, attempting to put his heroic ideals into action, is discomfited by realities in the shape of slapstick comedy.

Thus deeds, with a vengeance, comment on words; and Cervantes' formula is demonstrated again and again. Afterward there are more words, pleasant discussions, *"graciosos razonamientos"* — which naturally require the presence of an amusing companion, an interlocutor, a *gracioso*. The hero of cape-and-sword drama is squired by such a buffoon; the courtier is often burlesqued by the zany who serves him; Don Quixote's servant — like Figaro or Jeeves — is cleverer, in some vital respects, than his master. Much, possibly too much, has already been written on the dualism of Don Quixote and Sancho Panza as a symbolic representation of soul and body, past and present, poetry and prose, the inner dilemmas of psychology, or the all-embracing antitheses of metaphysics. We need only remind ourselves in passing that, within this eternal comedy team, Sancho Panza's role is to assert a sense of reality. The incident of the windmills provides him with his usual cue and his classical response. When the knight beholds these machines in the distance, and asks the squire whether he too does not behold those monstrous giants, it is Sancho's function to reply with another question: "What giants?" In his person the challenging voice of empiricism does its best and its worst to refute the aprioristic frame of mind, which has since become so closely identified with the Don that we sometimes term it *Quixotry*.

Now, on the comic stage, Sancho would have the final word. In the pictorial vision of Daumier, the pair coexist within the same frame of reference as the bourgeoisie and the caricatured intellectuals. Yet in a book, where words are the only medium, Don Quixote enjoys a decided advantage; the very weakness of his position in life lends strength, as it were, to his position in literature; in the field of action he may encounter discomfiture, but in the verbal sphere he soon resumes his imaginary career. When Sancho is skeptical about the basin and goes on to doubt the rewards of knighthood, the Don simply lapses into his autistic fantasies of wish-fulfillment; and his conversation during the next few pages spins out another romance in miniature. The most elaborate of the many little romances that run through his head and through the novel figures in his argument with the Canon of Toledo at the end of the First Part, and offers Cervantes occasion to develop his theory of the comic epic in prose. The Canon, on his side, is a more erudite humanist than Sancho Panza; but he casts the weight of his learning in favor of what the critics have labeled "probability"; and he pertinently distinguishes between fictitious and truthful histories (*historia imaginada, historia verdadera*).

Don Quixote's answer is a powerful statement of the appeal of romance. Freud would have diagnosed it as the purest indulgence in the pleasure-principle, the sheerest escape from the reality-principle. It is the daydream of a golden world of gardens and castles where art improves upon nature, where blandishing damsels await the errant adventurer and every misadventure leads toward a happy ending. It is a heady and concentrated restatement of the ever-appealing myth that, in Cervantes' day, incarnated its bland archetype in Amadís of Gaul. Amadís, like every true cavalier, was by definition a paragon who surpassed all other cavaliers; his invulnerable prowess was as unparalleled as the peerless beauty of his lady, Oriana, or the perfect faithfulness of his squire, Gandalín. He was predestined to triumph over an all but endless sequence of rivals and obstacles, and to be united with his heroine in an enchanted chamber which only the bravest and fairest could enter, somewhere out of this world on an uncharted island misleadingly named Terra Firma. Meanwhile the chronicle of his adventures and those of his progeny, prolonged through five generations and twenty-four volumes, furnished the primary source of inspiration for Don Quixote, whose pattern of behavior is — to speak it profanely — a kind of *imitatio Amadís*.

Imitation is the test that Cervantes proposes, knowing full well that when nature imitates art, art reveals its innate artificiality. Literally his hero reënacts episodes from the life-cycle of his own hero, as when he assumes the name of Beltenebros and undergoes penance in the Sierra Morena. But since he aspires to combine the virtues of other heroes — the Nine Worthies, the Twelve Paladins, the aggregate muster-roll of knight errantry — he must likewise emulate Ariosto's Orlando. And since Orlando went mad for love of the fair Angelica, Don Quixote must rage in order to prove his devotion to the fair Dulcinea del Toboso. The place-name he attaches to his kitchen-maid heroine is less aristocratic than anticlimactic, particularly when it is left to dangle as the refrain of one of the poems addressed to her. The process of emulation, dedicated to a whole set of models at once, going through their motions so pedantically and overstating their claims so fanatically, tends to reduce them all to absurdity. Because this tendency is deliberate, the prevailing method is that of parody: a marvelous gift, according to Ben Jonson, which makes a work "absurder than it was." But *Amadís de Gaula* could hardly have been absurder than it was; its innumerable sequels might almost have been parodies; while *Don Quixote* might be no more than another sequel, if it had no objective vantage-point from which to chart the deviations of its subjective course.

Its protagonist sallies forth at the outset, talking to himself — as will be his wont — about the historian who will have the honor of recording the exploits he is about to accomplish (I, ii). With a dizzying shift of the time-sense, he looks back from the future upon events which have yet to take place. From first to last the narration is colored by his own self-consciousness. A much later sally is introduced by this mock-heroic sentence: "Scarce had the silver morn given bright Phoebus leave with the ardor of his burning rays to dry the liquid pearls on his golden locks, when Don Quixote, shaking off sloth from his drowsy members, rose up and called Sancho his squire, that still lay snorting (II, xx)." Here, with the calculated anticlimax of the last word, all the mythological ornamentation sinks into bathos. Actuality, suddenly intervening, restores our perspective to a more firmly grounded base of observation. The high-flown monologue becomes a pedestrian dialogue, which in turn restates the dialectical issue of the book. Sancho Panza, the principal dialectician, is quite aware of that variance which makes his fall into a mere hole so utterly different from Don Quixote's exploration of the Cave of Montesinos: "There saw he goodly and pleasant visions and here, I believe, I shall see nothing but snakes and toads (II, lv)." The pleasant visions are abstract and remote; the snakes and toads are concrete and immediate; the variance is all in the point of view.

The psychological contrast is reflected in the stylistic texture from the opening page, where the first paragraph is straight factual exposition, while the second echoes two florid sentences from Don Quixote's reading. Diction shows the increasing influence of Sancho's viewpoint when — amid bouquets of poetic conceit and parades of learned authority, the regular mental context of Don Quixote — Cervantes apologizes for using the homely substantive *puercos*, and thereby calling a pig a pig. Once this sort of interplay has been established, Don Quixote himself can take the metaphorical step from the sublime to the ridiculous. When Sancho reports that Dulcinea's visage is slightly blemished by a mole, he can respond with an inappropriate amplification — "Though she had a hundred moles as well as that one thou sawest in her, they were not moles but moons and bright stars" — a pretty picture which outdoes even Shakespeare's hyperbolic gibes against the Petrarchan sonneteers (II, x). The gravity of his demeanor is matched by the grandiosity of his rhetoric, a manner of speaking broadly connoted by the rhetorical term *prosopopeya*. His dead-pan humor would not be humorous were some one else not there to see the joke, to watch the imitation becoming a parody by failing to meet the challenge at hand. As his purple passages are juxtaposed with Sancho's vernacular proverbs, the bookish and sluggish flow of his consciousness is freshened and quickened; flat assertion is rounded out, and soliloquy is colloquialized.

Cervantes, whose *Colloquy of the Dogs* we must not forget, was well schooled in those mixed modes of Erasmus and Lucian which — linking the early modern spirit to the late Greco-Roman — seem to express the self-questionings of a traditional culture during an epoch of rapid and far-reaching change. The literature of the Renaissance, which moves from one extreme to the other so readily, is the register of a violent effort to catch up with the expanding conditions of life. With its realization that certain themes are still untreated goes the feeling that certain techniques are becoming outmoded. The needed renewal and the strategic enlargement begin by adapting, experimenting, cross-fertilizing, and incidentally producing giants and dwarfs whose incongruous qualities merely bear witness to the overplus of creativity. Extraordinary combinations of language, such as macaronics, waver between Latinity and the vulgar tongues. Poetry, evoking the legendary past, varies its tone from nostalgia to facetiousness. Prose impinges, entirely unaware of its hybrid possibilities as an imaginative medium. A transitional sense of disproportion makes itself felt, not only in mannerist painting, but in complementary literary genres: mock-epic, which magnifies vulgarity, applying the grand manner to commonplace matters; and travesty, which minimizes greatness, reclothing noble figures in base attire.

It will easily be seen, from page to page, how Cervantes ranges between these two reductive extremes. One of his own descriptions of his style, at the beginning of the chapter before us, oscillates from high-sounding *("altisonante")* to trivial *("minima")*. This oscillation puzzled Shelton so much that he translated the latter word by one more congruent to the former: "divine" *(divina)*. However, Cervantes encompasses many such disparities, bridging the gap between style and subject by the continual play of his irony. Rabelais could revel in the *mélange des genres,* parodying the quest for the Holy Grail in the cult of the Holy Bottle. A lesser writer, Robert Greene, could live between two worlds and keep them apart: first-hand journalistic accounts of the London underworld and mannered pastoral romances set in some escapist Arcadia, with very little intermixture of styles. The immeasurable contribution of Cervantes was to broaden the province of prose fiction by bringing both realms together, not in a synthesis perhaps, but in the most durable antithesis that literature has known; by opening a colloquy between the romance and the picaresque, so to speak, between *Amadís de Gaula* and *Lazarillo de Tormes.* Spain, with its strongly marked chiaroscuro of contrasts, social as well as cultural, presented the pertinent matter of fact along with the far-fetched matter of fiction. The first-person narrative of the little beggar, Lazarillo, whose harsh masters taught him to cheat or be cheated, gave Cervantes the fructifying example for an exemplary novel to which *Don Quixote* refers, *Rinconete and Cortadillo* — a tale endearing to American readers as a Sevillian adumbration of *Tom Sawyer* and *Huckleberry Finn.*

II

Having proceeded discursively, after the fashion of Rocinante, we have come back to our starting point and are ready to set out once again. Our preliminary amble has not been wasted if it has confirmed our awareness of the "disorderly order" that regulates the imaginary gardens of Cervantes, and that may emerge from the passage to which we now return. After the gang of unfortunates bound for the galleys is released through the officiousness of Don Quixote, he is confounded by reality in the shifty person of their ringleader: a rogue indeed, the authentic picaroon, Ginés de Pasamonte. Ginés, among his other dubious traits, harbors pretensions as a man of letters; to beguile the time in prison, he declares, he has made a book out of the story of his life. This may strengthen the bonds of affinity that connect the present chapter with the life of Cervantes; for we know that the author was imprisoned, through some bureaucratic complication, during the period

when he was writing *Don Quioxte*; and he may be referring to
that circumstance, with his genius for rising above a situation,
when his prologue alludes to "some dark and noisome prison."
In any case, Don Quixote is curious about this particular product of incarcerated endeavors.

> "Is it so good a work?" said Don Quixote.
> "It is so good," replied Ginés, "that it quite puts down *Lazarillo
> de Tormes* and as many others as are written or shall write of that
> kind: for that which I dare affirm to you is that it treats of true acci-
> dents, and those so delightful that no like invention can be compared
> to them."
> "And how is the book entitled?" quoth Don Quixote.
> "It is called," said he, "*The Life of Ginés of Pasamonte.*"
> "And is it yet ended?" said the knight.
> "How can it be finished," replied he, "my life being not yet ended?"

To mention a work of fiction in the course of another work
of fiction can be a two-edged device. It can show up the book
that is mentioned, thereby sharpening the realism of the book
that does the mentioning. This is what Ginés does for his
own work at the expense of Lazarillo, and what Cervantes is
doing for *Don Quixote* at the expense of *Amadís de Gaula*,
expressly invoked by his own commendatory verses. Conversely, the invidious comparison can glance in the other direction, as in the case of many a derivative academic novel today:
the pale reflection of a dream of the shadow of Henry James.
But that is unmitigated imitation, and it produces a conventional literature, circumscribing novelists to the point where
even their titles must be quotations from other books. The
method of Cervantes utilized literary means to break through
literary conventions and, in the very process, invented a form
substantial and flexible enough to set forth the vicissitudes of
modern society. Parody, explicitly criticizing a mode of literature, developed into satire, implicitly criticizing a way of life.
Developing out of the debris of feudalism, the novel has waxed
and waned with the middle class. Yet in the twentieth century,
according to Thomas Mann's contemporary Faust, the arts
tend more than ever to parody themselves. The writer's problem, as André Gide has rephrased Cervantes' formula, is still

the rivalry between the real world and the representation we make of it.

It is significant that Gide's most serious novel, which likewise probes the theme of how novels come to be written, is called *The Counterfeiters*; and that Mann's last fragment — begun forty years before and completed only, in the peculiar sense of Ginés, by the author's death — is a reversion to the picaresque cycle, *Confessions of Felix Krull*. For trickery is inherent, as artists recognize, in their business of dealing with illusion. We do well then to scrutinize some of their tricks rather closely; and Cervantes is well justified in conveying this caveat, or insight, through the mouth of an incorrigible charlatan. After all, no one can express what is by nature inexpressible. Life itself is infinitely larger than any artistic medium. However, by revealing the limitations of their medium, writers like Cervantes heighten our consciousness of what existence means. The real story of Ginés de Pasamonte, comparatively more real than the imagined *Life of Lazarillo de Tormes*, is bound to be incomplete because life is endless. It lasts forever, as Tolstoy's peasant says just before he dies in *War and Peace*. In all sincerity, therefore, we cannot say *finis*; we can only write "to be continued." And so with Cervantes, like Ginés writing in prison, and breaking off his First Part with a provisory ending and a cautionary moral: Beware of fiction! It is fictitious; that is to say, it is false. Don't let it mislead you!

The ironic consequence of his warning was the creation of an archetype, a fictional personage destined to be far more influential than Amadís of Gaul. The remarkable success of the First Part was the precondition of the Second, which is consequently more deliberate in its artistry. By that time, the latter volume announces, the fame of its predecessor has spread so widely that any lean horse would be hailed as Rocinante. The earlier conclusion, in which so little was concluded, clearly invited some continuation. Before Cervantes could take up his own tale again, the interloper who signed himself "Avellaneda" brought out his notorious sequel: an imitation of a parody. Because the impersonation had to be imitative, it could not be organic; it could not live and grow as Cervantes' original would do in his Second Part. The mysterious Avellaneda, when Cervantes finally caught up with him, all but took the place of Amadís as a satirical target, and as a measure of the distance between echoed phrases and lived experiences. Adding insult to injury, he had not only plagiarized; he had also criticized his victim for not keeping his own brain-children in character, and — even more significantly — for introducing Ginés. That scoundrel had shown a comparable ingratitude when he rewarded his liberator with a shower of stones, absconding with Don Quixote's sword and — temporarily — Sancho Panza's ass. But the Second Part arranges a further encounter and, for the knight, an opportune revenge.

This involves our second illustration, a rather more extended example which need not be cited at length, since it figures so prominently in the celebrated episode of Master Peter's puppet-show. Poetic drama — another genre which Cervantes had practiced with indifferent results — is here reduced to its most elementary level, just as prose fiction was in the instance we have been discussing. The link between these two passages, as we learn from the next chapter, is Maese Pedro himself, who turns out to be none other than Don Quixote's old enemy, Ginés. Always the escape-artist, he is now an itinerant showman, and more of a dealer in deception than ever. One of his other exhibits happens to be a fortune-telling ape, whose roguish trick is subsequently exposed. Now Cervantes was obviously fond of animals; a dog-lover and a master of the beast-fable, he satirizes war in a parable about braying asses and courtly love in a serenade of cats; the dramatis personae of his book include a traveling menagerie; but the ape, above all, is the parodistic animal. When the lovelorn Dorothea joins the friendly conspiracy to bring the knight to his senses, she poses as the Infanta Micomica of Micomicón ("Princess Monkey-Monkey of Monkeyland"). Actually a damsel in distress, she acts the part of a damsel in distress; and the make-believe story she recounts to Don Quixote is the parody of a parody, her own story.

This monkey-business, if it may be so designated, accelerates to its climax through a sequence of scenes at the inn. There the incidental stories accumulate, and there the actual personages who tell or figure in them are interrelated through the fiat of romantic coincidence. Viktor Shklovsky has aptly described this meeting-place as "a literary inn," though another emphasis would interpret it as a social microcosm. On the one hand, the relationship between letters and arms is the appropriate topic of Don Quixote's discourse; on the other, the crude farce of the wineskins and the stern intervention of the Holy Brotherhood, searching for the importunate busybody who freed the convicts, underline the romance with a touch of reality. The central interpolation is a tale which comes out of the same bag of manuscripts as some of Cervantes' *Exemplary Novels* — or so the literary host very plausibly informs his guests. It is the tale of the so-called Curious Impertinent, an almost Proustian study in point of view, wherein Anselmo's universal suspicion functions as a sort of mirror-opposite for Don Quixote's ubiquitous credulity. Characterization of the protagonist gains in depth as he passes through the levels of the characters who surround him, in their assumed roles, with their recounted adventures — sometimes tales within tales. As in Chaucer's *Canterbury Tales*, the story-tellers take on an extra dimension against the formal backdrop of their stories.

Part I situates these episodes, within the tradition of the frame-story, at an extra remove from the reader. In Part II, as the narrator proudly explains, they are unified by the divagations of a single plot. Where the First Part centered upon an inn, which the hero insisted on taking for a castle, the Second Part leads to a long sojourn at a genuine castle, where the conversation is less inspired and the horseplay heavier than at any other juncture of the book. Castles in Spain, for non-Spaniards, have proverbially symbolized the veritable fabric of romance. "Castle-building," in the library at Waverley Honour, was the state of mind that engendered the latter-day romances of Sir Walter Scott. The terrain of Don Quixote, the arid region of La Mancha, overlaps Castille, which is quite literally the land of castles. But Cervantes' castle seems to mark an anticlimactic turning point, a release from mental imprisonment, the beginning of an undeception for the knight;

while it bewitches the squire, offering him a brief chance to
go his own way and to impose the rough justice of the common
man on the neighboring dependency of Barataria. Overshadowed by that glimpse of a democratic community, or the
disillusioning city of Barcelona just ahead, chivalric entertainment may well pall. Not that the Duke and Duchess have
spared any courtesy; they have humored their fantastic guest
with such labored vivacity that they are accused of being
madder than he; there has been more manipulation and masquerading, more play-acting and practical joking, at the castle
than at the inn.

The effectiveness of the play-within-the-play lies in making
the main drama more convincing: when the King interrupts the
Players in *Hamlet*, we feel that at last we have come to grips
with reality. One way of attaining this effect is to make the
theatrical figures unconvincing; and when these are puppets
rather than actors, wooden dolls imitating human beings,
everything undergoes a reduction of scale; their performance
becomes a mode of ridicule, as Bergson has suggested in his
essay on laughter. Hence, among the many stratagems that
Cervantes employs against the romance, none is more sharply
conceived nor more skillfully executed than the puppet-play.
His description of it commences in epic style, with the specta-
tors — Tyrians and Trojans — falling silent, and the youthful
reciter appealing to the authority of old French chronicles
and Spanish ballads (II, xxvi). The setting is a city whose
ancient name, Sansueña, suffuses a dreamy atmosphere. The
plot concerns the Princess Melisendra, imprisoned by the
Moors even as Cervantes himself has been, and her knightly
rescuer, Gaiferos, who must accomplish his task by fighting
the Moors as Cervantes has done — but with a difference, that
crucial difference between fantasy and actuality which it is his
constant purpose to emphasize.

For once Don Quixote has no need to superimpose his
fancies; he need only take the presentation literally. As a matter
of fact, he starts by criticizing certain details of Moorish local
color. Gradually he suspends his disbelief — which has never
been too strong — and enters into the spirit of the occasion so

actively that, before the others can stop him, he has begun
"to rain strokes upon the puppetish Moorism." The puppeteer,
Ginés alias Pedro, cries: "Hold, Señor Don Quixote, hold! and
know that these you hurl down, destroy, and kill, are not real
Moors but shapes made of pasteboard." And reality is restored
no less abruptly than it is when Alice cries out to the creatures
of Wonderland: "You're nothing but a pack of cards!" Pedro-
Ginés, the arch-manipulator, the ever versatile illusionist, laments his loss for an operatic moment or two, and then
shrewdly reckons it up: so much for Charlemagne split down
the middle, so much for Melisendra without a nose, and so
on down to the last marivedi, paid in full by Don Quixote in
coin of the realm. Such mercenary language contrasts with
another aspect of the show: the puppets were knocked down,
we are told, "in less than two credos." This is rather a figure of
speech than an article of belief; and the wax candles probably
have no ritual significance; yet it is worth remembering that
the word *retablo*, applied to the puppet-show, signifies primarily an altarpiece. I do not want to place undue stress on symbols which prove so brittle; but we cannot altogether ignore
the iconoclasm of Cervantes, since the Inquisition did not.

In the next chapter, when the narrator swears to his own
veracity as a Catholic Christian, the author himself feels
obliged to point out that this protestation comes from an un-
believing Moor (II, xxvii). Elsewhere he repeatedly warns us
that Moors are not to be trusted: they are "cheaters, impostors,
and chemists" (II, iii). Cervantes' fictional narrator is one of
these elusive infidels: an "Arabical and Manchegan historiographer" named the Cide Hamete Benengeli, who does not
appear in the opening pages of the book. Don Quixote completes his first sally, saunters forth again, challenges the Bis-
cayan, and is left sword in air by the break between the seventh
and eighth chapters. In a digression, Cervantes tells us that his
documentation has run out, and that we might well have been
left in suspense forever; again, as in the later colloquy between
Don Quixote and Ginés, life is conceived as an unfinished
book. Happily, in a bazaar at Toledo, Cervantes has chanced
upon an Arabic manuscript which will supply the rest of the

story; and from now on the Cide Hamete will be responsible for it, even as Captain Clutterbuck or Jedediah Cleishbotham would be responsible for Scott's narrations, and other pseudonymous narrators for Stendhal's and Manzoni's. Since the author presents himself as editor, assuming the intervention of a Spanish translator from the Arabic, the text stands at three removes from ourselves, enriched with afterthoughts like a palimpsest. This procedure has the advantages of enabling the author to digress more freely, to blame his source for indiscreet remarks, and to cultivate an air of authenticity.

But authenticity is deeply called into question on one problematic occasion, when the whole trend of the book is reversed, turning back from pragmatic demonstration to metaphysical speculation, or — in the more incisive phrase of Américo Castro — from a critique of fiction to a critique of reality. Can men's lives be so sharply differentiated from their dreams, when all is said and done? Can we live without illusion? we are asked. Don Quixote may be right, the rest of us wrong. Many of the philosophers, most of the poets, would take his side. Spanish imagination is not unique in having been fascinated by Calderón's refrain: *La vida es sueño*, life is a dream. Even Shakespeare conceded the possibility: "We are such stuff/As dreams are made on . . ." Who are we, in that event, to look down upon puppets imprisoned within the dream-city of Sansueña? May it not be that the images of ourselves created by writers, as Pirandello would urge, are more real than we are? For example, *Don Quixote*. The chapter that explores such ultimate doubts is admittedly apocryphal; it may be an intermixture of truth and falsehood, as pantomimed by Maese Pedro's ape. We are tempted to believe that Don Quixote's descent into the Cave of Montesinos is a return to the deep well of the past, the unconscious memory of the race, and that the mythical heroes sleeping there personify the ideals he struggled to practice, the ideology of the Golden Age. Yet the simple and brutal alternative persists that he may have been caught in a lie and have become a party to the general imposture.

In the absence of other witnesses, certainty continues to elude us. The best advice Don Quixote can report is the gambler's maxim spoken, curiously enough, by the flower and mirror of chivalry, Durandarte: *Paciencia y barajar*, patience and shuffle, go on with the game (II, xxiii). After the underground interview with the dead heroes, the next stage is the fable about the asses, and then the puppetry of Pedro-Ginés; and each successive chapter is a station on the pilgrimage of disenchantment. Disarmed, dismounted, and finally discomfited, the former knight is on his way homeward, when the sight of shepherds rouses his flagging impulses to their last wish-dream. Sancho, of course, has an important part in it:

"I'll buy sheep and all things fit for our pastoral vocation; and calling myself by the name of shepherd Quixotiz and thou the shepherd Pansino, we will walk up and down the hills, through woods and meadows, singing and versifying and drinking the liquid crystal of the fountains, sometimes out of the clear springs and then out of the swift-running rivers. . ." (II, lxvii).

But Don Quixote has come to the end of his life and, accordingly, of his book. It remained for other books to parody the pastoral romances, as his had parodied the romances of chivalry: notably a French disciple of Cervantes, Charles Sorel, who wrote a novel entitled *Anti-Romance*, and subtitled *The Wayward Shepherd* (*L'Anti-roman, ou le berger extravagant*). That would be another story; but perhaps the term *anti-romance* might be usefully borrowed to generalize a major premise of the modern novel, from Fielding, who began as Cervantes' professed imitator by lampooning Richardson, to Jane Austen, who sharpened her acute discriminations on Gothic romances and novels of sensibility:

Charming as were all of Mrs. Radcliffe's works, and charming even as were the works of all her imitators, it was not in them perhaps that human nature, at least in the midland counties of England, was to be looked for.

The time, the place, and the style of *Northanger Abbey* have little in common with Cervantes; but his protean formula has held, as it has been readjusted to varying situations through the lengthy record of Don Quixote's posthumous adventures.

One of the many female Quixotes has been Madame Bovary; one of the many Russian Quixotes has been Prince Myshkin. Heinrich Heine summed up the romantic movement as a school of Quixotry when he exclaimed: "Jean-Jacques Rousseau was my Amadís of Gaul!" In a parallel vein, it might be argued that Voltaire's Amadís of Gaul was Leibniz, that Tolstoy's was Napoleon, or Mark Twain's Baedeker. The number of specific instances would seem to indicate some broader principle, such as André Malraux has recently formulated in his illustrated treatise on the creative imagination. His dictum — that every artist begins with *pastiche* — is highly illuminating, so far as it goes; it has to be qualified only by recognizing that *pastiche* implies both activities which we have associated and distinguished, imitation and parody. The novelist must begin by playing the sedulous ape, assimilating the craft of his predecessors; but he does not master his own form until he has somehow exposed and surpassed them, passing from the imitation of art through parody to the imitation of nature.

Don Quixote and Moby-Dick

This article — with somewhat fuller bibliographical apparatus — was contributed to the quadricentennial volume, Cervantes across the Centuries, *edited by Angel Flores and M. J. Bernardete and published by the Dryden Press (New York, 1947), with whose permission it is republished. It was translated into Spanish for the Cervantes issue of* Realidad *(Buenos Aires), II, 5 (September–October, 1947). It was also the basis of a lecture on "Cervantes and Melville" in the commemoration at Harvard University on October 23, 1947. I should like to thank the Committee on Higher Degrees in American Civilization at Harvard for the opportunity to utilize Melville's annotated copy of* Don Quixote *and other items from the collection of his books and manuscripts in the Houghton Library. What I have said regarding the untraced role of Cervantes in American literature is happily no longer justified. An article by M. F. Heiser appeared, coincidentally with mine, in the* Hispanic Review. *And we may now also refer to the broad conspectus of Stanley T. Williams,* The Spanish Background of American Literature.

▰▰▰

I

The profoundest tribute to Cervantes is that which other writers have paid him by imitation and emulation. It goes too deep to be altogether reducible to terms of conscious literary influence; it springs from the almost Homeric circumstances that made him the first to master a genre which — through that very process of mastery — has come to predominate in modern literature. *Don Quixote* is thus an archetype as well as an example, the exemplary novel of all time. Not only has its characterization invited an endless round of sequels, from Avellaneda to Kafka, but its conception has enabled later novelists to unfix a whole series of preconceived ideas, with consequences that range from *Candide* to *War and Peace*. Each of the major European cultures, it may be said, has provided characteristic variations on the theme of Quixotry, *mutatis mutandis* adapting itself to the uses of French realism, British humor, German metaphysics, or even the exploration of the Russian soul. Scholars and critics have traced this chronicle of adaptation in fascinating detail. We must not infer, from the fact that Don Quixote's adventures in North America are still untraced, that Cervantes was unimitated or unemulated here.

That story would begin, if we sought to recount it, when the translations of Charles Jervas, Smollett, and others were imported along with the eighteenth-century English novel. The most significant early product of this cross-fertilization would be H. H. Brackenridge's *Modern Chivalry*, which first appeared in 1792. Not feudal but democratic institutions are there subjected to a genial criticism which, in some respects, anticipates Tocqueville. The chivalrous figure of Captain Farrago, a whimsical observer of human nature, is gradually eclipsed by the political career of his servant, the Irish bog-trotter, Teague O'Regan. Perhaps it would be self-explanatory to mention — along with the name of the author, Tabitha Tenney — the title of her book: *Female Quixotism, Exhibited in the Romantic Opinions and Extravagant Adventures of Dorcasina Sheldon*. This cautionary tale of an incorrigibly susceptible spinster, written in 1800, lacks the animation of its English forerunner, *The Female Quixote* by Charlotte Lennox, who coincidentally had been born in this country. With Washington Irving's *Knickerbocker History of New York*, we should come much closer to the mainstream of American letters. Irving himself, if not his Peter Stuyvesant, "had studied for years in the chivalrous library of Don Quixote." Among his later projects, for which he gathered documents, was a life of Cervantes. His interest in everything Spanish would be matched on more academic levels by the work of Ticknor, Prescott, and Longfellow.

At first glance it might seem that a culture which prided it-

self upon being so matter-of-fact and getting so close to nature
would spontaneously express itself in realism and naturalism.
Yet our greatest writers functioned in the atmosphere of
romanticism. The enchantments of the Gothic, rather than
the disenchantments of the picaresque, enlisted the genius of
Poe. Hawthorne, who had encouraged his sister to translate
Cervantes' *Exemplary Novels*, eschewed the contemporary form
of the novel for his own particular version of the romance —
for a tradition of fiction, half didactic and half poetic, which
he had derived from the religious allegory and the philosophical tale. In weighing the claims of the present against those of
the past, *The House of the Seven Gables*, like many of his
stories, gives a New England inflection to the argument of
Cervantes' antiromance. But the resolution of *The Marble
Faun* is predicated upon a nostalgic return to the storied ruins
of the old world. Following Hawthorne's footsteps, and writing
his biography, Henry James lamented the numerous ivy-
covered items of high civilization that were so conspicuous by
their absence from the American scene. Though James's passionate pilgrims seem Quixotic rather than Cervantesque, it
is the intrusion of mundane realities upon their personal ideal-
isms that constitutes the drama of their lives.

The opposite point of view, the new world's critique of
Europe, is bumptiously personified by Mark Twain's *Innocents
Abroad*. His tirade on "Castles and Culture" in *Life on the
Mississippi* attacked the nineteenth-century revival of medieval
architecture, and deplored the debilitating influence of Sir
Walter Scott upon the South. His *Connecticut Yankee in King
Arthur's Court*, designed as a streamlined revision of *Don
Quixote*, today appears more dated than its model. It is noteworthy, however, that when a school of American naturalists
finally arose, their leader turned out to be a lifelong admirer
of Cervantes. W. D. Howells has left a memorable description
of how, as a boy on a farm in Ohio, he was originally affected
by the narrative of the ingenious *hidalgo*. "I believe that its
free and simple design, where event follows event without the
fettering control of intrigue, but where all grows naturally out
of character and conditions, is the supreme form of fiction,"

Howells adds, "and I cannot help thinking that if we ever have a great American novel, it must be built upon such large and noble lines." A recent critic and novelist, Edward Dahlberg, has reaffirmed this belief; but it is precisely the effort to transcend a photographic naturalism, to visualize an enchanted helmet in a barber's basin, that he calls upon his contemporaries to make.

It is not so much the letter as the spirit of Cervantes that the critical realists of our own period call to mind. If the mock-heroine of Sinclair Lewis' *Main Street* recoils before the drabness of Gopher Prairie, she has a more immediate exemplar in Flaubert's female Quixote, Emma Bovary, dreaming at Yonville-l'Abbaye. James Farrell's anti-hero, Studs Lonigan, may not be a studious admirer of Amadís of Gaul; but the movies and tabloids have colored his fantasies to the point where all experience is a grim disillusionment. The mood of *desengaño* has seldom been probed more desperately than in the train of novels that followed the First World War: Ernest Hemingway's embittered account of the retreat from Caporetto, for example, ends by questioning all such abstract words as "glory" and "honor," and by accepting only place-names and concrete numbers. Nowhere is there a greater disparity than in America, Jean-Paul Sartre has recently observed, "between men and myths, real life and the collective representation of it." Hence the formula that Cervantes discovered is peculiarly applicable. In a broader sense, the arid region of La Mancha is timeless and placeless. It bears a striking resemblance to that expatriate wasteland which T. S. Eliot invokes, ever awaiting its wounded hero whose quest is the promise of ultimate fertility.

II

No American author, however, can more fitly be compared with Cervantes than Herman Melville. The harsh schools in which the two men educated themselves were immeasurably far apart: a whaling ship, Melville boasted, was both Yale and Harvard to him. Yet a sailor in the South Sea islands may learn, even as a soldier in Algerian captivity, to make life itself a commentary on book-learning. Melville's seafaring bookishness possessed the measurable advantage of also including *Don Quixote* within its ken. He has not registered for us, as Howells did, the actual impact of discovery; but *White-Jacket*, published in 1850, describes a Quixotic shipmate who read the book and only became more confirmed in his native Quixotism. The autobiographical hero of *Redburn*, published in 1849, runs truer to type: the young American's expectations of Europe, nourished upon a quaint old guidebook, are undeceived by the slums of Liverpool. In the same year Melville bought a copy of *Guzmán de Alfarache*; again, the following year, he borrowed *Lazarillo de Tormes*; he had previously demonstrated his thorough acquaintance with Smollett and other English masters of the picaresque.

At London, in December 1849, while arranging for the publication of *White-Jacket*, he picked up the Second Folio of Beaumont and Fletcher. According to the flyleaf, he spent New Year's Day, 1850, at sea; his homeward journey was lightened by reading these plays, several of which draw their plots or characters from Cervantes. To judge from his markings, he was particularly interested in *The Knight of the Burning Pestle*, which closely parallels the situation of *Don Quixote*. "A hit at Shakespeare in Hotspur," he notes in the margin, where the grocer's apprentice parodies the famous speech on honor, thereby bracketing two Elizabethan plays in which the chivalric way of life conflicts with more bourgeois standards of comfort and common sense. It is worth the trouble of gathering up these stray indications, because Melville was to spend the next year in the composition of *Moby-Dick*; and though his masterpiece — as we shall find — attests his profound admiration for Cervantes explicitly as well as implicitly, the Jervas translation of *Don Quixote* (Philadelphia: Blanchard and Lea) that survived in Melville's library was not actually printed until 1853, two years after *Moby-Dick*. "H. Melville, Sep. 18 '55" is penciled in his own hand on the verso of the flyleaf to the first volume. Pencilings throughout the two volumes seem to indicate that Melville, having purchased this new edition, gave the novel a careful rereading shortly thereafter.

A comprehensive study of Melville's reading would reveal

much about his writing, and even more about his thinking, especially during that later period when he seldom put his thoughts into his own words. He used his books as journals, choosing minds that reflected his own, and bringing out — by a sequence of annotations, underscorings, and checks — the latently Melvillian aspect of whatever he read. Such marks, in his copy of *Don Quixote*, are frequent and consistent. Some of them seem to be merely guideposts: notable chapters checked against the table of contents. Again, the backleaf of the second volume contains a list of references to the Cid Hamet; the man that spoke through Ishmael evidently had a special interest in Cervantes' Arabic narrator. But he was more interested, as marginal lines make clear, in discussions of knight-errantry. Agreeing with the humanitarian school of commentators, he emphatically approves of a sentence in Louis Viardot's introductory memoir: "Don Quixote is but the case of a man of diseased brain; his monomania is that of a good man who revolts at injustice, and who would exalt virtue." The object and inspiration of his quest, the fair Dulcinea, is often signalized by Melville's pencil. Her knight's defense of courtly love prompts Melville to append his most revealing note. Don Quixote's words are: "I have already often said it, and now repeat it, that a knight-errant without a mistress is like a tree without leaves, a building without cement, a shadow without a body that causes it." To which Melville, with an asterisk, adds:

or as Confucius said 'a dog without a master,' or, to drop both Cervantes & Confucius parables — a god-like mind without a God.

Thus the significance of Cervantes' absent heroine is momentarily transposed into Melville's key; she is the symbol of an elusive faith. And if she incarnates — or rather etherealizes — womanhood for Don Quixote, his relationship with his fellow men is symbolized in the person of Sancho Panza. From the initial pun on *hombre de bien*, which Jervas translates "an honest man (if such an epithet may be given to one that is poor)," Melville gives the squire his most serious regard. The social theme, even more than the philosophical, is the leitmotif he seems most anxious to score. Though he stresses democratic implications more heavily than his text may warrant, it must be admitted that Cervantes has furnished him with congenial passages on the dangers of authority and the blessings of liberty. With Don Quixote himself, Melville justifies the liberation of the convicts bound for the galleys, and sympathizes with the impoverished suitor at Camacho's wedding. He is impressed by the Spanish proverb, if not by Sancho's application: "There are but two families in the world, as my grandmother used to say, the *haves* and the *have nots*, and she stuck to the former." To this the sadder and wiser Sancho of the Second Part, on attaining his governorship, supplies a retort which Melville has also checked: ". . . while we are asleep, the great and the small, the poor and the rich, are all equal." Equality and love — the two themes blend in the meal with the goatherds that evokes Don Quixote's vision of the Golden Age. A double line marks Melville's enthusiasm for the knight's invitation to the squire:

> "That you may see, Sancho, the intrinsic worth of knight-erranty [*sic*], and how fair a prospect its meanest retainers have of speedily gaining the respect and esteem of the world, I will that you sit here by my side, in company with these good folks, and that you be one and the same thing with me, who am your master and natural lord; that you eat from off my plate, and drink of the same cup in which I drink; for the same may be said of knight-erranty, which is said of love, that it makes all things equal."

The light in which Melville must have reread Cervantes is caught in the introductory sketch of *The Piazza Tales*, where the enchantments of the Berkshire landscape remind him of "Don Quixote, that sagest sage that ever lived." By the end of that year, 1856, he had embarked upon a Mediterranean voyage, which was to stimulate further reminiscences in his *Journal up the Straits*: "At noon, off Algiers. In the vicinity beautiful residence among the hills. White house among gardens. Reminded one of passages in Don Quixotte [*sic*], 'Story of the Morisco.'" This episode — with the one that comes closest to Cervantes' own adventures, "The Captive's Story" — must have furnished more than a hint for Melville's powerful tale of a Spanish captain and a slave mutiny, *Benito Cereno*, with its atmospheric tension of mingled races and its sense of grim realities smouldering beneath romantic surfaces. But the greatest fiction is never an escape; it is a means of apprehending "more reality than real life itself can show," as Melville argued in the last novel he published, *The Confidence-Man*, which had just appeared when he returned to America in 1857. The truly original characters of literature, for him, are as rare and impressive as revolutionary philosophers or religious prophets. They illuminate everything around them "so that, in certain minds, there follows upon the adequate conception of such a character, an effect, in its way, akin to that which in Genesis attends upon the beginnings of things." Each of the three examples that Melville mentions — Hamlet, Don Quixote, and Milton's Satan — had such an effect, a creative impact, upon his own conceptions.

III

Melville's comments on *Don Quixote*, then, display a set of attitudes which he himself had crystallized five years before in *Moby-Dick*: a questioning of the nature of reality and an affirmation of the brotherhood of man. Nor can it be doubted that previous acquaintance with Cervantes' seminal work had suggested some of the technical features of his own. In its picaresque structure he found that free and simple design which, according to Howells, would characterize the great American novel. The course set by the *Pequod*, sailing across the high seas, continues and enlarges the pilgrimage of Rocinante, ambling along the highroads of La Mancha. The large, loose plot is integrated again by a single character: a monomaniac protagonist who, by dominating all that surrounds him, fulfills Melville's definition of literary originality. And though his style shows a temperamental affinity, rather than any specific indebtedness to the prose of the Castilian master, yet each achieves a richness of texture unique in his respective language by ranging freely from salty colloquialism to empurpled rhetoric. Though neither seriously pretended to be a man of learning, professional *Cervantistas* and Melvillians have demonstrated their own scholarship by documenting the hard-won humanism of the two, thereby indicating further analogies in the eclectic and independent use both novelists made of the traditional cultures that lay behind them.

No two novels would satisfy, better than *Don Quixote* and *Moby-Dick*, the Canon of Toledo's criteria for an epic in prose. Yet *Don Quixote* is a mock-epic, as well as an anti-romance: its Homeric catalogue introduces an army of sheep. Whereas the purpose of *Moby-Dick* is to cast a romantic and heroic glow over its subject: not to exorcise demons but to conjure them up, to speak of the Captain's mess as if it were Belshazzar's feast. For the later book, as for the earlier one, the point of departure is a library; a host of quotations on cetology, compiled by a sub-sub-librarian, replaces the authorities on chivalry; and whales are classified bibliographically in terms of folios, octavos, and duodecimos. On behalf of "the honor and glory of whaling" Melville stands ever ready to break a lance, split a helmet, and unhorse the gentle reader; he even undertakes to prove that whalemen liberated South America "from the yoke of old Spain." The doubloon nailed to the mast, "so Spanishly poetic," is transmogrified like the Helmet of Mambrino, while the Whiteness of the Whale signifies all things to all men. Where Cervantes undermines romance with realism, Melville lures us from a literal to a symbolic plane, turning nautical yarns into metaphysical flights and offering us "the Phaedon instead of Bowditch." His savage and sordid crew, under the influence of their phantom quarry, come to show "a certain generous knight-errantism," not unlike the Crusaders of old.

If, then to meanest mariners, and renegades and castaways, I shall hereafter ascribe high qualities, though dark; wave round them tragic graces; if even the most mournful, perchance the most abased, among them all, shall at times lift himself to the exalted mounts; if I shall touch that workman's arm with some ethereal light; if I shall spread a rainbow over his disastrous set of sun; then against all mortal critics bear me out in it, thou just Spirit of Equality, which hast spread one royal mantle of humanity over all my kind! Bear me out in it, thou great democratic God! who didst not refuse to the swart convict,

Bunyan, the pale, poetic pearl; Thou who didst clòthe with doubly hammered leaves of finest gold, the stumped and paupered arm of old Cervantes; Thou who didst pick up Andrew Jackson from the pebbles; who didst hurl him upon a war-horse; who didst thunder him higher than a throne! Thou who, in all Thy mighty, earthly marchings, ever cullest Thy selectest champions from the kingly commons; bear me out in it, O God!

The reverberating credo here enunciated is the avowal of Melville's belief in democracy itself, in the dignity of labor and the potentialities of every man to be president, genius, or hero. Hereupon the outcast narrator, Ishmael, proceeds from his "knights" to his "squires," from the mates to the harpooneers and finally the common seamen. Most of them, he tells us, are islanders, "each Isolato living on a separate continent of his own," and yet their individualistic energies are harnessed by the *Pequod*, "federated along one keel." The plight of the drowning castaway, set forth in Father Mapple's sermon on Jonah, conveys a terrifying sense of isolation. The same object-lesson was preached, in benignly classical rather than sternly biblical terms, with Don Quixote's apostrophe to the Golden Age: that primitive community where men lived happily together without owning property or waging war. When Sancho Panza became Governor of Barataria, he attempted to practice his master's preaching, and adumbrated the tragicomic pattern of democratic action. It is not without significance that his so-called island was actually a part of the mainland. His Melvillian counterpart is the harpooneer Queequeg, whose companionship resolves Ishmael's dilemma between society and solitude. Queequeg, a "George Washington cannibalistically developed," embodies the human condition as Melville had glimpsed it in *Typee* and *Omoo*: the peace and joy of "one insular Tahiti" which lies in the soul of man. That Queequeg's dark canoe, designed as a coffin, should be Ishmael's life buoy when the others meet death by water, is Melville's final paradox on life-in-death.

Cervantes, the realist, dissolved Don Quixote's fantasies in the bright light of the comic spirit; only the ambiguous Cavern of Montesinos left any room for illusion. For Melville, the idealist, visible objects are "pasteboard masks," and the tragedy is that man — in striking through them — fails to apprehend the mysteries they prefigure. For Captain Ahab, the white whale is "the monomaniac incarnation of all those malicious agencies which some deep men feel eating in them," all too tangibly evil in contradistinction to the evanescent goodness of Dulcinea. His mania fills him with a Quixotic consciousness of his mission: "I am the Fates' lieutenant. I act under orders." But if he can say, "my means are sane, my motive and object mad," the exact opposite may be said of Don Quixote, whose motives are admirable but in whose method there is madness. Neither is destined, like Bunyan's pilgrim, to attain his object: one, unhorsed, is trundled away in a cage, while the other, "dismasted," rages in a straitjacket. The fatal pride, the "irresistible dictatorship," the sinister hints thrown out — "that deadly scrimmage with the Spaniard afore the altar at Santa" — these tragic faults could be summed up in a Cervantesque epithet, *el curioso impertinente*. To make Don Quixote the butt of their jests, the others were always play-acting; to consecrate his ill-fated harpoon, Ahab stages a solemn drama; he enacts the role of Shakespeare's King Lear, in whose madness Melville detected the voice of truth. The sphinxlike heads of whales are Platonic and Kantian; the waves are Cartesian, the elements Spinozistic; but none of these natural philosophers will satisfy Ahab's doubts. To the end he is "a grand, ungodly, godlike man" — and afterwards his creator will observe that a knight without a mistress resembles "a god-like mind without a god."

The relation of *Moby-Dick* to *Don Quixote* is neither close nor similar; it is complementary and dialectical. One proposes worldly wisdom as the touchstone for an outworn set of ideals; the other, abandoning economic values, goes questing after a transcendental faith. Where Cervantes, whose skepticism was less fundamental, objectively jested at social inequalities, the failure of Melville's subjective idealism threw him back upon the only God he perceived — that Spirit of Equality which ends by leveling Ahab and confounding his quest in a shipwreck. The allegory and satire of *Mardi* had not clarified man's posi-

tion in the cosmos; they had merely implied that he was both
the pursuer and the pursued. With *Pierre*, immediately after
Moby-Dick, Melville dramatized the problem more explicitly;
he might have been referring to Ahab or Don Quixote when
he registered the doctrine "that in things terrestrial . . . a
man must not be governed by ideas celestial." When he wrote
The Confidence-Man, at about the time he was rereading *Don
Quixote*, he seems to have exchanged his Quixotry for mis-
anthropy. The theme is not illusion but delusion; the protagonist is not a dupe but a quack; and the moral is succinctly expressed in the barber's sign: "No Trust." Even so, the author
laments, in one of his many excursions on the art of fiction:
"After poring over the best novels professing to portray
human nature, the studious youth will still run risk of being
too often at fault upon actually entering the world."

What followed for Melville, at all events, was a period of
virtual literary retirement. Therein we find him, after fifteen
or twenty years, turning back to the subject once more — and,
on this last occasion, confronting it directly. Don Quixote is
the hero of a very brief poem left unpublished by Melville
among his "Jack Gentian" manuscripts. Its title, "The Rusty
Man," is joined to a parenthetical afterthought, a subtitle
transcribed by Raymond Weaver as " (By a soured one)."
Though the more recent editor of Melville's poems, Howard
P. Vincent, corrects several errors of earlier transcription, he
accepts this reading. But here the enigma of Melville's self-
characterization is reflected even in his handwriting. Another
practiced reader of it, Jay Leyda, suggests that Melville wrote
"timid" instead of "soured," which is no more in keeping with
his tone than with his hand. I should be tempted farther,
possibly emending "timid" to "tired"; but the heavily revised
manuscript, as I try to read it, seems to bear out Mr. Leyda's
conjecture. The poet conceives himself in the role of the dis-
appointed knight back among his books:

> In la Mancha he mopeth
>   With beard thin and dusty;
> He doteth and mopeth
>   In library fusty —

> 'Mong his old folios gropeth:
> Cites obsolete saws
> Of Chivalry's laws —
> *Be the wronged one's knight*:

Originally Melville seems to have concluded with a single additional line: "Seek the San Graal's light." But he deleted this conclusion and added five more lines, in which romantic altruism is tempered by cynical resignation:

> Die, but do right.
> So he rusts and musts,
> While each grocer green
> Thriveth apace with fulsome face
> Of a fool serene.

The most significant variants are "beggar's" which has been replaced by the more abstract "wronged one's" in the eighth line, and "philistine" for the less tendentious "grocer green" in the eleventh. The poem seems to trail off rather shakily; but that would seem to complete the identification; and Melville's ending is Cervantes' beginning.

Balzac and Proust

*In a series of exercises commemorating the hundredth anni-
versary of Balzac's death, this lecture was given at Columbia
University on March 17, 1950. A French translation was included in the* Hommage à Balzac *published under the auspices
of UNESCO and under the imprint of the* Mercure de France
*during that centennial year. Through the courtesy of the edi-
tors of that volume, the original English version is printed
here for the first time. An Italian translation by Luigi Berti
appeared in* Inventario, III, 4 *(Spring, 1951). More recently,
our impression of Proust's concern with Balzac has been
strengthened by the publication of new material from his*
cahiers. *The posthumous fragment edited by Bernard de
Fallois as* Le Balzac de Monsieur de Guermantes *(1950), which
finds a place among the other relevant fragments in the same
editor's* Contre Sainte-Beuve *(1954), is a strong link between
Proust's self-expressed critical opinions and the fictional use he
makes of Balzac in* A la recherche du temps perdu. *His rediscovered early novel,* Jean Santeuil *(1952), in its youthful bookishness, has a good deal to say about Balzac: a paragraph of
measured yet just appraisal placed in the mouth of the imaginary novelist, a chapter on the relationship between the lives
and the works of writers, and a number of incidental allusions
to characters in the* Comédie humaine. *The matter will be put
in another and broader context by the forthcoming study of
Walter Strauss on Marcel Proust as a literary critic.*

▬▬▬▬▬▬▬▬▬▬▬▬▬▬▬▬▬▬▬▬▬▬▬▬▬▬▬▬▬▬▬▬▬▬

I

The hundred years that have now elapsed since his death,
plus the thousands of miles that stretch between his grave at
Père-Lachaise and our commemoration in America, give a
better measure of Balzac's accomplishment than anything I

could add in the way of tribute or reappraisal. The most impressive testimonial has been his impact upon his medium, which every subsequent novelist of stature — from Dostoevsky to Dreiser — would attest. Sometimes this response has been a recoil, as it seems to have been with Flaubert, who started writing so soon afterwards that he could only realize his individuality by moving in other directions. But the usual course, as with Zola somewhat later, has been to assimilate Balzac's techniques and extend their application. In many ways it would not be inappropriate to look upon the novels of the past century as a collective supplement to the *Comédie humaine*. Some of them, however, are monuments in their own right, not so grand perhaps, but comparably great. Of these the one that comes closest to us, temporally and perhaps temperamentally, is *A la recherche du temps perdu*. And if we reverse our historical perspective, and ask ourselves which French writers look ahead to Proust, we may find it suggestive to look back toward Balzac.

My present venture is to cull a garland from Proust and hang it on the pedestal of Balzac. I am encouraged to do so by the fact that Proust's criticism is infinitely more valuable than mine; that he has never been much considered as a critic; and that, if anything could reflect further light on Balzac, it would be Proust's uniquely intensive focus. The conjunction may serve, at all events, to illuminate his own endeavors. There are, I believe, enough points of contact between them to establish a significant relationship, and yet the two men stand so far apart that any affinities must needs be elective. Granted that both belong to the same literary tradition, the ruling dynasty of modern fiction, a crude distinction sometimes asserts itself in terms of Balzac's antithesis: grandeur and decadence. Is their kinship no stronger than the attenuating line that relates a full-blooded founder to a last hemophilic scion? Life, for Proust, was what Balzac would have called *la vie élégante* in contradistinction to *la vie occupée*; assuredly the extremes of idleness and industry have never found more characteristic exponents. If our purpose were merely to differentiate them, we could rehearse the fable of the ant and the grasshopper, and then go on to balance such antitheses as debt and income, robustness and invalidism. But that would not explain why Proust, the worldling, devoted himself to the theme of isolation; why Balzac, so gregarious in his writings, produced them through an almost monastic regimen; why their minds seem to meet so often on the middle ground of paradox; or how to distinguish what is Balzacian from what is Proustian.

What is "Balzacian?" What is "Proustian?" The common denominator is that the two novelists lend their names to respective kinds of insight, special attitudes toward situations. All too often the attitude is naïvely confounded with the situation: *Balzacian* connotes a vulgar concern with money, and *Proustian* a morbid curiosity about sex. Thus the former becomes a loose synonym for *mercenary*, and the latter for *neurotic*. When Bloch, who is both, asks the narrator of Proust's novel about the family fortunes of Saint-Loup, he professes to be motivated by "a Balzacian point of view." The same phrase is used, somewhat more disinterestedly, by Saint-Loup himself and even the impeccable Swann. It seems to have been frequently invoked by Proust himself to designate the particular interest he took in genealogizing — an interest, as Lucien Daudet points out, which has subsequently been designated Proustian. What could be more Proustian or more Balzacian than Proust's excitement over the *lettre de faire part*, the funeral announcement of Balzac's stepdaughter, Countess Mniszech, with its genealogical clusters of Hanskis and Rzewuskis, Radziwills and Sapiehas, and other ornaments of the Polish nobility? Proust's friends had coined the verb *proustifier* to denote the elaborate compunctions with which, from time to time, he all but smothered them. At the other extreme, he instanced the Dreyfus affair as an example of nature imitating art and creating intrigues in the manner of Balzac. Like the natural historians they admired and emulated, both men are permanently identified with the species they discovered.

Both adjectives, therefore, stand primarily for the use of fiction as a means of discovery, an analytical instrument, and secondarily for two diverging and overlapping fields of analysis. Whenever we turn from Balzac to Proust, our emphasis shifts from social consciousness to psychological perception; yet these coigns of vantage, as we shall see, are complementary rather than antithetical. To indicate their essential continuity, let me quote a very Proustian observation from Balzac's *Traité de la vie élégante*. "In our society," wrote Balzac in 1830, "differences have disappeared and only nuances are left. The only barrier that separates the man of leisure from the businessman is poise, an elegant manner, the indescribable result of a finished education." If this were neither Balzac nor Proust, our next guess would be Veblen's *Theory of the Leisure Class*. "Hence the high price attached by the majority," Balzac continues, "to purity of speech, to grace of bearing, to a more or less easy way of wearing one's clothes, to the search for apartments . . ." *A la recherche des appartements* — no idle amusement then or now, but a rather more mundane search than the scientific research, the esthetic quest for *le temps perdu*. Not that the hermit of the Boulevard Haussmann was unconcerned with physical environment, worldly observance, or conspicuous consumption, any more than Balzac was really indifferent to *la recherche de l'absolu*. The foreword to the *Comédie humaine* subdivided the novelist's material into Men and Women and also — with pioneering explicitness — Things. Later novelists register the ever-increasing pressure of things upon the lives of men and women, and Proust — along with Henry James — is their elegiac poet.

A span of two to three generations separates Balzac's description from French society as Proust would describe it, yet the words I have quoted apply to Proust's subject-matter even more pertinently than to Balzac's. Retrospectively we are bound to notice differences which had not been altogether submerged in his day, and nuances which have since been greatly multiplied. Chronology can help to account for both, by reminding us that he was born in the year of Napoleon's *coup d'état*, while Proust was born in the year of the Commune. The glamor that aristocracy held for the latter was largely an emanation from the past. The virtue that the former saw in the bourgeoisie lay in its continuous struggle for recognition. Chronologically speaking, Swann's grandfather might have been a character in the *Comédie humaine*; but he would have moved in the financial circles of the Chaussée d'Antin, rather than among the forebears of his grandson's friends in the Faubourg Saint-Germain. In completing the chronicle of middle-class arrival, the convergence of the *deux côtés*, Proust airily assumes those dynamic processes of getting and spending into which Balzac enters with such avidity. And where the busy metropolis, Paris, exerts a centripetal force over Balzac's provincials, the existence of Proust's Parisians seems an endless vacation, a centrifugal journey to various watering-places, a nostalgic return to the countryside. It seems to follow that, if any social category is more fully represented in *A la recherche du temps perdu* than in Balzac's work, it is the servant class.

The familiar charge that Balzac — in spite of his relations with déclassée duchesses — "tried to depict social circles in which he was not entertained" is echoed by Proust's Marquise de Villeparisis, who speaks for the generation between Balzac's Princesse de Cadignan and his own Duchesse de Guermantes. On the other hand, the gowns of his Duchess are compared to those of Balzac's heroines, and all of the Guermantes prove to be avid readers of the *Comédie humaine*. Anecdotes tell us how Balzac used to talk about his characters as if they were historical personalities. Accepting them as such, Proust went a step farther, according to Jacques Truelle: he talked about Colonel Chabert and Cardinal Fleury and Dr. Cottard as if they co-existed on the plane of actuality. We are licensed, then, to proceed on the assumption that the dramatis personae of Balzac and Proust belong to one compact and continuous world, albeit that world has been changing and diminishing until — with Proust — it has become *le monde*: society in the capitalized and rarefied sense of the term. Within these selective limits, the change has been comparatively slight; the interval between the appearance of the Duchesse de Guermantes at the Opéra-Comique and Balzac's account of the Marquise d'Espard at the Théâtre des Italiens seems more like a week than a lifetime. Whether it is the Duc de Guermantes who jilts Madame d'Arpajon for the Marquise de Surgis-le-duc, or the Marquis d'Ajuda-Pinto who abandons the Vicomtesse de Beauséant in favor of the Comtesse de Rochefide, the Faubourg seems to persist in its classical patterns of behavior.

If lives were longer, we could almost believe that certain careers which began in the *Comédie humaine* survive into *A la recherche du temps perdu*. We could imagine that Madame Rabourdin, losing her looks but not her intellectual pretensions, went on with her salons after her second marriage to M. Verdurin; or that Raoul Nathan, pursuing the main chance through various realms of journalistic and erotic adventure, changed his name to Bloch at the time of the Dreyfus case. It may well be that certain roles are timeless, such as the dandy and the courtesan; but Henri de Marsay cuts a more dashing — if less convincing — figure than Charles Swann, and Odette de Crécy grows pale and languid by comparison with Valérie Marneffe. Proust himself joins in the game of seeking such counterparts for his characters, vaguely suspecting that one of his families — long before he knew them — had been at home in *Scènes de la vie de province*. But it is hard to believe that the Cambremers, whom Proust depicts as old-fashioned country gentry, are descended from the fisherman's family of the same name in the crudely powerful *Tragédie au bord de la mer*. It could probably be shown that every person in *A la recherche du temps perdu* has an opposite number in the *Comédie humaine*, but the converse would be decidedly untrue; for no other novels cover so much territory as Balzac's, and no other novelist challenges his primacy among what he termed "*artistes compréhensifs*."

The index of his successful efforts to "compete with the civil registry" is the *Répertoire*, the directory of characters compiled by MM. Cerfberr and Cristophe, a labor not unworthy of MM. Bouvard and Pécuchet. To contrast it with a similar index to Proust, compiled by Charles Daudet, is to juxtapose the telephone-book and the social register. Where Balzac's domain has a total population of more than two thousand, Proust's consists of about 230 — which is just about fifty less than the number indexed under the letter "C" in the handbook of Cerfberr and Cristophe. The cast is further reduced by Proust's subjectivity, his habit of questioning the objective reality of everyone except his first-person spokesman. Where Balzac dealt with individuals on a wholesale scale, Proust deliberately restricts his full treatment to himself; and consequently presents a criterion, not so much for quantitative measurement, as for qualitative evaluation. When the notion of a Proustian repertory was first proposed, he confessed that he blushed at the implied analogy, but expressed the clairvoyant hope that this undertaking would be "less literal" than its Balzacian model, and would leave more "room for the effect of impressions." His own conception has been forwarded better by Raoul Celly's *Répertoire des thèmes*, with its more Wagnerian mode of classification, than by the earlier volume of Charles Daudet. Since Proust is less concerned with human beings than with human relationships, his characterization is too elusive to be pinned down by the census-taker. As T. S. Eliot's *Cocktail Party* reminds us:

> What we know of other people
> Is only our memory of the moments
> During which we knew them.

Here is where Proust deviates from Balzac, whose characterization is so solidly grounded upon his conviction that the people he writes about exist independently of what at the moment he happens to be writing about them. He could hold this view because, of course, he had already written about so many of them and was continually planning to write more. When Proust comes to reconsider the nineteenth century, its critical awareness of itself, its incomplete yet organic art, including that of Wagner, *La Prisonnière* evokes the inspiration whereby Balzac, "viewing his works as both a father and a stranger, discerning in one place the fullness of Raphael and in another the simplicity of the Gospel, suddenly decided that it would shed a retrospective illumination over them . . . to gather them together into a cycle wherein the same personages would reappear." This last touch, this *coup de pinceau*, this peculiarly Balzacian device has been imitated occasionally by other writers whose work aspires to reproduce a world; but more often than not, the result has been a mechanical series of sequels, like *Jean-Cristophe* or *Les Hommes de bonne volonté*, where new installments do more to deaden the story than to keep it alive. And though Proust utilized Balzac's cyclic method, *le retour des personnages*, just as he drew upon Wagner's system of leitmotif, he had only to elaborate a single book while Balzac had to integrate a hundred. The difference in scope is a fair reflection of differing intentions: a self-consciousness which puts little trust in anything but impressions upon itself, as against an awareness of others which subordinates the text at hand to the all-enveloping context of our lives.

II

The parallel can be extended farther, but perhaps I have pushed it far enough to suggest that the works of both writers could be grouped very closely together in the imaginary museum of criticism, where personal considerations are neutralized and historical contingencies are transcended. History supplies its own connections, which are so direct — howbeit one-sided — that it may now be worth our trouble to trace a few of them. Proust, after all, could and did read and criticize Balzac, and his critical reading was gradually absorbed into the process of his creative writing. I have cited a crucial passage from his novel where he characteristically invokes his predecessor, and I shall point to others which are modeled on Balzac's example. For the moment, however, let us pause before a trifle which brings the two into closest juxtaposition: the parody of Balzac that Proust contributed to the *Figaro* in 1908. Since this was the first of a series, it had to convey the theme on which the later variations were played, and the theme could hardly have been more Balzacian. It just so happened that a swindler named Lemoine had defrauded the De Beers international syndicate by falsely claiming to have synthesized diamonds. Invention, promotion, chicanery, luxury, financial and sexual intrigue — merely to tell that story was to emulate Balzac; and Proust managed to narrate it to *"l'élite de l'aristocratie parisienne"* in the salon of the Princesse de Cadignan, *"cette carmélite de la réussite mondaine."*

Its first long, crowded sentence marches toward a culminating date, and those that follow are replete with epithets and superlatives, catalogues and allusions, rhetorical questions and cross-references, information and gossip, and other Balzacian twists of phrase and thought. When the parodist moves on to other writers, he does not forget his point of departure; he inspires Sainte-Beuve to take a sideswipe in passing, and Renan — applying the higher criticism — to question the authorship of the *Comédie humaine*, concluding on the basis of its unformed style and its dogmatic ideas that it could not have been written any later than two centuries before Voltaire. Since *pastiche* is a means of identification, as well as a mode of criticism, it is significant that, in Balzac, Proust met one of his most congenial subjects. Heretofore it has often been assumed that Balzac was, for Proust, a taste acquired late. To reread Proust's letters, stimulated by the new material in André Maurois' recent biography, is to reverse that assumption. It is said that his father quoted Balzac as frequently as his mother quoted Madame de Sévigné. Thence it is usually inferred that Proust, following his parental preferences, resisted Balzac until his maturer years. But his correspondence with his mother reveals an early and common interest in Balzac's novels, which he seems to have first discovered in the setting that he later celebrated as Combray. Proust grew up with Balzac, like so many others, and Balzac in his turn helped Proust to grow up.

When Proust, in his turn, undertook a monumental work of fiction, who could help him to shape it if not Balzac? Pierre Abraham has literally charted the curve of this influence by tabulating the number of occasions on which Balzac's name is mentioned in *A la recherche du temps perdu*. Having made my own count, and somehow arrived at a series of tabulations which vary somewhat from M. Abraham's, I cannot quite share his confidence in statistics. But my figures, such as they are, support his major premise; for they tend to run higher than his; and it may well be that a really perceptive investigator would emerge with even more impressive totals. Of M. Abraham's findings, the most important for us is that the highest number of references to Balzac occurs in the fourth and central novel of Proust's seven-part work, *Sodome et Gomorrhe*. The most questionable inference is that Proust dis-

covered Balzac midway in the composition of his own book.
This is partly based on M. Abraham's failure to observe that
Balzac was evoked at least twice in Proust's first novel, *Du
côté de chez Swann*. Yet the unpublished proofs for his second
volume, which Professor Feuillerat has examined, indicate
that many of these passages were added in the course of revision. Proust's original intentions were precious and experimental, subjective and metaphysical, remote from the traditional spheres of French fiction. As he wrote his way into his
story, and brought it within an objective frame of reference,
he gradually placed himself under the tutelage of Balzac.

What is quintessentially Proustian remains psychological: a
point of view which preoccupies itself with points of view, an
approach which Proust himself compared with X-ray. To
warrant that degree of intensity, he had to contrive substantial
characters, set up complex situations, and cultivate that sociological purview which is Balzacian mainly because Balzac ex-
ploited it more fully than other novelists. Paradoxically, it
may be more of a distinction to be common in that way than
to be rare in Proust's. The latter started with a lyrical note, an
impressionistic outlook of his own; what he lacked, what he
could acquire from Balzac, was the kind of narrative craftsmanship that is both conventional and indispensable. *A la recherche du temps perdu* develops, as the tale is told, into an
accumulating sequence of large dramatic scenes and long essay-
istic digressions in the manner of the *Comédie humaine*.
Through this development the amateur, Proust, becomes a
professional. He acknowledges his debt to the arch-profession-
al, Balzac, by evoking him more than others with whom the
personal link seems closer — more than Flaubert, Dostoevsky,
George Eliot, or any other novelist. Whenever a novel mentions
another novel, a certain tension is created, which tests the
authenticity and challenges the fictitiousness of both. Great
writers of fiction, like Cervantes, have made their reputations
by exposing the unconvincing qualities of lesser writers. Im-
mature novelists sometimes give themselves away by introducing literary conversation. It is to the credit of Proust that he
is not eclipsed by the implied comparison, and of Balzac that

he is unquestionably the favorite author of Proust's characters, if not of their author.

The most confirmed Balzacian among them, strikingly enough, is perhaps the most Proustian of them, the Baron de Charlus. Since he is the exacting arbiter of taste *à la* Guermantes, his fervid eulogies are praise indeed; and he never tires of pointing out analogies between the *Comédie humaine* and contemporary society. The fact that one of his relatives owns a garden which Balzac used as a background for one of his stories fills the Baron with ambivalent pride. He is also proud to possess a copy of *Le Cabinet des antiques*, with corrections in the author's own handwriting — a bibliographical item which is not without relevance to the *soirée* of the Princesse de Guermantes. There, when he meets a youth who bears the same name as its hero, Victurnien, he is swept off his feet by no mere antiquarian fervor. Later, when he expatiates to the narrator on his favorite novels, he employs the very phrase that Proust employed in a letter to René Boylesve, expressing his admiration for "the immense frescoes" of *Illusions perdues* and *Splendeurs et misères*. The preference, in other words, is Proust's. In the book M. de Charlus is called upon to defend it against Professor Brichot, who roundly declares that these are unlifelike shockers and that Balzac's so-called comedy is "not very human." The Baron retorts that the Professor does not know enough about life to recognize some of its melodramatic aspects. Balzac, on the contrary, "knew even those passions of which few people are aware, and which are studied only to be stigmatized."

An earlier version of the foregoing passage, which survives in Proust's notebooks, combines this defense of Balzac with attacks upon other writers — a caveat against the pursuit of literature which, at the final stage, is delivered by M. de Norpois. It would seem that Proust once intended to combine the characters of the diplomat and the baron. But the Baron de Charlus, himself a composite figure, outgrew Proust's plans. His living model, Robert de Montesquiou, having sponsored Proust in certain fashionable circles and introduced him to certain esthetic tastes, likewise confirmed him — as their correspondence shows — in the cult of Balzac. When Montesquiou, toward the end of his career, began to suspect that Charlus might turn out to be his portrait, Proust allayed those suspicions by pointing to a literary model: Balzac's characterization of the master criminal Vautrin. But privately, in commenting on Vautrin, Proust had already noted his resemblance to Montesquiou. Thus the chain of connection extends from Proust through Charlus to Montesquiou, and from Montesquiou through Vautrin to Balzac. Leaving aside the two novelists and their intermediary, Vautrin and Charlus are as widely separated as the underworld and the *élite*. Yet the convict holds a magnetic attraction for the snob. "It is the poetry of evil," writes Lucien de Rubempré in his farewell to Vautrin, "the genius of corruption." *La Dernière incarnation de Vautrin* hints quite explicitly at the sort of awareness for which Charlus praises Balzac: "The boldness of truth achieves combinations forbidden to art because they seem improbable or improper, unless the writer softens or abridges or castigates them."

Balzac's presentation of human experience was comprehensive enough to touch in passing upon the subject that would be Proust's obsession and revelation: homosexuality. Proust, as he uneasily approached it, thought of appealing to Balzac's authority; he thought for a while of printing, as a footnote, a paragraph on "the third sex" from the *Comédie humaine*. In the relations between Vautrin (*alias* the Abbé Carlos Herréra) and the young Corsican thief, Théodore Calvi, if not in Vautrin's sponsorship of Rubempré and Rastignac, he found a precedent for the infatuation of Charlus with the corrupt violinist, Morel. But Charlus does not need such specific examples; for, by "a mental transposition," he can identify himself with the Princesse de Cadignan. His source, in the last analysis, is Proust; and their relationship is that of third-person actor to first-person spectator; whereas Balzac, through identification with Vautrin, vicariously lives the careers of his younger heroes. This underlying pattern, which he terms "the moral phenomenon of the Double," shifts to a triangle as both writers face the phenomenon of Lesbianism. And where *Splen-*

deurs et misères des courtisanes gave readers a preliminary glimpse of Proust's Sodom, his Gomorrah is darkly fore-shadowed by *La Fille aux yeux d'or* — which occupies, inciden-tally, a place in Swann's library. The sensational adventure of Henri de Marsay, who loved Paquita Valdès and encountered an unexpected rival in the Marquise de San-Réal, is a far cry from the plight of Proust's narrator, whose love and jealousy are so largely the creatures of his mind. Yet Albertine, like Balzac's heroine, is the object of a triangular rivalry between heterosexual and homosexual passions.

Proust realizes that the side of the *Comédie humaine* on which he dwells is exceptional, *"hors de nature."* In *A la re-cherche du temps perdu* the exception is constantly threaten-ing to engulf the norm. Nevertheless Proust shares with Bal-zac a fundamental sense of normality, a social morality based upon the integrity of the family — from which, alas too often, they both are engaged in recording deviations. For Balzac the symbol of a society whose values were disintegrating is the prodigal father. Proust, who witnessed a later phase of that disintegration, symbolizes it in his conception of "the pro-faned mother." But here too Balzac unconsciously anticipates him, in that powerful scene from *La Cousine Bette* where Madame Hulot is forced, through her very devotion to her husband and children, into bargaining over her favors with the disdainful interloper, Crevel. As for her husband, the prodigal Baron Hulot, it is curious that — in the search for models and scramble for keys — no one has seen in him a proto-type of the Baron de Charlus. Each case follows, in outline, the same degradation, and even details of appearance are simi-lar. Both barons decline, from a state of aggressive dandyism, through several stages of physical dissolution, to the point where we finally behold them — white-bearded, hair undyed and waist uncorseted — forcing their lecherous attentions on a child. Since the sexual motivation is inverted with Charlus, he becomes an even more flagrant offender against social norms, and in fact is punished more abysmally.

Proust, of course, puts his emphasis rather upon the ma-ternal than the paternal role, and upon the irresponsibilities of children toward parents. Balzac, however, created another father, more sinned against than sinning; and if *Le Père Goriot* consciously echoes *King Lear*, it progresses toward a climax which heralds Proust. This is where the old man is on his deathbed, and one of his daughters is rushing off to the ball, while the other subsequently arrives too late. Proust reproduces that archetypal situation in one of his characteristic early stories, *La Mort de Baldassare Silvande*, where the youthful hero is dying and his heroine deserts him to attend a ball. He reverts to it again at the climactic moment of *Le Côté des Guermantes*, the episode of the Duchess's red slippers, where she and the Duke are so unwilling to interrupt a round of parties that they ignore the impending death of their best friend, Swann. Nonrecognition scenes of this sort recur throughout Proust's work, perhaps because he viewed the world as a semi-invalid, increasingly confined to his room while his friends danced away to their pleasures. Balzac, at the other extreme, perhaps because he felt the world too much with him, cast his wistful glance at those dedicated souls who managed to avoid it. Man's inhumanity to man, as depicted — let us say — in *Le Cousin Pons*, involves a network of intrigue, a tightening of the bonds of interest. Proust's depiction is not less sinister because it stresses the absence of ties, the breakdown of relations; because its comedy is so tragic, its humanity so inhumane.

III

These historical links and critical parallels could be strengthened and amplified considerably; but similarities, after a certain point, are less significant than differences or nuances; and if you are willing to accept the comparison between Balzac and Proust, I think we now have more to learn from the contrast. We have glimpsed how the one affected the formation of the other's work: would that the other might have had some effect on his forerunner! But history is unfair in this respect, and literary influence is unrewarding, since it cannot — except with contemporaries — be reciprocal. To be sure, the *Comédie humaine* is so all-inclusive that if you look through *Un Début dans la vie,* you will find that the name of Proust appears for a moment on a legal document which is whisked away. We cannot ask for the dialectical counterpart of what Proust gives us in theory and practice: a critique of Balzac. Any rereading of Balzac, however, is an implicit commentary on Proust; it is also a series of critical comments on the hundred years that now stand between Balzac and ourselves. Balzac, whose fifty-year span corresponds so neatly to the first half of the nineteenth century, must have been more at home in his time than Proust at the *fin du siècle.* Between them came M. Homais, who prided himself on keeping up with that century, and Flaubert who prided himself on rejecting it. Balzac not merely accepted it, he embraced it: its stupidity and brilliance, its misery and splendor, its decadence and grandeur.

Indeed, had he not professed some traditional allegiances, he might have swallowed the greatness without reservation and failed to recognize the weaknesses of his age. He wrote, so he said, in the light of two eternal verities: the Bourbon monarchy and the Catholic church. As if two eternal verities were not enough for any single lifetime, or possibly because one of those verities was — and continues to be — in a state of eclipse, he opened his hospitable mind to many others: quasi-religious, pseudo-scientific, magical. That these were bound to conflict, or to be exploded, is not important; what matters is the confident presupposition that all inquiries, zealously pursued, lead toward the truth. The ebbing of such confidence as this left Proust's more rigorous quest perplexed with uncertainties. His philosophical mentor, Bergson, taught him to seek reality in the ever changing flow of subjective experience. For Balzac it lay in the order of objective nature, as unified, classified, and organized by such scientists as Geoffroy Saint-Hilaire. Science, largely biological, was still regarded as natural history; and though its demonstration of kinships between humanity and the animal kingdom was embarrassing, it was far less disquieting in the long run than relativity, indeterminacy, and other advances in physics, both theoretical and applied. Balzac considered the anatomist Cuvier as much of a conqueror within his realm as Napoleon in Europe at large. This analogy, with its hint that conquest has its limitations, can be carried farther than Balzac intended; for he was prompted by their endeavors to undertake the *Comédie humaine*.

We can understand why Proust stood in such awe before the masterworks of the nineteenth century, and why it was bold and perhaps old-fashioned of him — on however reduced a scale — to attempt such an undertaking. The contrast is pointed more sharply by the response of Franz Kafka to anecdotes about Balzac's gold-headed and jewel-studded cane, which — according to Kafka — bore this dashing motto: "I break every obstacle." Kafka's comment is the heartcry of another century: "Every obstacle breaks me." It would be hard to state, with more poignant candor, the antithesis between the driving energies and monumental constructions of Balzac's day and the shored fragments and failing nerves of the year 1950. If anything was needed, after Proust's neurasthenia, to complete the nervous prostration of the hero, it was Kafka's protagonists, always suffering, never acting, whom we know quite as well as we know ourselves. From where we sit, or where we lie, we could admire worse heroes than Balzac's, though he himself is the first to warn us against them. *Vouloir*, will consumes them; *pouvoir*, power destroys them. Business and politics, molded by their will-to-power, have more than fulfilled Balzac's warning. But why, because power is an axiomatic source of corruption, should the will itself be abdicated? Why, in understandable revulsion from the cult of success, should we genuflect to Henry Adams's cult of failure? Balzac also underlined the distinction between *pouvoir* and *voir*, active and passive roles. It is typical of the present generation of critics that it emphasizes the passive, the spectatorial, the visionary side of Balzac: *Balzac voyant*.

This is an interesting but lesser facet of Balzac's genius, like the facet that especially interested Proust. Proust, as we have seen, was stimulated by Balzac to project his characters and dramatize his situations; but his inclination is to fall back upon himself, that is to say, upon his center of consciousness; and in two crucial episodes he does not hesitate to play that least heroic and most abject of roles, the *voyeur*. Whether the novelist is a *voyant* or a *voyeur*, a seer or an eavesdropper, a Dostoevsky or a Henry Miller, depends to a large extent upon the quality of his vision. As the novel retreats and specializes, from Balzac to Proust, it loses ground but gains intensity; analysis goes as far as it can to make up for synthesis. Refinement of taste is probably not the fullest compensation for loss of appetite; but if the defect of Balzac's quality is vulgarity, the quality of Proust's defect is sensibility. Reckoning the debits and credits, like one of Balzac's accountants, should we conclude that he offers us more matter with less art? That would be a nuance, rather than a difference, since there is so much art in Balzac and so much matter in Proust. Beyond the two ways of living that Balzac discriminates, the *vie élégante* and the *vie occupée*, he ends by suggesting a third way: *la vie d'artiste*. So with Proust, who moves on from the *côté de Méséglise* through the *côté de Guermantes* toward that artistic vocation which was first revealed to him by the steeples of Martinville.

At last, then, they come together on the plane where it is most appropriate for them to meet; and even here we note differences of tone between the professional Bohemianism of the one and the fashionable dilettantism of the other. What is a special preoccupation with Proust, again, is merely one of the many topics that Balzac takes in his encyclopedic stride. The *Comédie humaine*, like Balzac's quarters, is crowded with real and imaginary bric-a-brac. It also utilizes a device which becomes habitual with Proust: portraying a character by referring to a work of art. Hence Proust, in his *pastiche* of Balzac, can write of the Princesse de Cadignan: "Raphael alone would have been capable of painting her." This habit reaches its triumphant anticlimax in the final sentence of *Massimilla Doni*, where to the bedside of his faltering heroine Balzac summons not only the Sistine Madonna, but Bellini's angels, Dürer's virgins, Michelangelo's Day and Night, and innumerable anonymous monuments of sculpture and architecture. Proust, of course, displays more discrimination; but this game of correspondences is an old favorite with Swann; and when he ascends the staircase of Mme. de Sainte-Euverte, he mentally compares the servants to originals by Mantegna, Dürer, Goya, Cellini, and the Greeks. Just previously, almost as a kind of acknowledgment, he thought of Balzac in connection with one of the footmen. And afterwards, when the Vinteuil sonata begins, it echoes Balzac's fondness for musical accompaniments: the discussion of Rossini in *Massimilla Doni* or the Beethoven leitmotif in *César Birotteau*.

The triumph of art over life — Proust's major theme — is personified by his composer, Vinteuil, whose music soars to posthumous success, although his career — like that of the actress Berma — is victimized by an unfilial daughter. No consolation awaits Balzac's unhappy musicians, Pons and Schmucke; while the compositions of the luckless Gambara turn out to be the delusions of a madman. The ambiguity of misunderstood genius, so closely allied to madness, is definitively treated in *Le Chef-d'oeuvre inconnu*, where the perfectionism of the painter Frenhofer daubs at a single canvas until it is meaningless. It is almost as if Balzac were apologizing for the careless verve of his own immense productivity. Yet he has no patience with talents that compromise, like the sculptor Steinbock, or mediocrities that charm the bourgeoisie, like the portraitist Grassou. Life conspires, in the *Comédie humaine*, to get the better of art. The artist is not without honor, when Proust incarnates him in the painter Elstir — or, above all, in the man of letters, Bergotte. The literary market, as Balzac presents it in *Illusions perdues*, reduces Lucien de Rubempré to a lower condition than the prostitutes who sell themselves to support him. His failure is complete: artistic, moral, worldly. Art is not trade for Balzac, and who can say so more authoritatively? It is something out of this world: a mysterious talisman, not unlike the philosopher's stone that Balthasar Claës never quite succeeds in discovering, or the metaphysical system that Louis Lambert goes mad in vainly striving to construct.

For Proust too, art belongs to another and better sphere; but, possibly because he stood aloof from the sphere of business and deliberately retired from the sphere of fashion, his third world seems more accessible to human integrity. In connection with the Vinteuil septet, or again with the death of

Bergotte, he postulates a sort of Platonic myth: artists are citizens of an undiscovered country who work in obedience to its higher laws, not for worldly reward but for the same reason — whatever it be — that parents are kind to their children. This is not escapism; there is no escape from reality. Oscar Wilde, glibly supporting his famous paradox on the priority of art over nature, once remarked that the worst grief in his life had been the death of Lucien de Rubempré. Alluding to that remark in a letter, and again in *Sodome et Gomorrhe*, Proust dryly observes that Wilde's trial must have taught him the meaning of real grief. Similarly, reading *Illusions perdues* does not help M. de Charlus to shed his illusions; and Vautrin is no less romantic to him than Amadís of Gaul was to Don Quixote. Thus every novelist must draw his own distinctions between fact and fiction, as Balzac does between Lucien's career and the novel he writes in imitation of Scott. When Proust evokes the lost illusions of his youth, he associates them with the pastoral romances of George Sand. After many years and disillusionments, when a wedding announcement arrives, his mother greets it naïvely. "This is the reward of virtue," she says, "like the ending of a novel by Mme. Sand." But the narrator, conscious of what lies behind the happy invitation, takes a darker view. "This is the reward of vice," he thinks, "like the ending of a novel by Balzac."

Proust explained that the Dreyfus case ended happily, after twelve years of Balzacian intrigue, because it was basically fictitious and could therefore be resolved by poetic justice. Other men lead more tragic lives than Captain Dreyfus, he adds, because the evils that overtake them are based upon truth. Though Balzac more often than not allows evil to prosper and good to suffer, for reasons which he explains in his *Avant-propos*, the impression he leaves us with is more optimistic. He continues to believe ebulliently in so many things which Proust, finding them illusory, discards; while Proust, in his augmenting pessimism, clings more desperately to the one ideal of art. Yet Balzac abides the test of that retrospective touchstone. The crudity of his letters, of his life, is contrasted with the literary perfection of *La Cousine Bette* and *Le Curé de Tours*, when Proust — in his concluding volume, *Le Temps retrouvé* — parodies the journal of the brothers Goncourt. We have noticed how the entire work is strewn with generous acknowledgments, how consciously it develops themes and utilizes techniques adumbrated in the *Comédie humaine*. The irony of Balzac's situation, as Proust contemplates it, is that — although he never completed his masterpiece — art yielded to him the mystery it withholds from the perfectionist Frenhofer. "The secret of relief," the masterstroke for which Proust eulogized Balzac, lay in his discovery of the cycle: the use of recurrent characters to transcend the limits of the novel itself and bring his more comprehensive fiction to life. At the outset I translated a passage from his *Traité de la vie élégante*, where Balzac sounded like Proust. Let me now translate a passage from *Du Côté de chez Swann*, where Proust — *mutatis mutandis* — sounds like Balzac.

"O audacity!" Swann exclaims in response to a phrase of music, "perhaps as inspired as that of a Lavoisier or an Ampère, the boldness of Vinteuil experimenting, discovering the secret laws of an unknown force, driving the invisible team to which he entrusts himself, and which he will never behold, across unexplored territory toward the only possible goal!" So it is with Balzac. He possessed a keener sense of destination, a firmer control over movement, than most of those whose researches carry them into the realm of ideas; but not otherwise than Vinteuil or his own Daniel d'Arthez, he ultimately presents himself as "a candidate for posthumous honors." Neither Balzac nor Proust, nor for that matter any great novelist, has been welcomed into that by no means exclusive institution which assumes the critical responsibility of pronouncing certain French writers — during their lifetime — "immortal." Immortality as mortals confer it, as the late Paul Valéry envisaged it, is a *"consolatrice affreusement laurée."* When Proust put the finishing touches on his ultimate portrait of the artist, he asked himself whether Bergotte was really dead forever. His answer, his impassioned argument that human endeavor can be the master rather than the slave of time, is most concretely embodied in the rows of Bergotte's books, ranged against the dark windows in flickering candlelight. Nothing that we can add, in the transient role of posterity, supports such arguments more powerfully than the volumes of the *Comédie humaine*. Ranging across our shelves, reminding us that a large segment of time has been secured against time, they outshine the candles we burn in Balzac's memory.

Joyce's Sentimental Journey through France and Italy

The idea for this little excursion originated with Professor Henri Peyre, when he invited me to address his students at Yale University, November 13, 1947, on James Joyce's debts to French and Italian literature. A paper, abridged from my notes for that lecture, was read to a section of the Modern Language Association (Contemporary English Literature: The Writings of James Joyce) on December 29, 1948. This was printed in The Yale Review, XXXVIII, 4 *(Summer, 1949), and with the kind permission of the Yale University Press is reprinted here. The richness of the subject it all-too-sketchily outlines has lately been demonstrated by monographic investigations, such as Haskell Block's of Joyce and Flaubert and David Hayman's of Joyce and Mallarmé.*

▀▀

James Joyce is said to have cherished precedents and cultivated analogies, in his life as well as in his work. If tradition be defined as a living relationship with the dead, no writer has been more traditional. He therefore might not have objected to being linked, through the connotations of a title, with a predecessor whom he read and liked: another Irish-born sentimentalist, who journeyed through France and Italy, and turned out to be one of the virtuosi of English literature. But, having suggested a relation, I must add a qualification; for Joyce's journey was much more purposeful, far less wayward than Laurence Sterne's. And the sentiment or the sentimentality — depending upon whether or not you share it — had nothing to do with the countries and cities in which Joyce traveled and sojourned; it was carefully saved for the country he had left, the city to which each one of his books returns. He told Professor Heinrich Straumann that, wherever he went, he bore with him his native Dublin. He was in the habit of referring to it as "the seventh city of Christendom." In a letter to his Austro-Jewish-Italian friend, Italo Svevo, he specifies the other six: the list begins with a London suburb, Clapham Junction, and ends with "San Giacomo in Monte di Pietà (St. James by the Pawnshop)." In a sense he adumbrated his own career when he jotted in an early notebook: "Ireland — an afterthought of Europe."

It is worth remembering in this connection, though not without a qualm of self-conscious irony, that one of Joyce's contemplated careers was a professorship of Romance languages at his college in Dublin, now the National University. In *Exiles* he dramatized his dilemma: whether to bring European culture to Ireland or to create Irish culture on the Continent. When he had acted upon his decision, he supported himself as tutor, as translator, as teacher in a Berlitz school. One of the most pathetic objects in *Ulysses* is Chardenal's French primer, which Dilly Dedalus blushingly hopes will save her from the shabbiness that her father has brought upon their family. And one of Mr. Bloom's unrealized hopes is a series of Italian lessons imparted by Stephen Dedalus to Marion Tweedy Bloom. As linguist and pedagogue, Joyce had a professional grasp of what was not only his problem but finally his theme: the difficulty of communication in the modern world. In a sense we are all moral deafmutes, struggling to understand each other, like Mutt and Jute in *Finnegans Wake*. Like them we "spigotty anglease," we "phonio saxo"; some of us even "tollerday donsk" or "tolkatiff scowegian." But the words, when they come, are bristling and baffling: "Come on, fool porterfull, hosiered women blown monk sewer?" This — our impatience prompts us to say — is nonsense, meaningless babble, verbal chaos. But let us try the words again, listening this time in French: "*Comment vous portez-vous aujourd'hui, mon blond monsieur?*"

Hereupon the invader sets foot upon shore (or, on another plane of interpretation, the customer steps up to the bar), and out of the confusion of tongues emerges the perception that Joyce's many conflicts start from the basic incongruity between his Celtic race and his Norman name. His attitude toward the English language, which his spokesman, Stephen, considers a foreign tongue, helps to explain his stylistic virtuosity. As for the Irish language, we know how strongly Joyce reacted against every manifestation of nationalism; when the visiting Englishman in *Ulysses* addresses the old milk-woman in Gaelic, she mistakes it for French. Dr. Oliver Gogarty, though he has not yet managed to "Hellenize Ireland," has frequently reminded us that Joyce had small Greek. And Mr. Stuart Gilbert, though he writes engagingly of "the Latin Joyce," is in the awkward position of being a better classicist than his friend. Joyce's Latinity, though immense, was not profoundly classical; it was originally scholastic and ultimately neo-Latin. Meanwhile he studied Germanic languages, particularly Dano-Norwegian. If the reading of Dante in Italian was the experience that awakened his literary consciousness, it was actually the figure of Ibsen that inspired him to become a writer. Dante was "the first poet of the Europeans," but Ibsen was his latterday successor, and Joyce blamed "the spirit of the time" for driving him from the Florentine's orthodoxy to the Viking's iconoclasm.

Nothing linguistic was completely alien to him, but he had a special flair for French and Italian, and these were subjects in which he specialized at the university. His classmate, Constantine Curran, tells us that Joyce's French compositions were the pride of Père Cadic, their Breton instructor. The essay on James Clarence Mangan, which Joyce contributed to the college magazine, couples the names of Baudelaire and Verlaine with those of Shakespeare and Wordsworth. Conspicuous among a number of yellow-backed volumes, dating from this period and bearing Joyce's signature, are Verlaine's *Poètes maudits* and Flaubert's *Tentation de Saint-Antoine*. As the the only candidate presenting Italian in his time, Joyce suffered from the snickers of fellow students who attributed his scholarly zeal to the fact that the *Decameron* was even smuttier in the original than in English translation. Yet even so matter-of-fact a course as physics could point his curiosity in the same direction: he came away treasuring a phrase of Galvani, "enchantment of the heart (*incanto di cuore*)." He modeled his love poems on the *Vita Nuova* and, at Marsh's library, pored over Saint Francis and various "mild heresiarchs" of the *Trecento*. His continental interests were looked upon by his Irish Jesuit instructors as a kind of devil's advocacy. He could not agree with them that Louis Veuillot was a finer writer than Victor Hugo, or see the hand of Providence in the asphyxiation of Zola. On his side, Joyce defended the heresies of Giordano Bruno in friendly arguments with his Italian master, Father Ghezzi, a sympathetic little priest from Bergamo (who figures in *Stephen Hero* under the name of Artifoni, which is transferred to the music-master in *Ulysses*). Since Bruno was born in Nola, he could not inappropriately be invoked as "the Nolan." Under this Hibernian pen-name, he provided a text for Joyce's impatient manifesto, "The Day of the Rabblement," which went on to attack the Irish theater from the vantage point of European drama, and accused Yeats and Moore of floundering "in the backwash of that tide which has advanced from Flaubert . . . to D'Annunzio." Joyce's taste was confirmed by a holiday visit to London, where he saw a play of d'Annunzio acted by Duse. It became increasingly clear that he was destined to cross the Channel. The very sight of clouds moving westward reminded him of whence they had come — "Europe of strange tongues . . . memories and names."

The *Memoirs of Vidocq* and *The Count of Monte Cristo* had aided his boyish imagination to offset the parochial drabness of Dublin. Later he clothed it in associations from Guido Cavalcanti, Ibsen, and various favorites of his adolescence. After he went abroad he was able to contemplate it in unrelieved concreteness: *Ulysses* is dated from three other cities, "Trieste-Zurich-Paris." Zurich, where he lived during the First World War and died during the Second, is neutral ground for our purposes as it was for his. The other two were not less international and polyglot and unique. His sojourn at Rome, the seat of an authority which he had rejected, was inevitably transient. On the other hand, Trieste, though mainly Italian in culture, was an unassimilated colony of the Austro-Hungarian empire, especially suited to the irredentism of the Irish temperament. There his children, Giorgio and Lucia, were born and brought up to speak the prevailing tongue. On his final visit to Dublin, Joyce describes himself "spouting Italian by the hour." Returning home to Trieste, he not only taught English; he lectured on English authors at the Università Popolare; he collaborated in an Italian version of Synge's *Riders to the Sea* and chronicled Irish literature and politics for the local *Piccolo della Sera.*

"Trieste, ah Trieste, ate I my liver!" Through the double-talk of *Finnegans Wake* we can hear this plaint of a self-torturing Prometheus. "*Triste, ah triste, était mon livre.*" The book is never sad for very long; except for such moments, it is uproariously funny. But again, when its locale has shifted to Paris, the voice of a self-questioning Henri Quatre is heard to ask: "Was Parish worth that mess?" Reminiscences of the Latin Quarter, during Joyce's first expatriation, reverberate through *Ulysses*: the exiled Fenian typesetter, his Gallicized son Patrice, and Edouard Drumont's journalistic hatred of Queen Victoria. Even *Hamlet* (*pièce de Shakespeare*) is subjected to a *rive-gauche* reinterpretation, with incidental comments quoted from Mallarmé, Maeterlinck, and Dumas *fils* — or is it *père?* The metropolis of the arts, the cosmopolitan Paris where Joyce resided between the two wars, welcomed him to the roster of its distinguished citizens. If his later works eluded the obstacles that all but aborted his earlier ones, it was because they were printed and published in France. At a time when the *Revue des deux mondes* forbade its contributors to mention Proust and Gide, Joyce was hailed in its pages by Louis Gillet — who thereupon received a letter of protest from Edmund Gosse.

Paris was rich in associations which Joyce could share: he told Austin Clarke that he never crossed the Place Saint-Sulpice without thinking of Renan. If he had not supplied Stephen with an apt quotation from Villon, or permitted Mrs. Bloom to remember "Master François somebody supposed to be a priest," Joyce's French affinities would still be evident. Chiefly these were with the *symboliste* poets. He translated a poem by Verlaine into the idiom of the Celtic twilight, and a poem by James Stephens into French which sounds not unlike Verlaine.

Baudelaire's pantoum, *"Harmonie du soir,"* with its repeated lines and its punning rhymes, is untranslatable; but Joyce's "Night-piece" succeeds in catching the same dark mood by using the same ecclesiastical imagery. French novels seem to have bored Joyce less than English ones; he always enjoyed Maupassant, and once expected to be called "the Irish Zola." Nonetheless, his debt to the French naturalistic school has been minimized by such highly qualified critics as Valéry Larbaud. We can accept this *a fortiori* judgment with one strong reservation: the striking affinity in theory and practice, in the men and their work, between Joyce and Flaubert.

Joyce had read every line of Flaubert, according to Frank Budgen; yet specific echoes are less important here than parallel intentions. Certainly he gave the example in English of much that his French predecessor had exemplified in literature at large. When Joyce's Stephen speaks of flying by three nets, he indicates the triple allegiance — creed, country, position — that Flaubert renounced. The artist, behind or beyond his handiwork, is likened by both to God, invisible and omnipotent in His creation. Compare a story by Joyce — "Clay," for example — to Flaubert's *"Un Coeur simple,"* or the *Portrait of the Artist* to the *Education sentimentale;* or Gerty MacDowell's reveries to those of Emma Bovary, or the clichés of Leopold Bloom to those of Bouvard and Pécuchet. The midnight fantasy of *Ulysses* owes vastly more to the *Tentation de Saint-Antoine* than to Goethe's *Walpurgisnacht*: Mrs. Bloom in Turkish attire resembles the Queen of Sheba, the rationalistic grandfather plays Hilarion, and the face of Sweny the druggist blasphemously parodies Flaubert's culminating sunrise. Flaubert's experimentation, his documentation, his self-criticism, his perfectionism, are pushed to the ultimate in Joyce's *Finnegans Wake.* It was Joyce who perfected for our language *le style indirect libre,* Flaubert's modulated compromise between indirect discourse and first-person narrative.

Joyce is better known for a further development of style: the perfection of the so-called "stream of consciousness." In a book entitled *Life and the Dream,* which does not always distinguish very sharply between those categories, Mrs. Mary

Colum questions the usual ascription of this technique to Edouard Dujardin's novelette, *Les Lauriers sont coupés,* first published in 1888. Against her word we have merely Joyce's, who inscribed a copy of *Ulysses* to Dujardin, *"annonciateur de la parôle intérieure,"* and subscribed himself the impenitent thief (*"le larron impénitent"*). The older writer repaid the compliment by inscribing a new edition of his book to the *"maître illustre qui a dit à l'homme mort et enseveli: Lazare, lève-toi!"* From the role of thief to the role thereby implied must have been a dizzying elevation. If Joyce had any doubts of his mission, they must have been allayed by receiving this veneration not once but twice — both times from a man old enough to be his father. In the second edition of Italo Svevo's *Senilità,* — which, like *Les Lauriers sont coupés,* was republished through Joyce's friendly offices — he is thanked again for repeating the miracle of Lazarus. His encouragement stimulated Svevo, who had come to Joyce for English lessons in Trieste, to come out of retirement with *La Coscienza di Zeno.* Svevo, in turn, furnished Joyce with more than a hint for the psychology of Leopold Bloom; and correspondence reveals that his widow, Signora Livia Schmitz, served as one of the models for Anna Livia Plurabelle.

With this exception, Joyce had little interest in contemporary Italian literature. Shrewdly he warned a young "futurist" that the new movement had no future. With residence in France, his feeling for Italy concentrated upon two lifelong hobbies: grand opera and philosophy. His letter "From a Banned Writer to a Banned Singer" displays a *bravura* command of the operatic repertory. Here his admiration for Enrico Caruso and Giacomo Lauri Volpi comes second only to his friendship for the Irish tenor, John Sullivan — "Rico is for carousel and Giaco for luring volupy but Nino, the sweetly dulcetest, tuning-fork among tenors, for the best of all . . . ." Joyce's philosophical studies proceeded from the terminology — if not the theology — of the Franco-Italian Aquinas; they moved, via the empiricism of Nicholas of Cusa, toward the heresy of Bruno of Nola. "The Nolan," along with his Dublin antithesis, Browne, animates the metaphysical dualism of

Finnegans Wake. Its grand design — historical, mythological, philological — bodies forth the speculations of the Neapolitan philosopher, Giambattista Vico. "Mr. John Baptister Vickers" is credited for a production which — if we trust the program notes — is prompted by "Elanio Vitale *(élan vital)."* The promptings of this cosmic authority (Bergson), irreverently cited by Joyce as Bitchson, are supplemented by the anthropological applications of Lévy-Bruhl, whose name invites additional byplay. Joyce's reversion to primitive myth is well supported by modern scholarship: the French Hellenist, Victor Bérard, was his guide to the Homeric world.

His Florentine colleague, Francini-Bruni, reports Joyce's opinion that Italian literature began and ended with Dante. The bible from which he set out, to which he came back for "spiritual nourishment," was the *Commedia.* Its pattern, so luminously absent from *Dubliners,* is caricatured in "Grace," where Hell is drunkenness, Purgatory a hangover, and Paradise a Jesuit retreat. *Stephen Hero* conjures up a private *Inferno* for intellectually fraudulent classmates, as well as a *Paradiso* which is somewhat more Mohammedan than Dantesque. The heroine, however, rejects the uncourtly proposal that Stephen has left his Italian lesson to make; their last interview, noted in the *Portrait of the Artist,* turns on the "spiritual-heroic refrigerating apparatus, invented and patented in all countries by Dante Alighieri." As between the ever-virginal Beatrice and the earthier *Ewig-Weibliche,* the drama of *Exiles* reenacts the artist's established preference. *Ulysses,* wasting no regrets over "the isosceles triangle, Miss Portinari," evokes a majestic procession in *terza rima* under the newspaper heading of "Rhymes and Reasons." And *Finnegans Wake* finds exile and anticlericalism grotesquely manifested in *"Through Hell with the Papes,* by the divine comic, Denti Alligator."

Though Joyce's dream-vision was symbolically conceived and monumentally executed, he was well aware of the abysses that separate it from Dante's universe of discourse. "Look at this passage about Galilleotto," he confesses to the reader. "I know it is difficult. . ." It is easier if we recall a famous line, which Joyce misquoted from Dante with particular reference to himself. This is the line that names both the book and the author that first brought Paolo and Francesca together: *"Galeotto è il libro e chi lo scrive."* Our author, too, may be a fool as well as a go-between; he may even be, what Balzac called "a galley-slave to pen and ink," a *galeotto* in another sense. He also happens to have lived and worked in the Rue Galilée, and — like Galileo in his own way — to have widened our universe. Reading between the hieratic lines, we may glimpse some progress toward Goethe's hope that national literatures would blend into one world literature. The fact that *Ulysses* has been so widely translated is at least a sign that the barriers to international understanding are not insurmountable. Joyce's sentimental journey was neither a pilgrimage nor a crusade; it was his realization of Irish nationality within the widening perspectives of Latin tradition and Mediterranean culture. In short, it was a tale of two cities, Paris and Trieste; of French poetry and erudition, of Italian music and philosophy; of two older writers rediscovered by a younger disciple, Edouard Dujardin and Italo Svevo; of two timeless masters, Flaubert, invisible and omnipresent, and Dante, first and last.

Observations on the Style of Ernest Hemingway

These observations began as a book review and continued as explication de texte. The book involved was Ernest Hemingway: The Man and His Work, edited by John K. M. McCaffery, with a side-glance at Hemingway's introduction to In Sicily, by Elio Vittorini. The explication had its first hearing from the seminar in literary criticism at the Johns Hopkins University on October 19, 1950. The resulting conflation was published in The Kenyon Review, XIII, 4 (Autumn, 1951), from which it is reprinted with thanks and without changes. During the five years since, new honors and further adventures have befallen our subject; but if the analysis here submitted is valid, it is supported rather than modified by The Old Man and the Sea (1952); for in this latest substantial piece of Hemingway's writing, it might be said that he is neither at his best nor at his worst but at his most typical. The tale again is an expanded short story — indeed, to a large extent, a monologue. The situation is ideally calculated to project the actions and sensations of lonely struggle; and though the narrative conveys this excitement with something of the old muscularity, its firm contours are weakened by adipose passages of conversation and commentary. The hero, described by the author as "simple," turns out to be a garrulous character who talks to himself in the Hispanese of For Whom the Bell Tolls, translated or explained by Hemingway in a manner which is pedagogical, if not pedantic. The prediction that his work was ripe for academic study is finding fulfillment in articles and monographs which go beyond my most inflated expectations.

▬▬

I

"The most important author living today, the outstanding author since the death of Shakespeare," is Ernest Hemingway.

So we have lately been assured by John O'Hara in the *New York Times Book Review*. We should have to know what Mr. O'Hara thinks of the various intervening authors, of Shakespeare himself, and indeed of literature, in order to get the full benefit of this evaluation. It might be inferred, from his review of *Across the River and into the Trees*, that he holds them well on this side of idolatry. Inasmuch as Hemingway's latest novel tends regrettably to run certain attitudes and mannerisms to the ground, merely to describe it — if I may use an unsportsmanlike simile — is like shooting a sitting bird. Mr. O'Hara's gallant way of protecting this vulnerable target is to charge the air with invidious comparisons. His final encomium should be quoted in full, inasmuch as it takes no more than two short words, which manage to catch the uncertainty of the situation as well as the strident unsteadiness of Mr. O'Hara's tone: "Real class." That interesting phrase, which could be more appropriately applied to a car or a girl, carries overtones of petty snobbery; it seems to look up toward an object which, it admits in wistful awe, transcends such sordid articles of the same commodity as ordinarily fall within its ken. To whistle after Hemingway in this fashion is doubtless a sincerer form of flattery than tributes which continue to be inhibited by the conventions of literary discourse. Had Mr. O'Hara been a French symbolist poet, he might have said: *"Tout le reste est littérature."*

Yet Hemingway too, one way or another, is literature. If his preoccupation has been mortality, his ambition — spurred perhaps by having easily won such rewards as contemporaries offer — is nothing less than immortality. He doesn't speak of building a monument or even burning a candle, but he sometimes refers to playing in the big league or writing something that will not soon go bad. Shakespeare, as Colonel Cantwell acknowledges in *Across the River*, is "the winner and still the undisputed champion." But Mr. O'Hara's build-up seems to suggest that Hemingway is training for the title bout. At least there are confirmatory signs, to state the matter in milder and more bookish terms, that he is becoming a classic in his time. He has just become the subject of "a critical survey" which should be welcomed as the first of its kind, with the expectation that its shortcomings will probably be made good by a long shelf of future volumes devoted to *Hemingwayforschung*. Since the present volume has been pasted together from other publications, it does not pretend to originality; it offers a readable and typical selection of twenty-one reviews and articles. This sort of symposium, especially when it concentrates upon so compact a body of material, is bound to cross and recross familiar territory. It is no discredit to the contributors — in fact, it reinforces their positions — that they do not diverge from each other more variously. However, it raises questions reflecting upon the judgment and knowledge of the anthologist.

He does not seem to have cast a very wide net. Given the scope and impact of his author, we might fairly expect international representation. But, except for one Soviet contribution, the table of contents is one-hundred-percent American, thereby excluding such significant essays as the almost classical polemic of Wyndham Lewis or the more recent appreciation of Claude-Edmonde Magny. Closer to home, it is hard to see how the editor — whose introduction strives to conterbalance the negative emphasis of so much criticism — could have overlooked the handsome tribute and prescient revaluation by Robert Penn Warren in *The Kenyon Review*. Yet sins of omission, with anthologies, should always be considered venial; and we need not question the individual merits of the editor's inclusions. Some of them justify their place by being too little known and not readily accessible: notably Lincoln Kirstein's sensitive review of *Death in the Afternoon* and Edward Fenimore's informative article on the language of *For Whom the Bell Tolls*. But others, though not less notable, are not so readily justified: chapters from volumes still in print by Edmund Wilson, Alfred Kazin, and W. M. Frohock. It should also be pointed out that Malcolm Cowley has published better pieces on Hemingway than the profile that Mr. McCaffery reprints from *Life*. The editor might have done a more useful job by collecting Hemingway's unreprinted writings. These are not touched upon by the bibliography, which is therefore inadequate; and there are no notes to identify the contributors, though several of them require identification. Since the chronological arrangement is based on dates of books, rather than periodical publication, it is somewhat misleading.

Yet when these cavils have been duly registered, it should be acknowledged that the book remains faithful to its protagonist. Its qualities and defects, like his, are journalistic — and I use that term in no deprecatory spirit, for journalism has more often than not been the school of our ablest writers, from Mark Twain to Hemingway himself. I simply refer to the losing race that fiction runs against fact, the hot pursuit of immediate reality in which the journalist outstrips the novelist, and also the risks — artistic as well as physical — that the imaginative writer takes by competing on the reporter's ground. For one thing, the successful reporter is seldom content to remain a good observer; give him a by-line, and he starts writing about himself; and he ends by making news for his professional colleagues, the gossip columnists. From all accounts, including his own, it would seem that, as a correspondent in the last war, Hemingway saw action in more ways than one. It may be that his refusal to draw a line between actor and spectator is one of the secrets of his vitality. Herein it is reported by John Groth that "Hemingway's jeep driver knew him as Hemingway the guy, rather than Hemingway the famous writer." And John McCaffery devotes his particular enthusiasm to "Hemingway as a man among men." We see him plain; we hear and applaud his feats as soldier, traveler, sportsman, athlete, and playboy; and sooner or later we find ourselves asking why this consummate extrovert should have taken the trouble to become a famous writer.

If he was, as we are informed, "an okay joe" to his comrades in arms, he is something more complex to his fellow writers. Their collected opinions range from grudging admiration to fascinated suspicion. Though most of them make their separate peace with him, they leave a total impression which is fairly consistent and surprisingly hostile. The exception that proves the rule, in this case Elliot Paul, is the

warm admirer who demonstrates his loyalty by belaboring
Hemingway's critics. Few of them are able to maintain the
distinction, premised by Mr. McCaffery's subtitle, between
"the man" and "his work." Curiously enough, the single
essay that undertakes to deal with craftsmanship is the one
that emanates from Marxist Russia. The rest, though they incidentally contain some illuminating comments on technique,
seem more interested in recapitulating the phases of Hemingway's career, in treating him as the spokesman of his generation, or in coming to grips with a natural phenomenon.
All this is an impressive testimonial to the force of his
personality. Yet what is personality, when it manifests itself
in art, if not style? It is not because of the figure he cuts in
the rotogravure sections, or for his views on philosophy and
politics, that we listen to a leading *Heldentenor*. No contemporary voice has excited more admiration and envy,
stimulated more imitation and parody, and had more effect on the rhythms of our speech than Hemingway's has
done. Ought we not then, first and last, to be discussing the
characteristics of his prose, when we talk about a man who —
as Archibald MacLeish has written — "whittled a style for his
time"?

II

Mr. Hemingway, in his turn, would hardly be himself —
which he is, of course, quite as consciously as any writer could
be — if he did not take a dim view of criticism. This is understandable and, as he would say, right: since criticism, ever
seeking perspective, moves in the very opposite direction from
his object, which has been immediacy. His ardent quest for
experience has involved him in a lifelong campaign against
everything that tends to get in its way, including those more
or less labored efforts to interpret and communicate it which
may be regarded — if not disregarded — as academic. Those
of us who live in the shelter of the academy will not be put
off by his disregard; for most of us have more occasion than he
to be repelled by the encrustations of pedantry; and many of
us are predisposed to sympathize with him, as well as with

ourselves, when he tells us what is lacking in critics and scholars. That he continues to do so is a mark of attention which ought not to go unappreciated. Thus currently, in introducing a brilliant young Italian novelist to American readers, he departs from his subject to drive home a critical contrast:

The Italy that [Elio Vittorini] learned and the America that the American boys learned [writes Ernest Hemingway, making a skillful transition] has little to do with the Academic Italy or America that periodically attacks all writing like a dust storm and is always, until everything shall be completely dry, dispersed by rain.

Since Hemingway is sparing in his use of metaphors, the one he introduces here is significant. "Dryasdust" has long been the layman's stock epithet for the results of scholarly inquiry; while drought, as evoked by T. S. Eliot, has become a basic symbol of modern anxiety. The country that seems to interest Hemingway most, Spain, is in some respects a literal wasteland; and his account of it — memorably his sound track for the Joris Ivens film, *The Spanish Earth* — emphasizes its dryness. Water, the contrasting element, for Hemingway as for his fellow men, symbolizes the purification and renewal of life. Rain beats out a cadence which runs through his work: through *A Farewell to Arms*, for example, where it lays the dust raised by soldiers' boots at the outset, accompanies the retreat from Caporetto, and stays with the hero when the heroine dies — even providing the very last word at the end. It is rain which, in a frequently quoted paragraph, shows up the unreality of "the words sacred, glorious, and sacrifice and the expression in vain." In the present instance, having reduced the contemporary situation to a handful of dust, as it were, Hemingway comes back to that sense of reality which he is willing to share with Vittorini. In the course of a single sentence, utilizing a digressive Ciceronian device, *paralipsis*, he has not only rounded up such writers as he considers academic; he has not only accused them of sterility, by means of that slippery logical shortcut which we professors term an enthymeme; but, like the veteran strategist he is, he has also managed to imply that they are the attackers and that he is fighting a strictly defensive action.

The conflict advances into the next paragraph, which opens on the high note that closed the previous one and then drops down again anticlimactically:

Rain to an academician is probably, after the first fall has cleared the air, H_2O with, of course, traces of other things.

Even the ultimate source of nature's vitality is no more than a jejune scientific formula to us, if I may illustrate Hemingway's point by paraphrasing his sentence. Whereas — and for a moment it seems as if the theme of fertility would be sounded soon again — but no, the emphasis waxes increasingly negative:

To a good writer, needing something to bring the dry country alive so that it will not be a desert where only such cactus as New York literary reviews grow dry and sad, inexistent without the watering of their benefactors, feeding on the dried manure of schism and the dusty taste of disputed dialectics, their only flowering a desiccated criticism as alive as stuffed birds, and their steady mulch the dehydrated cuds of fellow critics; . . .

There is more to come, but we had better pause and ruminate upon this particular mouthful. Though we may or may not accept Hemingway's opinion, we must admit that he makes us taste his distaste. Characteristically, he does not countercriticize or state the issue in intellectual terms. Instead he proceeds from agriculture to the dairy, through an atmosphere calculated to make New Yorkers uncomfortable, elaborating his earthy metaphor into a barnyard allegory which culminates in a scatological gesture. The gibe about benefactors is a curious one, since it appears to take commercial success as a literary criterion, and at the same time to identify financial support with spiritual nourishment. The hopeful adjective "alive," repeated in this deadening context, is ironically illustrated by a musty ornithological specimen: so much for criticism! Such a phrase as "disputed dialectics," which is unduly alliterative, slightly tautological, and — like "cactus" — ambiguously singular or plural, touches a sphere where the author seems ill at ease. He seems more sure of his ground when, after this muttered parenthesis, he returns to his starting point, turns the prepositional object into a subject, and sets out again toward his predicate, toward an affirmation of mellow fruitfulness:

> . . . such a writer finds rain to be made of knowledge, experience, wine, bread, oil, salt, vinegar, bed, early mornings, nights, days, the sea, men, women, dogs, beloved motor cars, bicycles, hills and valleys, the appearance and disappearance of trains on straight and curved tracks, love, honor and disobey, music, chamber music and chamber pots, negative and positive Wassermanns, the arrival and non-arrival of expected munitions and/or reinforcements, replacements or your brother.

These are the "other things" missed by the academician and discerned by the "good writer" — whether he be Vittorini or Hemingway. It is by no means a casual inventory; each successive item, artfully chosen, has its meaningful place in the author's scheme of things. Knowledge is equated with experience, rendered concrete by the staple fare of existence, and wet down by essential liquids redolent of the Mediterranean; bed, with its double range of elementary associations, initiates a temporal cycle which revolves toward the timeless sea. Men, women, and dogs follow each other in unrelieved sequence; but the term of endearment, "beloved," is reserved for motor cars; while wavering alternatives suggest the movement of other vehicles over the land. Then come the great abstractions, love and honor, which are undercut by a cynical negation of the marriage ceremony, "disobey." Since chamber music sounds highbrow, it must be balanced against the downright vulgarity of chamber pots. The pangs of sex are scientifically neutralized by the reference to Wassermann tests, and the agonies of war are deliberately stated in the cool and/or colorless jargon of military dispatches. The final choice, "replacements or your brother," possibly echoes a twist of continental slang (*et ton frère!*); but, more than that, it suddenly replaces a strategic loss with a personal bereavement.

The sentence, though extended, is not periodic: instead of suspending its burden, it falls back on *anacoluthon*, the rhetoric of the gradual breakdown and the fresh start. Hence, the first half is an uncharacteristic and unsuccessful endeavor to complete an elaborate grammatical structure which soon gets out of control. The second half thereupon brings the subject as quickly and simply as possible to its object, which opens up at once into the familiar Hemingway catalogue, where effects can be gained *seriatim* by order rather than by construction. After the chain of words has reached its climactic phrase, "your brother," it is rounded out by another transitional sentence:

All these are a part of rain to a good writer along with your hated or beloved mother, may she rest in peace or in pieces, porcupine quills, cock grouse drumming on a bass-wood log, the smell of sweet-grass and fresh smoked leather and Sicily.

This time love dares to appear in its primary human connection, but only in ambivalence with hatred, and the hazards of sentimentality are hysterically avoided by a trite pun. And though the final images resolve the paragraph by coming back to the Sicilian locale of Vittorini's novel, they savor more of the northern woods of Hemingway's Upper Peninsula. Meanwhile the digression has served its purpose for him and for ourselves; it has given us nothing less than his definition of knowledge — not book-knowledge, of course, but the real thing. Thus Robert Jordan decides to write a book about his adventures in Spain: "But only about the things he knew, truly, and about what he knew." Such a book is Hemingway's novel about him, *For Whom the Bell Tolls;* and what he knew, there put into words, is already one remove away from experience. And when Hemingway writes about Vittorini's novel, unaccustomed though he is to operating on the plane of criticism, he is two removes away from the objects he mentions in his analysis — or should I call it a hydroanalysis? Critics — and I have in mind Wyndham Lewis — have called his writing "the prose of reality." It seems to come closer to life than other prose, possibly too close for Mr. Lewis, yet for better or worse it happens to be literature. Its effectiveness lies in virtually persuading us that it is not writing at all. But though it may feel like walks in the rain or punches in the jaw, to be literal, it consists of words on the page. It is full of half-concealed art and self-revealing artifice. Since Hemingway is endlessly willing to explicate such artful and artificial pursuits as bullfighting and military tactics, he ought not to flinch under technical scrutiny.

III

Hemingway's hatred for the profession of letters stems quite obviously from a lover's quarrel. When Richard Gordon is reviled by his dissatisfied wife in *To Have and Have Not*, her most embittered epithet is "you writer." Yet Hemingway's writing abounds in salutes to various fellow writers, from the waitress' anecdote about Henry James in *The Torrents of Spring* to Colonel Cantwell's spiritual affinity with D'Annunzio. And from Nick Adams, who takes Meredith and Chesterton along on fishing trips, to Hemingway himself, who arranges to be interviewed on American literature in *Green Hills of Africa*, his heroes do not shy away from critical discussion. His titles, so often quoted from books by earlier writers, have been so apt that they have all but established a convention. He shows an almost academic fondness, as well as a remarkable flair, for epigraphs: the Colonel dies with a quotation on his lips. Like all of us, Hemingway has been influenced by T. S. Eliot's taste for Elizabethan drama and metaphysical poetry. Thus Hemingway's title, "In Another Country," is borrowed from a passage he elsewhere cites, which he might have found in Marlowe's *Jew of Malta* or possibly in Eliot's "Portrait of a Lady." *A Farewell to Arms*, which echoes Lovelace's title, quotes in passing from Marvell's "To His Coy Mistress," echoed more recently by Robert Penn Warren, which is parodied in *Death in the Afternoon*. Hemingway is no exception to the rule that makes parody the starting point for realistic fiction. Just as Fielding took off from Richardson, so Hemingway takes off from Sherwood Anderson — indeed his first novel, *The Torrents of Spring*, which parodies Anderson's *Dark Laughter*, is explicit in its acknowledgments to *Joseph Andrews*. It has passages, however, which read today like a *pastiche* of the later Hemingway:

> Yogi was worried. There was something on his mind. It was spring, there was no doubt of that now, and he did not want a woman. He had worried about it a lot lately. There was no question about it. He did not want a woman. He couldn't explain it to himself. He had gone to the Public Library and asked for a book the night before. He looked at the librarian. He did not want her. Somehow she meant nothing to him.

A recoil from bookishness, after a preliminary immersion in it, provided Fielding's master, Cervantes, with the original impetus for the novel. In "A Banal Story" Hemingway provides us with his own variation on the theme of *Don Quixote*, where a writer sits reading about romance in a magazine advertisement, while in far-off Madrid a bullfighter dies and is buried. The ironic contrast — romantic preconception exploded by contact with harsh reality — is basic with Hemingway, as it has been with all novelists who have written effectively about war. The realism of his generation reacted, not only against Wilsonian idealism, but against Wilsonian rhetoric. Hence the famous paragraph from the Caporetto episode describing Frederic Henry's embarrassment before such abstract words as "glory" and "honor," which seem to him obscene beside the concrete names of places and numbers of roads. For a Spaniard, Hemingway notes in *Death in the Afternoon*, the abstraction may still have concreteness: honor may be "as real a thing as water, wine, or olive oil." It is not so for us: "All our words from loose using have lost their edge." And "The Gambler, the Nun, and the Radio" brings forward a clinching example: "Liberty, what we believed in, now the name of a Macfadden publication." That same story trails off in a litany which reduces a Marxist slogan to meaninglessness: "the opium of the people" is everything and nothing. Even more desolating, in "A Clean, Well-Lighted Place," is the reduction of the Lord's prayer to nothingness: "Our nada who art in nada . . ." Since words have become inflated and devalued, Hemingway is willing to recognize no values save those which can be immediately felt and directly pointed out. It is his verbal skepticism which leads toward what some critics have called his moral nihilism. Anything serious had better be said with a smile, stranger. The classic echo, "irony and pity," jingles through *The Sun Also Rises* like a singing commercial.

There is something in common between this attitude and the familiar British habit of understatement. "No pleasure in anything if you mouth it too much," says Wilson, the guide in "The Short, Happy Life of Francis Macomber." Yet Jake, the narrator of *The Sun Also Rises*, protests — in the name of American garrulity — that the English use fewer words than the Eskimos. Spanish, the language of Hemingway's preference, is at once emotive and highly formal. His Spanish, to judge from *Death in the Afternoon*, is just as ungrammatical as his English. In "The Undefeated" his Spanish bullfighters are made to speak the slang of American prizefighters. Americanisms and Hispanisms, archaic and polyglot elements are so intermingled in *For Whom the Bell Tolls* that it calls to mind what Ben Jonson said of *The Faerie Queene*: "Spenser writ no language." Hemingway offers a succinct example by translating *"Eras mucho caballo"* as "Thou wert plenty of horse." It is somewhat paradoxical that a writer, having severely cut down his English vocabulary, should augment it by continual importation from other languages, including the Swahili. But this is a facet of the larger paradox that a writer so essentially American should set the bulk of his work against foreign backgrounds. His characters, expatriates for the most part, wander through the ruins of Babel, smattering many tongues and speaking a demotic version of their own. Obscenity presents another linguistic problem, for which Hemingway is not responsible; but his coy ways of circumventing the taboos of censorship are more of a distraction than the conventional blanks. When he does permit himself an expression not usually considered printable, in *Death in the Afternoon*, the context is significant. His interlocutor, the Old Lady, requests a definition and he politely responds: "Madam, we apply the term now to describe unsoundness in abstract conversation or, indeed, any overmetaphysical tendency in speech."

For language, as for literature, his feeling is strongly ambivalent. Perhaps it could be summed up by Pascal's maxim: "True eloquence makes fun of eloquence." Like the notorious General Cambronne, Hemingway feels that one short spontaneous vulgarism is more honest than all those grandiloquent slogans which rhetoricians dream up long after the battle. The disparity between rhetoric and experience, which became so evident during the First World War, prompted the 'twenties to repudiate the genteel stylistic tradition and to accept the American vernacular as our norm of literary discourse. "Literary" is a contradiction in terms, for the resultant style is basically oral; and when the semiliterate speaker takes pen in hand, as Hemingway demonstrates in "One Reader Writes" — as H. L. Mencken demonstrated in "A Short View of Gamalielese" — the result is even more artificial than if it had been written by a writer. A page is always flat, and we need perspective to make it convey the illusion of life in the round. Yet the very fact that words mean so much less to us than the things they represent in our lives is a stimulus to our imaginations. In "Fathers and Sons" young Nick Adams reads that Caruso has been arrested for "mashing," and asks his father the meaning of that expression.

"It is one of the most heinous of crimes," his father answered. Nick's imagination pictured the great tenor doing something strange, bizarre, and heinous with a potato masher to a beautful lady who looked like the pictures of Anna Held on the inside of cigar boxes. He resolved, with considerable horror, that when he was old enough he would try mashing at least once.

The tone of this passage is not altogether typical of Hemingway. Rather, as the point of view detaches itself affectionately and ironically from the youth, it approximates the early Joyce. This may help to explain why it suggests a more optimistic approach to language than the presumption that, since phrases can be snares and delusions, their scope should be limited to straight denotation. The powers of connotation, the possibilities of oblique suggestion and semantic association, are actually grasped by Hemingway as well as any writer of our time. Thus he can retrospectively endow a cheap and faded term like "mashing" with all the promise and poetry of awakening manhood. When Nick grows up, foreign terms will hold out the same allure to him; like Frederic Henry, he will seek the actuality that resides behind the names of places; and Robert Jordan will first be attracted to Spain as a professional philologist. But none of them will find an equivalence between the word and the thing; and Hemingway, at the end of *Death in the Afternoon*, laments that no book is big enough to do final justice to its living subject. "There was so much to write," the dying writer realizes in "The Snows of Kilimanjaro," and his last thoughts are moving and memorable recollections of some of the many things that will now go unwritten. Walt Whitman stated this challenge and this dilemma, for all good writers, when he spoke of expressing the inexpressible.

IV

The inevitable compromise, for Hemingway, is best expressed by his account of Romero's bullfighting style: "the holding of his purity of line through the maximum of exposure." The maximum of exposure — this throws much light upon the restlessness of Hemingway's career, but here we are primarily concerned with the holding of his purity of line. It had to be the simplest and most flexible of lines in order to accommodate itself to his desperate pursuit of material. His purgation of language has aptly been compared, by Robert Penn Warren, to the revival of diction that Wordsworth accomplished with *Lyrical Ballads*. Indeed the question that Coleridge afterward raised might once again be asked: why should the speech of some men be more real than that of others? Today that question restates itself in ideological terms: whether respect for the common man necessitates the adoption of a commonplace standard. Everyone who writes faces the same old problems, and the original writers — like Wordsworth or Hemingway — are those who develop new ways of meeting them. The case of Wordsworth would show us, if that of

Hemingway did not, that those who break down conventions tend to substitute conventions of their own. Hemingway's prose is not without precedents; it is interesting to recall that his maiden effort, published by *The Double Dealer* in 1922, parodied the King James Bible. He has his forerunners in American fiction, from Cooper to Jack London, whose conspicuous lack was a style as dynamic as their subject-matter. The ring-tailed roarers of the frontier, such as Davy Crockett, were Colonel Cantwell's brothers under the skin; but as contrasted with the latter's tragic conception of himself, they were mock-heroic and serio-comic figures, who recommend themselves to the reader's condescension. Mark Twain has been the most genuine influence, and Hemingway has acknowledged this by declaring — with sweeping generosity — that *Huckleberry Finn* is the source of all modern American literature.

But Mark Twain was conducting a monologue, a virtual *tour de force* of impersonation, and he ordinarily kept a certain distance between his narrative role and his characters. And among Hemingway's elder contemporaries, Ring Lardner was a kind of ventriloquist, who made devastating use of the vernacular to satirize the vulgarity and stupidity of his dummies. It remained for Hemingway — along with Anderson — to identify himself wholly with the lives he wrote about, not so much entering into them as allowing them to take possession of him, and accepting — along with their sensibilities and perceptions — the limitations of their point of view and the limits of their range of expression. We need make no word-count to be sure that his literary vocabulary, with foreign and technical exceptions, consists of relatively few and short words. The corollary, of course, is that every word sees a good deal of hard use. Furthermore, his syntax is informal to the point of fluidity, simplifying as far as possible the already simple system of English inflections. Thus "who" is normally substituted for "whom," presumably to avoid schoolmarmish correctness; and "that," doing duty for "which," seems somehow less prophetic of complexity. Personal pronouns frequently get involved in what is stigmatized, by teachers of freshman composition, as faulty reference; there are sentences in which it is hard to tell the hunter from his quarry or the bullfighter from the bull. "When his father died he was only a kid and his manager buried him perpetually." So begins, rather confusingly, "The Mother of a Queen." Sometimes it seems as if Hemingway were taking pains to be ungrammatical, as do many educated people out of a twisted sense of *noblesse oblige*. Yet when he comes closest to pronouncing a moral, the last words of Harry Morgan — the analphabetic hero of *To Have and Have Not* — seem to be half-consciously fumbling toward some grammatical resolution: "A man . . . ain't got no hasn't got any can't really isn't any way out. . ."

The effectiveness of Hemingway's method depends very largely upon his keen ear for speech. His conversations are vivid, often dramatic, although he comes to depend too heavily upon them and to scant the other obligations of the novelist. Many of his wisecracks are quotable out of context, but as Gertrude Stein warned him: "Remarks are not literature." He can get his story told, and still be as conversational as he pleases, by telling it in the first person. "Brother, that was some storm," says the narrator, and the reader hears the very tone of his voice. In one of Hemingway's critical digressions, he declares that he has always sought "the real thing, the sequence of motion and fact which [*sic*] made the emotion. . ." This seems to imply the clear-cut mechanism of verbal stimulus and psychological response that Eliot formulates in his theory of the objective correlative. In practice, however, Hemingway is no more of a behaviorist than Eliot, and the sharp distinction between motion and emotion is soon blurred. Consider his restricted choice of adjectives, and the heavy load of subjective implication carried by such uncertain monosyllables as "fine" and "nice." From examples on nearly every page, we are struck by one which helps to set the scene for *A Farewell to Arms*: "The town was very nice and our house was very fine." Such descriptions — if we may consider them descriptions — are obviously not designed for pictorial effect. When the Colonel is tempted to call some fishing-boats picturesque, he corrects himself: "The hell with picturesque.

They are just damned beautiful." Where "picturesque" might sound arty and hence artificial, "beautiful" — with "damned" to take off the curse — is permissible because Hemingway has packed it with his own emotional charge. He even uses it in *For Whom the Bell Tolls* to express his esthetic appreciation of gunfire. Like "fine" and "nice," or "good" and "lovely," it does not describe; it evaluates. It is not a stimulus but a projected response, a projection of the narrator's euphoria in a given situation. Hemingway, in effect, is saying to the reader: *Having wonderful time. Wish you were here.*

In short, he is communicating excitement; and if this communication is received, it establishes a uniquely personal relationship; but when it goes astray, the diction goes flat and vague. Hemingway manages to sustain his reputation for concreteness by an exploring eye for the incidental detail. The one typescript of his that I have seen, his carbon copy of "The Killers" now in the Harvard College Library, would indicate that the arc-light and the tipped-back derby hat were later observations than the rest. Precision at times becomes so arithmetical that, in "The Light of the World," it lines up his characters like a drill-sergeant: "Down at the station there were five whores waiting for the train to come in, and six white men and four Indians." Numbers enlarge the irony that concludes the opening chapter of *A Farewell to Arms* when, after a far from epic invocation, a casual introduction to the landscape, and a dusty record of troops falling back through the autumn, rain brings the cholera which kills "only seven thousand." A trick of multiplication, which Hemingway may have picked up from Gertrude Stein, is to generalize the specific episode: "They always picked the finest places to have the quarrels." When he offers this general view of a restaurant — "It was full of smoke and drinking and singing" — he is an impressionist if not an abstractionist. Thence to expressionism is an easy step: ". . . the room whirled." It happens that, under pressure from his first American publishers, the author was compelled to modify the phrasing of "Mr. and Mrs. Elliott." In the original version, subsequently restored, the title characters "try to have a baby." In the modified version they "think of having a baby." It could be argued that, in characterizing this rather tepid couple, the later verb is more expressive and no more euphemistic than the earlier one; that "think," at any rate, is not less precise or effectual than "try." But, whereas the sense of effort came naturally, the cerebration was an afterthought.

If we regard the adjective as a luxury, decorative more often than functional, we can well understand why Hemingway doesn't cultivate it. But, assuming that the sentence derives its energy from the verb, we are in for a shock if we expect his verbs to be numerous or varied or emphatic. His usage supports C. K. Ogden's argument that verb-forms are disappearing from English grammar. Without much self-deprivation, Hemingway could get along on the so-called "operators" of Basic English, the sixteen monosyllabic verbs that stem from movements of the body. The substantive verb *to be* is predominant, characteristically introduced by an expletive. Thus the first story of *In Our Time* begins, and the last one ends, with the story-teller's gambit: "there was," "there were." In the first two pages of *A Farewell to Arms* nearly every other sentence is of this type, and the third page employs the awkward construction "there being." There is — I find the habit contagious — a tendency to immobilize verbs by transposing them into gerunds. Instead of writing *they fought* or *we did not feel*, Hemingway writes "there was fighting" and "there was not the feeling of a storm coming." The subject does little more than point impersonally at its predicate: an object, a situation, an emotion. Yet the idiom, like the French *il y a*, is ambiguous; inversion can turn the gesture of pointing into a physical act; and the indefinite adverb can indicate, if not specify, a definite place. Contrast, with the opening of *A Farewell to Arms*, that of "In Another Country": "In the fall the war was always there, but we did not go to it any more." The negative is even more striking, when Frederic Henry has registered the sensations of his wound, and dares to look at it for the first time, and notes: "My knee wasn't there." The adverb is *there* rather than *here*, the verb is *was* rather than *is*, because we — the readers — are separated from the event in space and time. But the narrator has lived through it, like the Ancient Mariner, and now he chooses his words to grip and transfix us. *Lo!* he says. *Look! I was there.*

v

Granted, then, that Hemingway's diction is thin; that, in the technical sense, his syntax is weak; and that he would rather be caught dead than seeking the *mot juste* or the balanced phrase. Granted that his adjectives are not colorful and his verbs not particularly energetic. Granted that he commits as many literary offenses as Mark Twain brought to book with Fenimore Cooper. What is behind his indubitable punch, the unexampled dynamics of Hemingway's style? How does he manage, as he does, to animate this characteristic sentence from "After the Storm"?

I said "Who killed him?" and he said "I don't know who killed him but he's dead all right," and it was dark and there was water standing in the street and no lights and windows broke and boats all up in the town and trees blown down and everything all blown and I got a skiff and went out and found my boat where I had her inside of Mango Key and she was all right only she was full of water.

Here is a good example of Hemingway's "sequence of motion and fact." It starts from dialogue and leads into first-person action; but the central description is a single clause, where the expletive takes the place of the observer and his observations are registered one by one. Hence, for the reader, it lives up to Robert Jordan's intention: "you . . . feel that all that happened to you." Hemingway puts his emphasis on nouns because, among parts of speech, they come closest to things. Stringing them along by means of conjunctions, he approximates the actual flow of experience. For him, as for Marion Tweedy Bloom, the key word is *and*, with its renewable promise of continuity, occasionally varied by *then* and *so*. The rhetorical scheme is *polysyndeton* — a large name for the childishly simple habit of linking sentences together. The subject, when it is not taken for granted, merely puts us in touch with the predicate: the series of objects that Hemingway wants to point out. Even a preposition can turn this trick as "with" does in this account of El Sordo waiting to see the whites of his enemy's eyes:

Come on, Comrade Voyager . . . Keep on coming with your eyes forward . . . Look. With a red face and blond hair and blue eyes. With no cap on and his moustache is yellow. With blue eyes. With pale blue eyes. With pale blue eyes with something wrong with them. With pale blue eyes that don't focus. Close enough. Too close. Yes, Comrade Voyager. Take it, Comrade Voyager.

Prose gets as near as it can to physical conflict here. The figure enlarges as it advances, the quickening impression grows clear and sharp and almost unbearable, whereupon it is blackened out by El Sordo's rifle. Each clipped sentence, each prepositional phrase, is like a new frame in a strip of film; indeed the whole passage, like so many others, might have been filmed by the camera and projected on the screen. The course of Harry Morgan's launch speeding through the Gulf Stream, or of Frederic Henry's fantasy ascending the elevator with Catherine Barkley, is given this cinematographic presentation. *Green Hills of Africa* voices the long-range ambition of obtaining a fourth and fifth dimension in prose. Yet if the subordinate clause and the complex sentence are the usual ways for writers to obtain a third dimension, Hemingway keeps his writing on a linear plane. He holds the purity of his line by moving in one direction, ignoring sidetracks and avoiding structural complications. By presenting a succession of images, each of which has its brief moment when it commands the reader's undivided attention, he achieves his special vividness and fluidity. For what he lacks in structure he makes up in sequence, carefully ordering visual impressions as he sets them down and ironically juxtaposing the various items on his lists and inventories. "A Way You'll Never Be" opens with a close-up showing the debris on a battlefield, variously specifying munitions, medicaments, and left-overs from a field kitchen, then closing in on the scattered papers with this striking montage-effect: ". . . group postcards showing the machine-gun unit standing in ranked and ruddy cheerfulness as in a football picture for a college annual; now they were humped and swollen in the grass. . . ." It is not surprising that Hemingway's verse, published by *Poetry* in 1923, is recognizably imagistic in character — and perhaps his later heroics are foreshadowed by the subject of one of those poems, Theodore Roosevelt.

In her observant book, *L'Age du roman américain*, Claude-Edmonde Magny stresses Hemingway's "exaltation of the instant." We can note how this emphasis is reflected in his timing, which — after his placing has bridged the distance from *there* to *here* — strives to close the gap between *then* and *now*. Where Baudelaire's clock said "remember" in many languages, Robert Jordan's memory says: "Now, *ahora, maintenant, heute*." When death interrupts a dream, in "The Snows of Kilimanjaro," the ultimate reality is heralded by a rising insistence upon the word "now." It is not for nothing that Hemingway is the younger contemporary of Proust and Joyce. Though his time is neither *le temps perdu* nor the past nostalgically recaptured, he spends it gathering roses while he can, to the ever accelerating rhythm of headlines and telegrams and loud-speakers. The act, no sooner done than said, becomes simultaneous with the word, no sooner said than felt. Hemingway goes so far, in "Fathers and Sons," as to render a sexual embrace by an onomatopoetic sequence of adverbs. But unlike Damon Runyon and Dickens, he seldom narrates in the present tense, except in such sporting events as "Fifty Grand." Rather, his timeliness expresses itself in continuous forms of the verb and in his fondness for all kinds of participial constructions. These, compounded and multiplied, create an ambiance of overwhelming activity, and the epithets shift from El Sordo's harassed feelings to the impact of the reiterated bullets, as Hemingway recounts "the last lung-aching, leg-dead, mouth-dry, bullet-spatting, bullet-cracking, bullet-singing run up the final slope of the hill." More often the meaning takes the opposite turn, and moves from the external plane into the range of a character's senses, proceeding serially from the visual to the tactile, as it does when the "Wine of Wyoming" is sampled: "It was very light and clear and good and still tasted of the grapes."

When Nick Adams goes fishing, the temperature is very tangibly indicated: "It was getting hot, the sun hot on the back of his neck." The remark about the weather is thereby extended in two directions, toward the distant source of the heat and toward its immediate perception. Again in "Big Two-Hearted River," Nick's fatigue is measured by the weight of his pack: ". . . it was heavy. It was much too heavy." As in the movies, the illusion of movement is produced by repeating the same shot with further modification every time. Whenever a new clause takes more than one step ahead, a subsequent clause repeats it in order to catch up. Repetition, as in "Up in Michigan," brings the advancing narrative back to an initial point of reference. "Liz liked Jim very much. She liked it the way he walked over from the shop and often went to the kitchen door to watch him start down the road. She liked it about his moustache. She liked it about how white his teeth were when he smiled." The opaque verb "like," made increasingly transparent, is utilized five more times in this paragraph; and the fumbling preposition "about" may be an acknowledgment of Hemingway's early debt to Gertrude Stein. The situation is located somewhere between a subjective Liz and an objective Jim. The theme of love is always a test of Hemingway's objectivity. When Frederic kisses Catherine, her responses are not less moving because they are presented through his reflexes; but it is her sentimental conversation which leaves him free to ask himself: "What the hell?" At first glance, in a behavioristic formula which elsewhere recurs, Colonel Cantwell seems so hard-boiled that motions are his only emotions: "He saw that his hand was trembling." But his vision is blurred by conventionally romantic tenderness when he contemplates a heroine whose profile "could break your . . . or anyone else's heart." Hemingway's heroines, when they aren't bitches, are fantasies — or rather, the masculine reader is invited to supply his own, as with the weather in Mark Twain's *American Claimant*. They are pin-up girls.

If beauty lies in the eye of the beholder, Hemingway's purpose is to make his readers beholders. This is easily done when the narration is conducted in the first person; we can sit down and drink, with Jake Barnes, and watch Paris walk by. The interpolated chapters of *In Our Time*, most of them reminiscences from the army, employ the collective *we*; but, except for "My Old Man," the stories themselves are told in the third person. Sometimes, to strengthen the sense of identification, they make direct appeal to the second person; the protagonist of "Soldier's home" is "you" as well as "he" — and, more generally, "a fellow." With the exception of Jake's confessions, that is to say *The Sun Also Rises*, all of Hemingway's novels are written in the *style indirect libre* — indirect discourse which more or less closely follows the consciousness of a central character. An increasing tendency for the author to intrude, commenting in his own person, is one of the weaknesses of *Across the River*. He derives his strength from a power to visualize episodes through the eyes of those most directly involved; for a page, in "The Short, Happy Life of Francis Macomber," the hunt is actually seen from the beast's point of view. Hemingway's use of interior monologue is effective when sensations from the outer world are entering the stream of a character's consciousness, as they do with such a rush at El Sordo's last stand. But introspection is not Hemingway's genre, and the night-thoughts of *To Have and Have Not* are among his least successful episodes. His best are events, which are never far to seek; things are constantly happening in his world; his leg-man, Nick Adams, happens to be the eye-witness of "The Killers." The state of mind that Hemingway communicates to us is the thrill that Nick got from skiing in "Cross Country Snow," which "plucked Nick's mind out and left him only the wonderful, flying, dropping sensation in his body."

VI

If psychological theories could be proved by works of fiction, Hemingway would lend his authority to the long contested formula of William James, which equates emotion with bodily sensation. Most other serious writers, however, would bear witness to deeper ranges of sensibility and more complex processes of motivation than those he sees fit to describe. Some of them have accused Hemingway of aggressive anti-intellectualism: I am thinking particularly of Aldous Huxley. But Huxley's own work is so pure an example of all that Hemingway has recoiled from, so intellectual in the airiest sense, and so unsupported by felt experience, that the argument has played into Hemingway's hands. We have seen enough of the latter to know that he doesn't really hate books — himself having written a dozen, several of which are, and will remain, the best of their kind. As for his refusal to behave like a man of letters, he reminds us of Hotspur, who professes to be a laconic philistine and turns out — with no little grandiloquence — to be the most poetic character in Shakespeare's play. Furthermore, it is not Hemingway, but the slogan-mongers of our epoch, who have debased the language; he has been attempting to restore some decent degree of correspondence between words and things; and the task of verification is a heavy one, which throws the individual back on his personal resources of awareness. That he has succeeded within limits, and with considerable strain, is less important than that he has succeeded, that a few more aspects of life have been captured for literature. Meanwhile the word continues to dematerialize, and has to be made flesh all over again; the first-hand perception, once it gets written down, becomes the second-hand notation; and the writer, who attains his individuality by repudiating literary affectation, ends by finding that he has struck a new pose and founded another school.

It is understandable why no critique of Hemingway, including this one, can speak for long of the style without speaking of the man. Improving on Buffon, Mark Schorer recently wrote: "[Hemingway's] style is not only his subject, it is his view of life." It could also be called his way of life, his *Lebenstil*. It has led him to live his books, to brave the maximum of exposure, to tour the world in an endless search for wars and their moral equivalents. It has cast him in the special role of our agent, our plenipotentiary, our roving correspondent on whom we depend for news from the fighting fronts of modern consciousness. Here he is, the man who was there. His writing seems so intent upon the actual, so impersonal in its surfaces, that it momentarily prompts us to overlook the personality behind them. That would be a serious mistake; for the point of view, though brilliantly intense, is narrowly focused and obliquely angled. We must ask: who is this guide to whom we have entrusted ourselves on intimate terms in dangerous places? Where are his limitations? What are his values? We may well discover that they differ from our assumptions, when he shows us a photograph of a bullfighter close to a bull, and comments: "If there is no blood on his belly afterwards you ought to get your money back." We may be ungrateful to question such curiosity, when we are indebted to it for many enlargements of our vicarious knowledge; and it may well spring from the callowness of the tourist rather than the morbidity of the *voyeur*, from the American zest of the fan who pays his money to reckon the carnage. When Spain's great poet, García Lorca, celebrated the very same theme, averting his gaze from the spilling of the blood, his refrain was *"Que no quiero verla!"* ("I do not want to see it!").

Yet Hemingway wants to see everything — or possibly he wants to be in a position to tell us that he has seen everything. While the boy Nick, his seeing eye, eagerly watches a Caesarian childbirth in "Indian Camp," the far from impassive husband turns away; and it is later discovered that he has killed himself. "He couldn't stand things . . ." so runs the diagnosis of Nick's father, the doctor. This, for Nick, is an initiation to suffering and death; but with the sunrise, shortly afterward, youth and well-being reassert themselves; and the end of the story reaffirms the generalization that Hazlitt once drew: "No young man ever thinks he shall die." It is easy enough for such a young man to stand things, for he is not yet painfully involved in them; he is not a sufferer but a wide-eyed onlooker, to whom the word "mashing" holds out mysterious enticements. Hemingway's projection of this attitude has given his best work perennial youthfulness; it has also armed his critics with the accusation that, like his Robert Cohen, he is "a case of arrested development." If this be so, his plight is generalized by the Englishman Wilson, who observes that "Americans stay little boys . . . all their lives." And the object of Wilson's observation, Francis Macomber, would furnish a classic case-history for Adler, if not for Freud — the masculine sense of inferiority which seeks to overcome itself by acts of prowess, both sanguinary and sexual. Despite these two sources of excitement, the story is a plaintive modulation of two rather dissonant themes: *None but the brave deserves the fair* and *The female of the species is more deadly than the male*. After Francis Macomber has demonstrated his manhood, the next step is death. The world that remains most alive to Hemingway is that stretch between puberty and maturity which is strictly governed by the ephebic code: a world of mixed apprehension and bravado before the rite of passage, the baptism of fire, the introduction to sex.

Afterward comes the boasting, along with such surviving ideals as Hemingway subsumes in the word *cojones* — the English equivalent sounds more skeptical. But for Jake Barnes, all passion spent in the First World War, or for Colonel Cantwell, tired and disgruntled by the Second, the aftermath can only be elegiac. The weather-beaten hero of *Across the River*, which appears in 1950, is fifty years old and uneasily conscious of that fact; whereas "the childish, drunken heroics" of *The Sun Also Rises* took place just about twenty-five years ago. From his spectacular arrival in the 'twenties, Hemingway's course has paralleled that of our century; and now, at its midpoint, he balks like the rest of us before the responsibilities of middle age. When, if ever, does the *enfant du siècle*, that *enfant terrible*, grow up? (Not necessarily when he grows a beard and calls himself "Mr. Papa.") Frederic Henry plunges into the Po much as Huck Finn dived into the Mississippi, but emerges to remind us even more pointedly of Fabrice del Dongo in Stendhal's *Chartreuse de Parme*, and of our great contemporary shift from transatlantic innocence to old-world experience. Certain intimations of later years are present in Hemingway's earlier stories, typically Ad Francis, the slaphappy ex-champ in "The Battler." Even in "Fifty Grand," his most contrived tale, the beat-up prizefighter suffers more than he acts and wins by losing — a situation which has its corollary in the title of Hemingway's third collection, *Winner Take Nothing*. The ultimate article of his credo, which he shares with Malraux and Sartre, is the good fight for the lost cause. And the ultimate protagonist is Jesus in "Today is Friday," whose crucifixion is treated like an athletic feat, and whose capacity for taking punishment rouses a fellow-feeling in the Roman soldiers. The stoic or masochistic determination to take it brings us back from Hemingway to his medium, which — although it eschews the passive voice — is essentially a receiving instrument, especially sensitized for recording a series of violent shocks.

The paradox of toughness and sensitivity is resolved, and the qualities and defects of his writing are reconciled, if we merely remember that he was — and still is — a poet. That he is not a novelist by vocation, if it were not revealed by his books, could be inferred from his well known retort to F. Scott Fitzgerald. For Fitzgerald the rich were different — not quantitatively, because they had more money, but qualitatively, because he had a novelistic interest in manners and morals. Again, when we read André Gide's reports from the Congo, we realize what *Green Hills of Africa* lacks in the way of social or psychological insight. As W. M. Frohock has perceived, Hemingway is less concerned with human relations than with his own relationship to the universe — a concern which might have spontaneously flowered into poetry. His talents come out most fully in the texture of his work, whereas the structure tends to be episodic and uncontrived to the point of formlessness. *For Whom the Bell Tolls*, the only one of his six novels that has been carefully constructed, is in some respects an over-expanded short story. Editors rejected his earliest stories on the grounds that they were nothing but sketches and anecdotes, thereby paying incidental tribute to his sense of reality. Fragments of truth, after all, are the best that a writer can offer; and, as Hemingway has said, ". . . Any part you make will represent the whole if it's made truly." In periods as confusing as the present, when broader and maturer representations are likely to falsify, we are fortunate if we can find authenticity in the lyric cry, the adolescent mood, the tangible feeling, the trigger response. If we think of Hemingway's temperamental kinship with E. E. Cummings, and of

Cummings' "Buffalo Bill" or "Olaf glad and big," it is easy to think of Hemingway as a poet. After the attractions and distractions of timeliness have been outdated, together with categorical distinctions between the rich and the poor, perhaps he will be remembered for a poetic vision which renews our interrupted contact with the timeless elements of man's existence: bread, wine, bed, music, and just a few more of the concrete universals. When El Sordo raises his glance from the battlefield, he looks up at the identical patch of the blue sky that Henry Fleming saw in *The Red Badge of Courage* and that looked down on Prince Andrey in *War and Peace*.

LONG VIEWS

Society as Its Own Historian

Under the title, "Social Aspects of the Nineteenth-Century Novel," this was the Philip Maurice Deneke Lecture delivered at Lady Margaret Hall, Oxford University, on May 21, 1953. I wish to thank the Misses Deneke for their hospitable invitation, Professor Lord David Cecil for his gracious introduction, and the Oxford University Press for allowing its rights of publication to be anticipated here. An earlier version of this lecture was delivered at Smith College and elsewhere under the title, "The Epic of the Middle Class."

▀▀

The visitor at Oxford, like the stranger at Athens, knows very well that he is a barbarian. This wholesome piece of self-knowledge is made quite palatable by the extraordinary hospitality with which he is nonetheless made to feel at home. Occasions are even provided, like the present one, when it is specified that: "Usually the lecturer invited shall be a foreigner lecturing in his own language." Hence I need not apologize for addressing you in my own demotic dialect of your language. Indeed, as an American, I could almost feel as if I were being promoted from a state of savagery to a state of barbarism. But when I think of the civilized traditions that the Philip Maurice Deneke Lecture has already gathered to itself, under the gracious auspices of Lady Margaret Hall; and when I think of my distinguished predecessors, both continental and British, and then of myself; then, most sincerely and seriously, I am overwhelmed by a sense of anticlimax. And so must you be; but, if I may say so, I would not have it otherwise; for anticlimax is the first premise of my subject, the nineteenth-century novel.

It is anticlimactic when a Homeric catalogue heralds an army of sheep, or when a Petrarchan litany celebrates the charms of a kitchenmaid, or when — in many other combinations — the knightly idealism of Don Quixote is undermined by the bourgeois realism of Sancho Panza. And if, for the father of the novel, Cervantes, the golden age of chivalry was already a distant dream, how much more distant must it be from the great age of the novel, the iron age of the nineteenth century — not to mention the age of uranium into which we have thus far somehow managed to survive. Men have always told each other stories, and I trust they always will; but the forms of fiction have varied greatly from one period to the next. If the epic presupposes a heroic age, then the difference between the epic and the romance is a difference between a heroic age and an age of chivalry, between the tribal and feudal ways of life: a society organized upon a warlike basis and one organized around the medieval cult of the Virgin, the Christian reverence for womanhood, and an increasing emphasis on the relations between the sexes.

It would be too much and too little to say that the ancient world was, like Ernest Hemingway's collection of short stories, a world of *Men without Women*. But those epical heroines whom we seem to remember best — Andromache, Penelope, Dido — seem warranted in complaining of neglect on the part of their men-folk. Whereas Boileau pointed out that such classical heroes as Brutus and Cato, under the effeminizing influence of the romance, became gallants and ladies' men. "Arms and the man I sing," so Vergil begins his epic. And how does Ariosto begin his romance? He will sing, so he tells us, "Of ladies and knights, of arms and amours." Not only was fiction written of women, but increasingly it was written for and by women. That singular anomaly, the lady novelist, in the rather masculine person of Madame de Staël, declared at the end of the eighteenth century that the novel could no longer confine itself to the sphere of love; that vanity, ambition, avarice, and other more worldly themes awaited novelists in the nineteenth century. Meanwhile an English lady novelist who had lived in France during the Revolution, Madame d'Arblay *née* Fanny Burney, declared that life was not the same after that great event; and that henceforth literature would be different.

After the Third Estate had come to power, the novel could come into its own. Hitherto it had been regarded as an illegitimate stepchild, a paradoxical hybrid; when traditional forms were wedded to modern themes, the result was mock-epic or antiromance; when Furetière spoke of "a bourgeois romance" or Fielding of "a comic epic in prose," they were speaking of contradictions in terms. Thanks to such efforts as theirs, which were seldom more than half-serious, during the seventeenth and eighteenth centuries the novel transcended its original limitations. Thanks also to the development of printing — as well as to the spread of literacy, which by this time was spread pretty thin — verse rather than prose came to be the medium of fiction, and private individuals rather than public figures came to constitute its subject-matter. Thus the novel, with writer speaking directly to reader, became the most immediate and personal mode of the arts. Taking its potentialities seriously, Hegel characterized it as *das bürgerliche Epos,* the epic of the middle class; while Zola was later to proclaim it as the *genre par excellence,* the predominant literary form of the nineteenth century. In the twentieth century this predominance is attested by publishers and booksellers, who often divide their stock into fiction and nonfiction, with fiction the larger category of the two.

This may suggest another characteristic of the novel: it tends, more expressly than most other kinds of artistic production, to be a commodity. At a time when so many novelists seem to write with one eye on the reading public and the other on the cinema audience, and so many critics seem to be motivated by the hope of being quoted on the jackets of the novels they review, there is no need to labor the point. It is only fair to recognize, however, that a certain commercial impetus has affected the novel throughout its course. The romantic movement may be interpreted, in the most narrowly literary terms, as a conscious effort to revive the romance. Yet the Great Unknown who wrote the Waverley Novels, who preferred to be known as the Laird of Abbotsford and not as a partner in the unlucky firm of Ballantyne,

Sir Walter Scott led a dual existence: he was both the last minstrel and the first best-seller. Hence the quality of his books is so uneven; roughly speaking, the most romantic are the least satisfactory. His historical romances of other countries and of the far-away past seem much dimmer to us than his regional novels, which so vividly preserve the Scotland of a generation or two before his time.

By covering that ground, by pointing out the local landmarks, moving from court to cottage, from the picturesque landscapes of the highlands to the pedestrian aspects of everyday life, Scott was more than an antiquarian; he was virtually a sociologist; and, certainly, he was the forerunner of the realists. Acknowledging this contribution, Balzac appreciated Scott's duality, which he crystallized in a pun: *"ce trouvère moderne,"* or alternatively *"ce trouveur moderne."* In other words, Scott could either be viewed nostalgically, as a medieval troubador, or somewhat more technically as a modern inventor. In contrast with the romance, which bears the weight of Latin tradition in its very name, the novel flaunts its resolve to be up-to-date. Its name means news; it means something new; wherefore Goethe defined it as "an unusual and unexpected event." While the romance may well be a twice-told tale, the novel must be a novelty, the creation of its time. And since its age is neither heroic nor chivalric but flatly bourgeois, it depends upon a system of human relations which is neither military nor courtly but essentially mercantile. Such a system — if we may call it that — repudiating feudal allegiances and tribal obligations alike but still recognizing the bonds of interest, is our free society where individual freedom is constrained mainly by the intermittent tightening of the cash nexus.

Now where the values of the epic were based upon war, and those of the romance upon love, the values of the novel are grounded on property. Its underlying rhythm is that which is beaten into the ground by the horse of Tennyson's Northern Farmer: "Proputty, proputty, proputty." Property is the basis of civilization, according to — among others — Fenimore Cooper, who on occasion could show as much gusto in defending landlords as his Leatherstocking displayed in attacking Indians. And, of course, John Galsworthy could retrospectively state that his purpose in chronicling *The Forsyte Saga* was to preserve the middle class in its own juice, "the sense of property." In the great manifesto of realism, the foreword to *The Human Comedy* — announcing that society was about to become its own historian and that the novelist would simply be its secretary — Balzac divided the whole field into three subjects: men, women, and things. This is, to say the least, a very drastic oversimplification; and I particularly hesitate to entertain it here, after the welcome of a critical and scholarly interpreter who has revealed to us so many of the delicate shadings and subtle motivations in English novels of the nineteenth century.

The hypothesis is worth entertaining, however, so long as we do not allow it to become a thesis. So long as we realize that the social aspect is merely one important side of a literary form which is marked by its many-sidedness, so long as we do not expect material considerations to explain everything, it is surprising — and rather disconcerting — how much they can explain. And it is surprising how well Balzac's three categories, men, women, and things, correspond to our three phases of fiction as historically considered: epic, romance, and novel. Where the epic centers on men in action, and where the romance centers on the relationship between men and women, the novel subordinates men and women to things. As we follow the progress of the novel, we witness a process through which things assume the saddle, and ride mankind at an ever accelerating pace. Very tentatively, very sketchily, and with due awareness of much that evades formulation, I should like to illustrate these assumptions, first, with respect to men; second, not excluding men, with respect to women; and third, not excluding other things, with respect to things in themselves.

Starting with men, by your leave, we may take as our starting point Thackeray's pathetic and self-revealing complaint: how difficult, how all but impossible it is for the author of *Pendennis*, for the novelist of the nineteenth century to create a MAN! And capital letters emphasize Thackeray's longing, inhibited by the genteel femininity of the Victorian epoch, for the more virile epoch of the eighteenth century and of manly Harry Fielding. This throws a certain light upon the subtitle of *Vanity Fair, A Novel without a Hero* — a subtitle which might aptly have served for a good many contemporaneous novels. "I want a hero," Byron's invocation for *Don Juan*, is just as significant of its time as were the respective invocations of the *Aeneid* and the *Orlando Furioso* for theirs. It is the cry of a century which is often considered a century of hero-worship, the quest of an age forever seeking and never quite finding what Lermontov styled *A Hero of our Time*. If ever it did find him, it found him flawed; and a whole subjective literature grew up out of the radical flaws of characters who were heroes only in the technical sense of the term.

Yet history gave the nineteenth century a hero who was himself an avid reader of novels, whose lengthened shadow falls across the literature of the time, Napoleon Bonaparte. As the great exemplar of the career open to talents, his talent opened the way for many careers, and encouraged many careerists, literary and otherwise. "To accomplish with the pen what he has done with the sword" — such were the words engraved on Napoleon's bust in Balzac's study. The career of his Rastignac or Rubempré, or of Stendhal's Julien Sorel for that matter, is typical of the generation that first felt this impact — little Napoleons of the law-courts and the theological seminaries, of the Bourse and the boudoir. Nor was the Napoleonic complex limited to a single generation or to France: it animated the criminal student Raskolnikov, hero or villain of Dostoevsky's *Crime and Punishment*. If the strong personality now sought an outlet in crime, rather than war, it was because the battlefield was no longer looked upon as an appropriate field for heroics.

When Hector volunteered to meet Achilles, individuals could manifest their prowess heroically. But all that had been strategically changed by the scale of modern warfare, the development of long-range artillery, the civilian conscription of vast and anonymous armies. The Battle of Waterloo figures in *Vanity Fair* mainly as a series of off-stage noises, which accompany the serio-comic departure of Jos Sedley from Brussels. In *Les Misérables* Victor Hugo muses grandiloquently, and takes us on a conducted tour of the battlefield, many years after the event. For the first-hand experience of the combatant, our primary authority is Stendhal, and we must consult his *Charterhouse of Parma*. His hero's hero, inevitably, is Napoleon; but young Fabrice del Dongo arrives on the scene too late to affect the outcome of the Emperor's last campaign. Shunted back and forth across the field, Fabrice hardly knows which side is which; taken under the wing of an elderly *vivandière*, he is fortified by brandy; then he shoots his man and, like a hunter, runs to his quarry. It is not until he buys a newspaper, in a neighboring town on the following day, that he finds an answer to his questions: was it a battle in which he had just participated? and was it perchance the Battle of Waterloo?

With the developing tactics and widening scope of more recent wars, the ironies and disillusionments of the novelist have become more bitter and more devastating than the mock-heroics of Stendhal. Fabrice is disillusioned to discover that the heroes of his time are lesser men than the knights of Ariosto. So modern writers, convincing themselves that they have come too late into a world too old, become praisers of the past. Their lament is characteristically expressed by this entry from the journal of the brothers Goncourt: "Everything goes to the people and deserts the kings. Even literature descends from royal misfortunes to private misfortunes. From Priam to Birotteau!" From Priam to Birotteau — what a falling-off is there! We have come down in the world most anticlimactically when we have descended from the tragic figure of the King of Troy, himself the father of fifty heroes, to the wholesale and retail perfumer who is the mock-hero of Balzac's *Grandeur and Decadence of César Birotteau*. Yet if, in his grandeur — issuing a Napoleonic challenge to his rivals, the manufacturers of macassar oil — César is a comic figure, he becomes sympathetic — if not tragic — in his decadence, when bankruptcy makes him the victim of the system he represents.

In general, as represented in the novel, your solid citizen is more to be scorned than pitied, more sinning than sinned against. At best he is little more than a figure of fun, like Monsieur Prudhomme or George F. Babbitt. At worst he is that paragon of bumbling complacency, that model of nineteenth-century provinciality, created by Flaubert to stand as a horrible example for all future centuries, Monsieur Homais. Here we encounter — if not an animus on the part of the writer — a refusal to accept the bias of his class, from which he stands apart in order to criticize. Usually it is the middle class; and where, if not there, would he find mediocrity? But, for Flaubert, it is really a state of mind: the bourgeois, by Flaubert's definition, is whoever thinks meanly (*"quiconque pense bassement"*). The bourgeoisie, on the other side, commits itself more and more to a philistine attitude toward the arts; and, as the rift widens, the artist feels more and more objectively warranted in his use of harsh colors and sharp lines. When the realistic painter, Courbet, was reproached for the ugliness of his portraits, he merely shrugged and replied: *"Les bourgeois sont ainsi!"*

To turn from men to women, in this context, is to turn from the mock-heroic to the antiromantic. It is rather a jolt to be reminded that those handsome and eligible young officers, who figure as dancing partners and possible suitors for Jane Austen's heroines, were on furlough from the Napoleonic campaigns. Romantic, as well as heroic, considerations are thus subordinated to more worldly ones; if war is mechanized, love is domesticated. Take, as an experiment, one of Jane Austen's novels; and turn, not to the last page — what will happen there is obvious — but to the first. You are fairly sure to find the same two themes, marriage and money, sounded there, and afterwards developed in strict polyphony. They are subsumed, with an epigrammatic sweep, in the introductory sentence of *Pride and Prejudice*: "It is a truth universally acknowledged, that a single man in possession of a good fortune must be in want of a wife."

In comparison with Jane Austen, the Brontë sisters treat the theme of love with tolerable warmth — in Emily Brontë's case, with a warmth that waxes all but intolerable. Yet the proposal of Mr. Rochester to Jane Eyre leaves something to be desired in the way of ardor: "You — poor and obscure and small and plain as you are — I entreat you to accept me as a husband." It was the reverberation of her response — "To the finest fibre of my nature, sir" — that shocked contemporary readers. It was shocking of Jane Eyre to respond so warmly, to confide so breathlessly in the reader, to tell her love; this was low; the tone was most ungovernesslike. It was proper enough for the governess — or indeed the housemaid — to marry the squire, if she behaved demurely. Since the days of Pamela and her brother, Joseph Andrews, novelists had been gaining access to the gentry through the servants' quarters. But it is harder for us to understand the outraged reviewer who surmised that, if the pseudonymous author of *Jane Eyre* was not really a man, it must be some woman who by her behavior had forfeited the companionship of all the respectable members of her sex. Times had changed, fifty years later, when Thomas Hardy described Tess of the d'Urbervilles as *A Pure Woman Faithfully Presented*. How Tess could be seduced and give birth to an illegitimate child, and then commit adultery and murder, and still remain a pure woman, is a question which may best be left to the capricious determination of those ironic gods whom Hardy was constantly apostrophizing.

The old-fashioned heroine faced the alternative of a happy ending, which could only be marriage, or an early death, either to escape from a fate which was worse or else to pay the penalty for not having escaped. Now it was discovered that marriage was not necessarily happy. The theme of adultery, though not altogether unknown, was explored more painstakingly than before. That marriage was not the end of everything, that the woman of thirty had a charm of her own, that romance could never quite be superannuated, is said to have been a discovery of Balzac's. The superiority of the wife to the husband, the plight of the superior wife or the misunderstood woman, *la femme incomprise,* was so well established by George Sand that, when a Madame La Farge disgracefully murdered her middle-aged, middle-class husband, the public sympathy was on her side. The test case is that of Madame Bovary; and though her romantic imagination ranged far beyond her husband, the mediocre doctor who brooded over his Norman patients while she dreamed of lovers in Italy, her nemesis was not love but debt; having proceeded from Rodolphe to Léon, she might have gone on to take another lover, had not the merchant Lheureux sent out his bills and the bailiffs moved in.

If love affairs are dealt with unromantically, as battles are dealt with unheroically, we may trace this astringent influence to its source, the Midas-touch that turns all things to dross. There is no special need to assume that human nature was changing. We need only admit how invariably human relations have adapted themselves to changes in culture: the necessities of war, the observances of love, the commitments of property. Consequently, speaking in terms of quantity and of its perennial encroachment on quality, we see values converted to prices. When Jane Austen speaks of "fortune" — a word which connotes so many vicissitudes — or when Trollope speaks of "living" — which should be limitless in its connotations — what is denoted, in either case, is simply "income." It is this process of cultural deflation, as it withers ideals and reduces individuals to a state of disillusionment, which the novelist — whether he considers himself a realist or a naturalist — makes it his task to comprehend and interpret. Like Balzac's money-changer, Gobseck, he subtracts the discount from life; he exhibits life with the discount subtracted. If the only hero of *The Human Comedy* is the franc, as has been maintained, then its typical character, the miser Grandet, is literally made of money — for his very name is an anagram of *d'argent.*

Happily, we may no longer be able to agree with Karl Marx, when he characterizes England as "the fortress of landlordism"; but, in his day, it must have seemed an impregnable citadel of vested interests; and its nineteenth century was, in the phrase of E. M. Forster, "the age of property." Over this period ownership shifted crucially, from landed property to invested capital; and capitalism, like everything else on earth, has its imaginative symbols. If history did not teach us that the old farms were dying out, and that the country estates were being mortgaged, we should know from reading *Castle Rackrent, The Bride of Lammermoor,* or *Wuthering Heights.* The haunted castles of fiction were not situated in the clouds; one of them, as the Marquis de Sade knew well, was the Bastille. It is not by chance that the *Communist Manifesto* begins as if it were a Gothic novel: "A specter is haunting Europe . . ." The great exception, you may say, is Trollope. Trollope, said Hawthorne, is just as solid as roast beef and ale. But the passage of years lends poignance to the metaphor; and when you come to read *The Way We Live Now,* you suspect that the ale has been watered and the beef has hung too long. No one has regarded the novel more frankly as a commodity than Trollope did in his *Autobiography.* And when we read there of his improvident father, his radical mother, and his expatriate brother, we sense the compulsion that prompted that mirage of false security which he named "the imaginary county of Barsetshire."

Vainly such idealists as George Eliot sought to reverse the direction. The history of fiction takes a picaresque road which leads it from the country to the city. The novel is intrinsically an expression of the culture of cities and their denizens, the burghers or bourgeoisie. The metropolis, progressively begrimed and industrialized, presents a fascinating but corrupting vista, a setting which dwarfs and stunts its dramatis personae. Though Dickens frequently takes his cockneys on a holiday, though he wistfully pines for coaching days and clearer air, we must remember that his Christmas decorations frame such grim pictures as that which he gives us of Coketown in *Hard Times.* When he depicts a typical estate, he calls it *Bleak House,* and connects it with the even grimmer mansion of Chesney Wold; both houses in turn are connected with the most dubious piece of real estate in London, the dilapidated tenements of Tom-All-Alone's; and that connection leads by various entanglements of the law to the Court of Chancery, the very arcanum of property. The accumulation of things, their tangible yet illusory nature, is symbolized by the junkshop of Mr. Krook, the mock Lord Chancellor, who expires mysteriously in the smoke and grease of spontaneous combustion.

The announced intention of *Bleak House* is to dwell upon "the romantic side of familiar things," to cast a more or less poetic glow on more or less prosaic material. This is apparent throughout, from the grimly impressive opening where the fog, with the tread of some prehistoric monster, creeps through the mud and gaslight up Chancery Lane. The only scene I know to match against it is that descent into hell which opens *Le Père Goriot*, where Balzac conducts us step by step into that vale of suffering between the slopes of Montmartre and the heights of Montrouge, and utters the Dantesque warning that we must abandon hope if we would enter the Parisian underworld. As a young romanticist, in *Notre-Dame de Paris*, Victor Hugo had taken a bird's-eye view of medieval Paris; as an older realist, in *Les Misérables*, he took his readers through the sewers of the modern city. But Hugo's convict-hero, Jean Valjean, carrying Marius on his shoulder, is more humanitarian than human — especially when we compare him with the absent-minded, bearlike, bespectacled Pierre Bezuhov in *War and Peace*, carrying a scrofulous child through the smoking ruins of Moscow. To become a hero, Pierre must abandon his property, must leave his mansion and leave it by the back door; and with him Tolstoy's conception of the besieged and deserted city attains a grandeur which transcends the bourgeois and strives again toward the heroic.

Pierre is happiest when he looks up at the sky, and sees that astronomical phenomenon which men have the temerity to call the Comet of 1812; in much the same way, his wounded friend Prince Andrey finds serenity in the midst of the Battle of Austerlitz, by fixing his gaze on a patch of blue overhead; and Tolstoy, at such moments, takes us out of the

realm of history into the orbit of the wider universe. Man's
environment is more broadly conceived as the century wears
on. The milieu in which the novelist situates his characters
is not so much society as it is nature. His concern, as George
Meredith voices it, is to write "the natural history of man."
Naturalism, supplanting realism as a critical slogan, continues the tendency but darkens the picture. The term
realism, borrowed from art, implies a descriptive technique:
the detailed notation, the photographic imitation of life, so
closely paralleled by Daguerre's recent invention. The term
naturalism, related to science, carries a philosophical implication: a materialistic method, a deterministic outlook, a
view of man victimized by his environment. Where Hugo, or
even Dostoevsky, views him with humanitarian sympathy as
the victim of society, Hardy views him as the plaything of
nature, the victim of a cosmic joke. But, as Hardy suggests,
there are two kinds of conflict: that between individuals and
human institutions, and that between individuals and things
inherent in the universe.

If any historical figure casts his shadow upon the literature
and thought of the latter half of the nineteenth century, it
is a professional naturalist, Charles Darwin. The controversy
over Darwin's theory of evolution came to a head, here at
Oxford, in a famous debate between Professor Huxley and
Bishop Wilberforce; and I scarcely need to remind you how
the chairman, a novelist as well as a politician, summed up
the question. Is man an ape, or is he an angel? It was, of
course, to the Bishop that Disraeli inclined, when he public-
ly espoused the cause of the angels. But, after all, Disraeli
was a notorious reactionary. When we recall the angels of
nineteenth-century fiction — the little Nells, the little Evas
— and then a more recent novel by Professor Huxley's
grandson, in which the endeavors of humanity are reduced
to the chattering of apes in Hollywood, we may well conclude
that Disraeli chose the losing side. No more serious challenge
to the orthodox notion of human nature had arisen since
Renaissance astronomy helped to girdle the earth and thereby favor the rise of the trading classes, the era of the private

individual. It was no longer a question of being lower than the angels; it was a question of keeping man's head above the level of the apes. That is still the question, as naturalism continues to put man in his place, with a pessimistic unction which circumstances conspire to justify.

The problem, for Meredith again, was "to build a road between Adam and Macadam": to utilize civilization as a means for reconciling man and nature. The reign of things has two phases, one commercial, the other scientific. Commerce and science combine to produce technology, the slave that seeks to be master. *Robinson Crusoe*, written in pioneering days of the bourgeoisie, had asserted man's mastery over things. Mrs. Shelley's Gothic fable of *Frankenstein* came closer to the shape of things to come, as it turned out, than all the obsolescent fantasies of Jules Verne and H. G. Wells. At some step or other, on the highroad to the utopian future, an unexpected turning point occurs: as soon as mechanical things seem to gain control over things organic, the machine becomes the common enemy and nature becomes man's ally. Charlotte Brontë describes the Luddites wrecking their looms in *Shirley*; Samuel Butler's Erewhonians revolt and destroy their machines; and D. H. Lawrence rounds out a cycle which takes the countryman through industrialism and back to a cult of primitive vitality.

When Zola set forth the havoc wrought by the Franco-Prussian War in *Le Débâcle*, he left his readers with a ray of hope: a last glimpse of the bloody battlefield, where vegetation is springing up anew. Similarly, after the strike and the explosion in *Germinal,* the incessant pumping finally stops; the great beast has ceased to breathe; the machinery sinks through the mine-shaft into the earth; and suddenly it is spring; the seeds are germinating; and again Zola ends by stressing the endless renewal of the seasons. By tracing the rise and fall of his Rougons and Macquarts through twenty volumes, Zola attempted to record *The Natural and Social History of a Family under the Second Empire.* But this comprehensive heading balances the respective claims of nature and of society more evenly than Zola's particular novels seem to do, as we reread them today. His views on nature have long since dated, whereas his visions of society have proved to be prophetic. His human sympathies have stood the test much better than his experimental pretensions, and scientific failure is outweighed by historical achievement.

The history of the Rougon-Macquart family, in its grandeur and decadence, was one of many fictional attempts to trace the genealogy of the century. A more succinct account was adumbrated by Zola's more fastidious colleagues, Edmond and Jules de Goncourt. They portray a generic man of letters, *Charles Demailly*, who writes a generic novel, which he therefore entitles *The Bourgeoisie*. As it is sketched for us, it seems to present three successive generations through three different types; the grandfather, the man of property, has a son who is sentimental, expansive, and idealistic; and this central figure has a son in his turn, who is cynical, skeptical, and effete. Crossing the Channel, we find the same three ages presenting themselves, with a difference and a similarity, in Samuel Butler's *Way of All Flesh*: first, the founder of the family fortunes, who combines business with religion by selling prayer-books; second, the heavy father, Theobald Pontifex, a high priest of mid-Victorianism; and third, the autobiographical Ernest, the young intellectual, the prodigal son. Looking back at the nineteenth century from the first year of the twentieth, Thomas Mann's *Buddenbrooks* offers a chronological parallel traced through the decline of a family of German burghers.

Thus the vantage-point of the *fin du siècle* permits us to take a conspectus of the whole period. Our three generations are known to literary history as romantic, realistic, and naturalistic. Through a more personal set of associations, we have recognized the first as Napoleonic and the third as Darwinian. It is fitting that the middle generation, that comfortable plateau between an ascent and a declivity, should be presided over by a woman, Queen Victoria. From another point of view, we could subdivide the century into halves, and watch the tension between crabbed age and youth, which finally breaks out into overt conflict in *The Ordeal of Richard Feverel*, or the ideological duel between the aging liberal and the youthful revolutionary in Turgenev's *Fathers and Sons*. After the solid comforts of the mid-century fade and dissolve, novelists take a nostalgic view of property. To evoke "the poetry, as it were, of something sensibly *gone*" was the confessed aim of Henry James in *The Spoils of Poynton*. James, without waiting for Proust, made himself the elegiac poet of things — which have their veritable holocaust at Poynton, when the fine old house is sequestrated and the rare old furniture goes up in flames. It remained for a younger and more hard-boiled American, F. Scott Fitzgerald, to reverse a proverb and point the moral: "The victor belongs to the spoils."

In emphasizing the tyranny of things, the influence of external factors over the lives of men and women, we are not forgetting the persistence of love and war, the importance of *Anna Karenina* as well as *War and Peace*. The all-too-clear loss of human dignity and stature gains some compensation perhaps, when the mind goes underground with Dostoevsky, and deepens its insight into some of the obscurer aspects of the human condition. If modern life is a strange disease, as your poet-critic would diagnose it, then modern literature makes the best of a difficult situation by improving its diagnostic technique and its pathological knowledge. Judging between the rival claims of free will and necessity, Tolstoy argued that every man has two lives, one individual, the other elemental. And though Tolstoy deflates the Napoleonic myth as decisively as Cervantes exploded the legend of chivalry, he creates a collective hero in the idealized figure of the peasant, Platon Karataev, to demonstrate how individual lives participate in elemental movement. Perhaps because Tolstoy had no connection with the middle class, because he was born into the aristocracy and ultimately threw in his lot with the peasantry, he escapes the limitations of the novelistic approach and seems to gravitate toward the epical.

In our twentieth century, where matter itself can be so fortuitously exploded, nothing encourages us to assume that civilization is resting securely on its basis of property. As culture accordingly changes, as the novel wanes with the fortunes of the middle class, what new direction is there for fiction to take? It has already taken two sharply diverging directions. Leaving the middle class to stew in its own juice, the sense of property, the novelist has identified himself with the proletarian on the one hand, and with the artist on the other. His solitary and self-conscious position was already proclaimed when Herman Melville asked his readers to call him Ishmael, or when Samuel Butler called himself "a literary Ishmaelite." But for that very reason, he could also make common cause with outcasts and other underdogs. The art of the nineteenth century had for its purpose, wrote Dostoevsky anent Victor Hugo, "the rehabilitation of the oppressed pariah." Men and women had been treated as things; their very souls were treated as property, when Gogol scoffed at serfdom in *Dead Souls*. But when Harriet Beecher Stowe attacked Negro slavery in *Uncle Tom's Cabin*, she apologized for introducing a subject "hitherto ignored by the associations of polite and refined society." The function of the novel has been a continual extension of the literary franchise to social classes hitherto ignored.

To the middle class, and then to the proletariat. It was not Marx, it was Disraeli who pointed out that England comprised two nations, the rich and the poor; and even if, in *Sybil*, the labor leader turns out to be the disguised son of a peer and the trade-unions meet in ruined castles by moonlight, there were others to sharpen the distinction and attack the bourgeoisie from the other side. If the artist, as Thomas Mann believes, is "a burgher gone astray," he has strayed far from his middle-class origins and across the line that divides philistines from bohemians. The tense relation between the novel and the middle class came to an open break, with the suppression of *Madame Bovary* and the trial of Flaubert. Flaubert's conclusion, that hatred of the bourgeoisie is the beginning of virtue, has become the point of departure for many a subsequent novelist, and notably for James Joyce. Joyce, on the one hand, exploits the personality of the artist, and cultivates the art of the novel for art's sake, to a point beyond which it seems impractical — if not impossible — to go. On the other hand, no one has shown more sympathy for the downtrodden citizen, or reconstructed so fully or so minutely the actual conditions of city life. With *Ulysses* our wheel comes full circle, revolving back toward the epic, and to an epos which presupposes the fall of a city: *Fuit Ilium.*

Pausing in latter-day admiration before Balzac's *Human Comedy* and other imposing and incomplete monuments of the previous hundred years, Marcel Proust discerned their special quality in a certain perspective toward their time, a certain ability to step back from it and rise above it, which he termed *autocontemplation.* This should not be confounded with *autocritique,* a term which has more lately been used to designate those painful occasions on which writers denounce themselves and renounce their independence; nothing could be farther removed from genuine criticism or contemplation, not to say introspection. This habit of mind, this self-contemplation explains a certain disparity between form and substance, the paradox of noble works created out of ignoble material. If life is really like that, if *les bourgeois sont ainsi,* then it is only the mediocre artist who tries to prettify the picture, and only the mediocre critic who censures it because it is not pretty enough. The epoch whose testament we have been reading, doubtless had many faults; but it had the redeeming virtue of self-criticism, in the broadest and most meaningful sense of the term: the virtue that makes it possible for a culture to be broader and wiser and more humane than the society on which it is founded.

A perfect society, by definition, has no use for a self-critical literature; but no society ever achieved a state of perfection by liquidating its critics. However, it is not for me to stress a principle which is so much better grasped in England than in most other countries of the world today. The quality that Maxim Gorky noted in the great writers of the nineteenth century was a refusal to accept the values of their own class, as chroniclers of its development and its decline. Whatever you name this tendency, "revolutionary romanticism" or "critical realism" or "the liberal imagination," whatever the terminology, it seems to mean something like what Proust means by self-contemplation. Though it is hard to think of two contemporaries who diverge more widely than Proust and Gorky, the novelist as artist and the novelist as proletarian, their divergence may help us to summarize the psychological depth and the social breadth of our subject, the novel in both its analytic scope and its esthetic richness. It should also remind us that, though many themes of nineteenth-century fiction are now as defunct as Queen Victoria, the attitudes it continues to assert constitute a hard-won inheritance. The struggle to sustain this critical heritage, to maintain a society which is capable of being its own historian, may well be the epic theme of the twentieth century.

Symbolism and Fiction

These remarks were tentatively put forward in a symposium on literary criticism at the University of Wisconsin on May 9, 1952. The notes were later written out and presented as a paper to the Peters Rushton Seminar on Contemporary Prose and Poetry at the University of Virginia on May 11, 1956. Through special arrangement, a separate edition has been issued by the University of Virginia Press, Charlottesville.

▬▬▬

A few years ago we welcomed to our Department a colleague who had never before taught English literature. As a poet he had practiced it; as a lawyer he had once taught law; and as Assistant Secretary of State he may even have prepared himself to cope with the complexities of academic life. Why should I not mention the honored name of Archibald MacLeish? Mr. MacLeish was anxious to meet the minds of the college generation, and incidentally to test the observation that William Faulkner had supplanted Ernest Hemingway as their literary idol. His first assignment required his class, as a sort of touchstone, to read and report on Mr. Hemingway's "Big Two-Hearted River." They had not read it; but you have, and you remember that it is hardly a story at all; it is simply a sketch about a boy who goes fishing. Its striking quality is the purity of its feeling, its tangible grasp of sensuous immediacy, the physical sensation that Mr. Hemingway is so effective at putting into prose. The students did not seem to feel this quality. They liked the story; they wrote about it at length; but in their protocols, to a man, they allegorized it. Each of those fish that Nick Adams had jerked out of Big Two-Hearted River bore for them a mystical significance, which varied according to its interpreter — Freudian or Jungian, Kierkegaardian or Kafkaesque. May I leave these silvery, slippery trout dangling there in the water to incarnate the fascination and the elusiveness of our subject?

American literature would all be childishness, the innocent wonderment of the schoolroom — according to one of its most perceptive interpreters, D. H. Lawrence — if it did not invite us to look beneath its bland surface and to find a diabolic inner meaning. The reaction of Professor MacLeish's students might suggest that we do not enjoy the surfaces enough, that we have become too morbidly preoccupied with the subliminal. In our restless search for universals, we may be losing sight of particulars: of the so-called quiddity, that "whatness" which characterizes a work of art, the truth of an object to its peculiar self. Literature is not a game of charades. Yet Lawrence's reinterpretation helped to rescue, out of the indiscriminate attic of children's books, the greatest classic in American literature; and *Moby-Dick* has plenty of deviltry at its core. When a lightning-rod man intruded upon Mark Twain, the upshot was a humoristic sketch. When a lightning-rod man intruded upon Herman Melville, the consequence became part of his lifelong quarrel with organized religion. It may now remain for some intrepid young allegorist to demonstrate, in some little magazine, that Mark Twain's sketch is nothing less than a cryptographic adumbration of a Rosicrucian tract.

At this juncture it may prove useful to be reminded that *Moby-Dick* itself, like "Big Two-Hearted River," is a simple story about a fishing trip. Basically, it is just another yarn about the big fish that got away. So is Mr. Hemingway's last book, *The Old Man and the Sea*, even though critics have seen themselves symbolized in the sharks that prey on the Old Man's gigantic catch. *Moby-Dick*, at all events, is a whopper; and, like all whoppers, it has the capacity to be expanded and elaborated *ad infinitum*. In the process of elaboration, Melville has introduced his linked analogies and dark similitudes, sometimes deliberately and — it would also seem — sometimes intuitively. He himself seemed scarcely conscious of certain implications which Nathaniel Hawthorne pointed out, and which thereupon fell into place — as Melville acknowledged — in "the part-and-parcel allegoricalness of the whole." (Or did he write "of the whale?" Melville's handwriting, in his famous letter to Mrs. Hawthorne, is indeterminate at this crucial point.) One of his chapters, anatomizing the beached skeleton of a whale, tells us that some of its smaller vertebrae have been carried away to make children's rattles. And so, he goes on to moralize, almost anticipating the reception of his book, so the most momentous enterprises can taper off into child's play.

Mr. Faulkner, being our contemporary, has not suffered very much from the innocence of his readers. On the contrary, the title of his last novel, *A Fable*, proclaims his own ambition to universalize a message of some sort, impelled perhaps by the sense of international responsibility that seems to go along with the Nobel Prize. But let us revert to a more modest example of his story-telling skill, with which we may feel more at home, *The Bear*. This is another story about a hunting trip; it sticks to his region and it securely belongs, along with *The Adventures of Huckleberry Finn* and *The Red Badge of Courage*, among those wonderful American stories in which a boy reaches manhood through some rite of passage, some baptism of fire, an initiation into experience. We may not have noticed, and we should therefore be grateful for the critical comment that points it out, a possible resemblance between the youthful Ike McCaslin and the epic heroes of Homer and Vergil. But we may be less grateful than puzzled when the same Kenyon Critic informs us that *The Bear* is an allegory of "the transition from pagan to Christian culture, if not from the Old to the New Testament." We may even begin to suspect that the commentator lacks a sense of proportion, if not a sense of humor.

Needless to say, these lacks would not be considered serious enough to disqualify him from practicing criticism as it is frequently practiced today. Criticism is a child of the time, and it changes as times change. The catchwords of critics have tended to echo the ideals of their respective periods. Thus a whole epoch is summed up in the term "decorum," and another by the shibboleth "sublime." What is our key word? "Ambiguity" is not my own suggestion; it is an obvious recommendation from our contemporary masters of critical terminology. Their stronghold, be it Axel's castle or Kafka's, is not the old allegorical castle of love or war, of perseverance or indolence; it is a citadel of ambiguity. Since the numerous types of ambiguity presuppose as many levels of meaning, it might be more up-to-date to call this castle a skyscraper, and to call our typologists of ambiguity — borrowing a compendious adjective from *Finnegans Wake* — "hierarchitectitiptitoploftical." As an instance of such hierarchitectitiptitoploftical criticism, without pretending to be citing at random, I might cite a recent interpretation of James Joyce's *Portrait of the Artist as a Young Man*. Here at the outset Cranly, the friend of the artist, is said to be not only John the Baptist but likewise Judas and Pilate — a wide and exacting and not exactly compatible range of roles for a secondary character.

Part of the difficulty would seem to spring from the critic's addiction to the copula. Some of our literary reviews, in this respect, might just as well be written in Basic English. Suggestive allusions tend to become flat assertions. Something, instead of suggesting some other thing, somehow *is* that other thing; it cannot mean, it must be. Everything must be stated as an equation, without recognizing degrees of relationship or the differences between allusion and fact. Now, as the name of his protagonist indicates, Joyce is fond of alluding to prototypes. Cranly is ironically linked with John the Baptist as a kind of predecessor; and to the extent to which every betrayer of his friend is a Judas and every avoider of moral responsibility is a Pilate, he may be said to have momentarily figured in both of those positions. But what are we then to make of the Artist as a Young Man? A Jesus? There is a sense in which the life of every good Christian is, or should be, an imitation of Christ. But Stephen Dedalus expressly chooses to imitate Satan: *"Non serviam!"* The comment is therefore not an ambiguity nor an ambivalence nor a tension nor an irony nor a paradox. It is a contradiction or — to use a very old-fashioned term — an impertinence; and there are times when reason can do no more than imitate Dr. Johnson and kick the stone.

Such interpretations are dismissed as "cabalistics" by the introduction to one of the many current studies of Franz Kafka. But when we turn from this introduction to the study itself, having been all but convinced that its author is uniquely sane and that Kafka's other commentators are uniformly mad, we find that he too has a frenzied glint in his eye and a cabalistic theory of his own: all of Kafka is to be explained by the incidence of the number two. Two is an important number, of course, when we come to think about it; and when we start to look for it, it appears to be so ubiquitous that it explains not only Kafka but everything else. The only matter it does not explain is the difference between Kafka and everything else. And that, I fear, is the trouble with much that passes for psychoanalytic criticism: it reduces our vocabulary of symbols to a few which are so crudely fundamental and so monotonously recurrent that they cannot help the critic to perform his primary function, which is still — I take it — to discriminate. Nature abounds in protuberances and apertures. Convexities and concavities, like Sir Thomas Browne's quincunxes, are everywhere. The forms they compose are not always enhanced or illuminated by reading our sexual obsessions into them.

Isolating text from context in the name of "close reading," we can easily be led astray. So sensible a critic as Edmund Wilson has argued that Henry James's "Turn of the Screw" should be read as a psychological projection of its governess's frustrations. Subsequently it has been shown by Professor Robert L. Wolff — a professional historian on a Jamesian holiday — that the manifest content of the alleged fantasy came from a sentimental illustration in a Christmas annual to which James had also contributed. What is needed today perhaps, what readers and writers might well join together in forming, would be a Society for the Protection of Symbols from Critics. But I do not want to labor a point which is, indeed, that all too many points may have been labored already. Having labored a little in the symbolistic vineyard, I share the curiosities and admire the ingenuities of many of my fellow laborers. If these remarks have the intonation of a caveat, they should also have the overtones of a *mea culpa*. When, however, this hieratic tendency draws back upon itself the leveling criticism of the philistines who are always with us, thereby exacerbating the war of attrition between the quarterlies and the weeklies, we must all be concerned one way or another.

A primrose by a river's brim is, obviously, one thing to J. Donald Adams and quite another thing to Kenneth Burke. For the leveling critic the flower in the crannied wall may be simply that and nothing more. A rose itself, the emblem of romance and so much more, the *rosa sempiterna* of Dante, the *rosa mystica* of Hopkins or Yeats, the garden of T. S. Eliot's agony, the thorn of which Rilke may actually have died in aromatic pain — well, a rose is a rose is a rose. And *Moby-Dick* is a book which exists on a plane of comparison with the novels of Captain Marryat. Without capitulating to that simplistic view, we could well afford to concede that not every literary surface happens to mask a darker meaning. Every work of art may be a form of symbolic action, as Mr. Burke keeps patiently reminding us; and behind the reminder stands Coleridge's conception of the artist as a creator of symbols. When Hamlet could not accuse Claudius directly, he approached him by means of the play-within-the-play — "tropically." So Ernst Jünger, during the Nazi regime, was able to attack it symbolically in his fantastic tale, *From the Marble Cliffs*. But there are symbols and symbols. "My tropes are not tropes," says King Media to the philosopher Babbalanja in Melville's *Mardi*, "but yours are." That is the issue: when is a trope not a trope, and what is it then?

It should do us no harm to admit that art continues to have its simpler vehicles, such as love lyrics or works of sculpture, designed to convey feelings rather than ideas. When Mr. Mac-Leish's students dredged up such grimly subaqueous intimations from the limpid waters of the Big Two-Hearted River, they were essentially engaged in revealing themselves. Furthermore, they were reflecting the outlook of our age — an age which, as it looks back toward the nineteen-twenties from the vantage-point of a full generation afterward — seems to be looking across an enormous gulf. Writing at the end of that fabulous decade, Mr. Wilson terminated his *Axel's Castle* with a kind of farewell to the symbolists: to Yeats and Joyce and Proust and several other supreme individualists, and to those rare artificial worlds of their private creation. But symbolism proved much too deeply rooted to take the hint and retire. In the meanwhile, a call for a "science of symbolism" had been issued by C. K. Ogden and I. A. Richards. Exploring the personal and the collective unconscious, Freud and Jung had shown how primitive myths survive through oneiric fantasies. Furthermore, public events have intervened in our lives to strengthen the authority of symbols. Hence the movement, broadening its base, has been going forward — or is it backward? For symbolism, in the Hegelian worldview, characterizes the earliest phase of culture.

One of the signs of revival has been the popularity of Suzanne Langer's *Philosophy in a New Key*, with its stimulating argument that modern logic, semantics, metaphysics, and various schools of thought in the social sciences run parallel to the course of symbolism among the arts. But the key in which all this is pitched, by virtue of Mrs. Langer's synesthetic metaphor, is by no means new. It is so old that we might properly call it a "mode"; and it leads us back to other modes of thinking which are rather prelogical than logical, rather magical than scientific, rather transcendental than empirical. Mrs. Langer's two philosophical masters, Ernst Cassirer and Alfred North Whitehead, were both profoundly aware that symbolism is inherent in the very processes of language and thought. So was Quintilian: "*Paene quicquid loquimur figura est.*" We could hardly speak or think or vote without symbols; we live and die by them; we should hesitate to cross the street at a traffic intersection, were it not for their unambiguous accord. All art, in this sense, is more or less symbolic. More or less, and whether it is more symbolic or less may be determined by historical as well as by esthetic considerations.

Take an illustration which William Butler Yeats admired because it happened to be "out of nature," because it belonged to "the artifice of eternity." Take "such a form as Grecian goldsmiths make" — a Byzantine icon. Such a religious image had to be stylized and conventionalized along the lines that were sanctioned and prescribed by the Church of the East. Its style could be considered more symbolic than the painting of the West; for Western painters, freed from the conventions and prescriptions and restrictions of Iconoclastic dogma, could come closer and closer to life — even as material actuality was becoming secular and realistic. At the eastern extreme, the taboo of the Jewish and Mohammedan religions against the making of graven images sponsored an art which was decorative and functional but not precisely significant, as in a prayer-rug. "In a symbol," wrote Thomas Carlyle in his handbook for symbolists, *Sartor Resartus*, "there is both concealment and revelation." But if everything were revealed, then nothing would be symbolized; and if everything were concealed, then too nothing would be symbolized. Thus a symbol is a sort of excluded middle between what we know and what we do not know — or better, as Carlyle put it, a meeting point between the finite and the infinite.

Art is always an imitation, never quite the real thing. It cannot represent without symbolizing. By its devices of synecdoche or metonymy, it gives us the part for the whole or the attribute for the object. It never gives us a perfect replica; on the other hand, it never gives us a complete abstraction. What has been ineptly termed "nonobjective painting" proves — if nothing else — that there is really no such thing as pure design. In the dramatic moralities, Vanity is a highly feminine creature and the Vice is full of boyish mischief. Life itself is bound to be mixed up with any artistic representation of it; yet even the "slice of life" of the naturalists had to be framed by symbolic conceptions, as in the fiction of Emile Zola or his American disciple, Frank Norris. Think of Norris' titles, *The Pit, The Octopus* — not to mention the monstrous tooth of McTeague. Banish the symbol, and it returns as a simile: the mine-shaft transformed by *Germinal* into a perpetually crouching beast. The London fog, with its natural aura of obfuscation, becomes a metaphorical vehicle for Dickens' critique of the law-courts in *Bleak House*. And Flaubert concentrates with such intensity on the details of materialistic circumstance that, in *A Simple Heart*, the stuffed parrot of his old servant-woman is apotheosized into the Paraclete.

Generally speaking, art seems to oscillate between two poles, the symbolistic and the realistic — or, we might say, the typical and the individual. In its westward movement it has kept pace with the development of human individuality. In its eastward purview it glances backward toward Byzantium, and toward an order of mind which derives its strength from the opposing principle of typicality. This polarity is recognized by philosophy in the habitual problem of the One and the Many, and it has innumerable repercussions in the political and sociocultural areas. Through some such oscillation, we have been moving — at least until lately — in the direction set by the Greeks. A humanistic literature, such as theirs, is not primarily regulated by symbolism. Homer and Sophocles made use of symbols, yes; but the *Odyssey* is a story about a man named Odysseus; it is not an ironic commentary upon a day in the life of a man named Leopold Bloom; while Oedipus, since he verily married his mother, was presumably the one recorded man who did not suffer from the frustrations of the Oedipus complex. The world of Odysseus and Oedipus was concrete; it was here and now as long as it lasted. Ages with less pride in the dignity of mankind would preach contempt for this world, along with hope for another and better one hereafter. The visible things of this earth, in the doctrine of Saint Paul, shadow forth the invisible things of God. As Christopher Cranch, the transcendentalist poet, expressed it: "Nature is but a scroll, — God's handwriting thereon." It is held that the artist, like the prophet, should have the insight to read and translate these divine hieroglyphics. Such is the state of mind that makes for symbolism, both in creating and in interpreting a hermetic art.

The two points of view, the otherworldly and the humanistic, clashed in the conflict between Christian asceticism and the pagan classics, which Saint Augustine resolved by formulating a masterly distinction between the spirit and the letter. If the letter kills, the spirit brings new life; and if a text is literally profane, it may be read figuratively and endowed retrospectively with a spiritual significance. The Song of Songs reads suspiciously like an erotic poem; yet the Rabbis admitted it to the sacred canon by pronouncing it to be an allegory of

God's love for Israel. Similarly the Fathers, for whom the Old Testament prefigured the New, accepted it as an expression of Christ's love for the Church. Following Augustine, through this retroactive procedure known as "figuration," the *Aeneid* could be taken as a pilgrimage of the soul adventuring among divers moral hazards. Thereafter Dante could take Vergil as his guide for a series of literal adventures through the next world. Dante, as he acknowledged, was also following Saint Thomas Aquinas, who — in answering the preliminary questions of his *Summa Theologica* — had sustained the doctrine that although the scriptures were literally true, they could be interpreted as figures on three ascending levels of spiritual meaning.

But though the *Divine Comedy* is polysemous, as it is expounded in Dante's dedicatory letter to Can Grande della Scala, the poem cannot pretend to literal truth; the Florentine poet, after all, was making believe that he himself had journeyed through hell and purgatory and paradise; the "allegory of poets" is not the "allegory of theologians." The next step would be taken by the more worldly Boccaccio, who in his life of Dante supported the validity of poetic truth. Elsewhere he went even farther, with the affirmation that theology is God's poetry. It has remained for latter-day symbolists to round out the cycle by affirming that poetry is man's theology. With the humanism of the Renaissance and the Enlightenment, the other world seems gradually to recede. Nominalistic reality shifts to the foreground; things are valued for themselves, and not for what they may prefigure. The shift from the type to the individual has its protagonist in *Doctor Faustus*, Marlowe's early sketch for Goethe's portrayal of modernism in action. Faustus is one poet who is not content to compare his mistress with famous beauties. Metaphors will not do and symbols are not enough; he must attain the object of his comparison. He must have the one and only Helen of Troy, and he does so *in propria persona*; but the reality proves to be as elusive as the symbol.

Poetry with its metaphors, metaphysics with its analogies, bridge a gap between seen and unseen worlds. The breakdown of the bridge is that dissociation of which Mr. Eliot has written so feelingly; and it is more than a "dissociation of sensibility"; it is a break in the whole chain of being. Hume's critique of analogy might be regarded, under this aspect, as a philosophical counterpart of neoclassical poetic diction. A symbol, on the other hand, is a connecting link between two different spheres; for the original word in Greek meant throwing together, a violent fusion, the very act of association. When man stands upon his own feet, proudly conscious of the achievements of his fellow men, he lives most fully and his art embodies the fullness of his life, his basic sense of reality. Then the *Aeneid* is not a *pélérinage de la vie humaine*, but the epic of a hero; the Song of Songs is not an allegory but a chant of love; and Shakespeare's tragedies are dramas of physical action and psychological conflict, not ballets of bloodless images or ceremonials for a dying god. In times which seem to be out of joint, when man is alienated from his environment, the heroic seems less immediately attainable and love itself may dim to a Platonic vision. A failure of nerve is accompanied by a retreat from reality.

Arthur Symons characterized the symbolistic movement of the nineteenth century as a perfervid effort to escape from materialism. It is much easier to comprehend what the symbolists were escaping from than what they were escaping to. Their problem was, and it certainly remains, to establish a viable set of intimate associations with another sphere. Some of them felt they had solved it personally through religious conversion; others frankly used their visionary imaginations, often abetted by stimulants and even by mental disorders. Whereas the traditional symbolist had abstracted objects into ideas, the self-proclaimed *symboliste* — as Jean Moréas announced in his manifesto of 1886 — sought to invest the idea in concrete form. Hence his emphasis was on the object itself rather than its conceivable signification, on the denseness of the imagery rather than the pattern of the thought, on concealment rather than revelation in Carlyle's terms. But since the symbol was never clearly acknowledged as the key to any higher plane of existence, poets could not be blamed when it became a fetish cultivated for its own sake. Literature could not be expected to transcend itself by its own bootstraps; and yet, with Mallarmé, the esthetic process became the principal subject for symbolization. So it is with Proust; but when it is manifested in connoisseurship of ecclesiastical architecture, the symbols are already fraught with a transcendence of their own.

The unvoiced premise of *symbolisme*, which is not far from that of orthodox mysticism, had been handed on by the German idealists to the New England transcendentalists. For Baudelaire, moving out of the woods of naturalism back toward the church, nature was a temple with trees for pillars. Man walks through this forest of symbols which seem to know him better than he knows them, and the words he hears there are confused. "*Les parfums, les couleurs, et les sons se répondent.*" Color and sound and other sensory impressions are linked together through correspondences, associative patterns whose final sanction is not discernible to the senses. Some of these were suggested by Rimbaud in his well-known sonnet on the vowels, but not everyone would accept his linkages. Different sounds would suggest different colors to different readers; and that is the essential dilemma of *symbolisme*. For all its efforts to reorder the universe, to categorize the diversity of experience, its influence has been unregenerately individualistic. Remy de Gourmont, the critical interpreter of the movement, aptly presents it as — among other things — the ultimate expression of individualism in art.

How far it stands apart from its medieval prototype might be measured by consulting the *Rationale* of Durandus, the thirteenth-century manual of Christian symbolism, as embodied in the sacramentalism of the Catholic church. Living tradition was — and is — practiced daily there, through the cruciform structure of the edifice, its orientation, ritual, and liturgy, the relation of the church year to the life of Christ, the reënactment of the last supper in the Eucharist. Through that rite of communion the paschal lamb, originally the sacrifice of the Jewish Passover, had become the commonest symbol for Jesus. The audience at fifteenth-century Wakefield, witnessing their *Second Shepherds' Play*, could not irreverently grasp a serio-comic parallel between the infant in the manger and the stolen sheep of the farcical underplot. This is an authoritative example of the technique of symbolic association. Conversely, we witness the effect of dissociation in *Madame Bovary*, when the great Cathedral of Rouen looks reprovingly down upon the lovers fleeing in their cab, and its disregarded sermons in stones exemplify all the values that Emma and Léon are flouting. It is a far cry from George Herbert's *Temple* to Baudelaire's.

"A symbol remains vital," the late Karl Vossler has written, "only when its representation is accompanied by faith." The number seven was no abstraction for Dante; behind it loomed the power of the Seven Sacraments, the Seven Deadly Sins, the Seven Gifts of the Holy Ghost. But when we turn away from the supernatural, in naturalistic suspension of belief, what — if anything — are we to make of Thomas Mann's conjurations with the same digit in *The Magic Mountain?* The seven chapters of the novel itself, the seven tables in the dining room of the Berghof sanitorium, which has seven letters in its name, as have its seven principal guests in their names, and all the recurrent multiples of seven — these are endowed with no more efficacy than the novelist's deliberate manipulation of coincidence. Whereas, if we now reconsider our fish, we find that it is alphabetically associated with the initial letters of the Greek words for "Jesus Christ, Son of God, the Savior," which can be read acrostically as *ichthys*. As such it served in the catacombs, where overt symbols would have been dangerous, to conceal the Christian revelation. In the terms of Durandus, it was a positive rather than a natural symbol, or — as Yeats would say — arbitrary rather than inherent.

It is the inherent, the natural symbol that Coleridge seems to have in mind when he asserts that it always partakes of that reality which it renders intelligible. The cross of the lamb, as opposed to the fish, may well be termed an emblem, as distinguished from a sign. But Saint Augustine can transform a sign into an emblem, when he mystically envisions Jesus Christ as a fish swimming through the depths of mortality. This distinction between emblems and signs corresponds with that which has been drawn since Goethe, more broadly and often invidiously, between symbolism and allegory. The symbolic is the only possible expression of some essence, according to Yeats, whereas the allegorical may be one cut of many. In the latter case, we are less engaged by the symbol itself than by what is arbitrarily symbolized. Yet when the fish is not a religious acrostic but Captain Ahab's whale, it is emblematic; and then, as W. H. Auden duly warns us, we must not expect a one-to-one correspondence. For what we then encounter is not an allegorical reference to something else in some particular respect, but a multiplicity of potential cross-references to other categories of experience.

These formulations could be tested by turning again to *Moby-Dick* and applying the polysemous method, the fourfold scheme of interpretation that Dante invited his readers to follow, which extends the meaning beyond the literal to the three figurative levels — allegorical, moral, and anagogical. Later allegories may not be as multileveled as the *Divine Comedy*; it is hard to discern more than three planes in the *Faerie Queene* or two in the *Pilgrim's Progress*. Under the subsequent impact of realism, the allegorical and the anagogical tend to wither away; the moral blends with the literal or drops out altogether, as writers turn from the Celestial City to Vanity Fair. But the Middle Ages maintained the sharp differentiation formulated in a Latin distich which can be conveniently paraphrased: the literal tells us what happens, the allegorical what to believe, the moral what to do, and the anagogical whither to strive. Thus, literally *Moby-Dick* is concerned with the voyage of the *Pequod*, the subject of whaling, the science of cetology; allegorically with society on shipboard, the parable of Ahab's "irresistible dictatorship"; morally with a series of object-lessons, such examples as the monkey-rope, the ligature of brotherhood that binds Ishmael to Queequeg; and anagogically . . . "*Quo tendas?* whither art thou striving?"

That is the question, and Melville offers no categorical answer. Dante knew, or believed he knew, the object of his journey; no traveler, to be sure, had returned to map out the topography of the next world; but Dante's account was based

on the *terra firma* of assumptions universally shared, while
Melville put out to sea in lone pursuit of "the ungraspable
phantom of life." He was enough of a transcendentalist to
ponder the meaning of this "great allegory, the world," enough
of an iconoclast to strike through the pasteboard mask of outer
appearances, and enough of a skeptic to respect the uncharted
mystery beyond it. But the anagoge, which for Dante is the
fulfillment of providential design, for Melville remains an
ultimate question mark. His overwhelming whale has been
identified with — among other concepts — nature, fate, sex,
property, the father-image, God Himself. It has meant various
things to varying critics because it is Melville's enigma, like
the doubloon nailed by Ahab to the mast, which signifies
dollars to the Second Mate, the Zodiac to the First Mate, and
the universe to the Captain. Shall we ever identify Moby-Dick?
Yes, when we have sprinkled salt on the tail of the Absolute;
but not before.

In one of his prophetic moments Melville even anticipated
atomic fission, describing the tail of the whale as if it were a
cyclotron. "Could annihilation occur to matter," Ishmael exclaims, "this were the thing to do it." However, the atomic is
just as far beyond our scope as the cosmic; and we cannot
necessarily count upon the rock of dogma for that firm founda-
tion on which Durandus constructed his medieval symbology.
Are we then at the mercy of sheer subjectivity, of the irrespon-
sible caprice of the overingenious critic, making symbols mean
what he wants them to mean? Or have we still some criteria
at our disposal, technical means for determining the relevance
— if not the truth — of any given comment? Here I would
venture to suggest that students of literature might profitably
emulate the researches now being carried on in the plastic
arts under the heading of Iconology. Some of us have been
collecting images, but not interpreting them very satisfactorily;
others have been tracing the history of ideas, without paying
much attention to formal context. Could we not hope for a
discipline which would bring the tools of critical analysis to
bear upon the materials of textual documentation, concentrating upon the thematic relationship between the idea and the

image? Shall we ever discover the archetype behind them both except through comparative study of its most impressive manifestations?

This is more easily called for than provided. The leaders of the Iconological School are brilliantly conspicuous for their combination of discernment and learning. We shall not have literary iconologists in our Departments of English until our discerners have picked up a little learning and our learners have somehow acquired a little discernment. In the interim, are there not a few reasonable game laws, which we might undertake to observe whenever we go fishing? Or — to state the problem more pragmatically — could we not agree upon a code of fair-trade practices, which might conduce to a closer meeting of critical minds? Granted that divergence of opinion is salutary — indeed necessary — for the evaluation of a work of art, and that the very suggestiveness of some masterworks is most richly attested by the variety of interpretations accruing to them. Yet the work itself is always greater than the sum of its interpretations; and unless these are grounded within some frame of objective reference, we have no basis for differentiating between perception and deception. After all, criticism — in a Baconian phrase — is reason applied to imagination. Doubtless the fourfold method of exegesis, which Dante appealed to and Saint Thomas propounded, would be somewhat hierarchical for our day. Nevertheless, in more democratic terms, the common consent of educated readers might be gained at four descending levels of acceptance.

The first, which raises no questions, would be strictly conventional. No one has any doubt what Hawthorne intends by the accepted symbol of the eagle over the door of the Custom House in the introductory chapter of *The Scarlet Letter*; and Melville's eagle soaring over the Catskills, though less official, is a bird of the same feather. The second use of the symbol is explicit, as when Melville glosses the monkey-rope or moralizes up and down the deck in *Moby-Dick*; or, best of all, Hawthorne's scarlet letter itself — how similar in appearance, how different in connotation, from the "crownèd A" of Chaucer's Prioress! Third, and here we cross an equatorial line, the implicit. "Thou too sail on, O ship of state!" is highly explicit, not to say conventional. But the good ship *Pequod* — like the frigate *Neversink* in *Whitejacket, or The World in a Man-of-War* — is a little world in itself; and when it goes down, what are we to make of the eagle that goes down with it or that rather sinister emblem, the hand with a hammer? Melville's "Tartarus of Maids" is explicitly a humanitarian sketch of a New England factory, and implicitly an obstetrical allegory of woman's fate. What is implied, in contrast to what is explicated by the author himself, can be possibly gaged by what are known in Shakespearean commentary as "fervors" and "recurrences."

These are patterns of repetition and emphasis, which in some fortunate cases can be reinforced by the facts of biography and the insights of psychology. Jay Leyda's *Melville Log* not only supplements the romances and tales, but fills in some missing segments of their imaginative configuration. Without such external evidence we could draw no sharp line between the implicit and, fourth, the conjectural level — or, for that matter, between the conjectural and the inadmissible. But once we admit degrees of plausibility, we may entertain, for whatever enhancement it may be worth, any conjecture likely to enrich our apprehension of the part-and-parcel allegoricalness of the whole. Does it enrich our apprehension of the later novels of Henry James if we construe them as Swedenborgian allegories? There is one tangential fact in support of this argument: the Swedenborgianism of the elder Henry James. And that is outweighed by the clearest expressions of intention, as well as by the internal consistency of the author's habits of thinking and writing. Therefore the purported symbolism is not conventional nor explicit nor implicit; it is, at best, conjectural; and since it obscures rather more than it illuminates, it should probably be discarded as inadmissible. Let us look for figures in the carpets, and not in the clouds.

And let us return, for the last time, to the whale. Surely no other literary symbol has invited and evaded so much conjecture; surely Melville intended to keep up guessing up to the bitter end and afterward. His book does not resemble life the less because it leaves us in a state of suspense. But just as insecurity seeks authority, just as complexity seeks simplification, just as pluralism seeks unity, so our critics long for the archetypal because they are bedeviled by the ambiguous. Groping amid ambiguities, they become increasingly hot for certainties; and symbols, they desperately hope, will provide the keys. So every hero may seem to have a thousand faces; every heroine may be a white goddess *incognita;* and every fishing trip turns out to be another quest for the Holy Grail. However, that boy of Hemingway's, fishing in Big Two-Hearted River, is not a type but an individual. He is not Everyman; he is Nick Adams; and, like every other single human being, he is unique. The river in which he fishes is neither the Nile nor the Liffey; it is a stream which runs through the Upper Peninsula of the state of Michigan. The sun that beats on his back is the same old planet that has generated myths since the world began. But the feeling it evokes is the existential conjunction of the scene, the moment, and human sensibility. Literature can give us many other things; but it gives us, first and last, a taste of reality.

The War of Words in English Poetry

The experience of teaching a course in English poetry to a class of French university students is one which brings out, and perhaps makes the teacher excessively conscious of, certain linguistic variances. I tried to extract a lesson from such an experience, and to pass it on informally to several American groups, originally to the Graduate English Society of Columbia University on April 2, 1954. But I have not put it into writing before, and I print it now with some reservation. I share the dissatisfaction of poets and linguists with the classical terms of prosody, and only use them as a kind of arbitrary shorthand. I suspect that phonemic analysis will provide much better tools for testing the problem that, meanwhile, I would merely wish to exemplify.

Any discussion of literature enjoys one advantage over discussions of the other arts, of the natural sciences, or of the more conceptual disciplines; for when we are dealing with objects composed of words, whether we are talking or writing about them, we can always exhibit them by quoting. Our illustration is the thing itself, not a reproduction or a diagram, nor are we using verbal means to approximate the nonverbal. On the other hand, since we use words to deal with words, there is always some danger of confounding our medium with our material. Literary criticism, in its recent state of self-consciousness, is nothing if not word-conscious; but sometimes its very immersion in problems of style seems to have had an untoward stylistic effect; too much of it might be cavalierly summed up as bad writing about good writing. Moreover, in its sweeping reaction against philological scholarship, it has disregarded basic facts of language.

The penalty has been not only frequently misreading but even occasional failure to appreciate the full esthetic significance of a passage. Philology, on its side, has been more strictly concerned with norms of usage than with idiosyncrasies of style. But stylistics, as we hopefully call the analytic study of literary expression, must know the normative in order to recognize the idiosyncratic.

Literary history tends to assume that a language is invented and developed by its writers. Actually, important as their contributions may be, these are largely determined by the nature of the stuff they work with, which they have inherited from their predecessors and must share with their nonliterary contemporaries. Any linguistic construct owes its existence to the preëxistence of many others; hence it can never be adequately considered in isolation. Indeed poetry, the most deliberately controlled and elaborately organized phase of language, is peculiarly subject to the influences of external circumstance. The physical aspect of a given word — phonetic, syntactic, orthographic — colors its semantic, if not its lexical, meaning. Rationally we may still feel, as Pope did, that the sound must seem an echo to the sense; but in practice the sense often seems to echo the sound. The interrelationship between sound and sense, the relation between the structure of language and the meaning of poetry, is a rich field now being investigated by the eminent Slavic philologist, Roman Jakobson. The results of such an investigation should prove consequential for students of English verse, our understanding of which has suffered too long from the unnatural and temporary divorce between linguistic and literary studies, particularly in the neglected sphere of prosody.

My present purpose is to call attention to one of the most distinctive characteristics of the English language, and to the special consequences it has had for poetic style. The principles involved are so well established that they can be very simply restated along the way; what should concern us more directly are the applications, with regard to both diction and versification. To test my particular point we shall have to gather quotations briefly sampling the scope and variety of the whole subject — a task not uninviting because it will leave us with, if nothing else, a sort of chrestomathy. But, before we start, perhaps I ought to apologize for my title, if it has struck a note of alarm or suggested barrages of propaganda, exchanges of billingsgate, or futile rodomontades. The habit of speech that I shall be tracing and trying to formulate might have been presented as linguistic tension, verbal dissociation, dynamic adjustment and/or dialectical interaction. The very choice between such timely jargon and the well-worn catchword I have preferred, as I hope to make clear, is a foretaste of my theme. The war of words in English poetry has been a continuous series of internal conflicts which, to qualify an overstatement, might be better characterized as lovers' quarrels than as overt battles.

To the many historic conquests of England, together with the consequent racial strains, we are indebted for that "great diversity" which Chaucer attests, that copiousness so dear to sixteenth-century rhetoricians, the enormous range and the extraordinary richness of the English vocabulary. Its various components can be traced back to their respective cultural strata: Celtic, Roman, Anglo-Saxon, Norman French, and mainly the latter two. If this were merely a matter of etymology, it could be left to the philologists; but since it also involves morphology, the sound and shape of words as well as their derivations, it has considerable importance for poets. Now the overwhelming majority of the words that we commonly employ are of Germanic stock. We think of them as indigenous, and of the others as borrowed. The brothers Fowler, who can be rather Podsnappian in their purism, would advise writers to take this attitude as a rule of thumb: "Prefer the Saxon word to the Romance." And yet *The Triumph of the English Language* — as lately documented by Richard F. Jones's survey of the growth of linguistic awareness — has been a gradual sophistication of native barbarism, originally considered much too crude for eloquence, through the enrichment of ornate and elegant borrowings. "Sounding words" were needed, as Dryden argued, to supplement "our old Teuton monosyllables."

Statistics lend cogent support to these lines of generalization. To begin from the bedrock of the English Bible, it has
been estimated that ninety-four per cent of its words are
Germanic in origin; and since this percentage is based on the
Authorized Version, the figure would run even higher for
Tyndale's earlier translation. For Shakespeare himself, despite the immensely varied resources of his word-hoard, the
gross proportion does not run much lower: he falls back on
Germanic words about ninety per cent of the time. The
clearest comparison might be with Gibbon, as the prime exponent of Latinate English, who nonetheless is dependent upon
the Teutonic to the degree of seventy per cent. Actually, we
seem to have gone beyond him in current technical prose, where
the Saxon component has sometimes registered as low as sixty
per cent, so that — historically speaking — we might conclude
that the language had become more and more Latinized. However, that tendency is counterbalanced by another which is
known as Zipf's Law, and which — like many laws — seems to be
an elaborate formulation of what is already recognizable to
intuition or common sense: namely, the inverse correlation
between the length and use of words. With frequencies which
are mathematical, people tend to use short and simple words
more than long and complex ones. The norm, the Anglo-
Saxon substratum then, must be our point of departure and
point of return, though the cycle leads over foreign territory.

Approaching a poem in Old English through the volubility
of modern speech, we are struck most forcibly by its terseness.
"þæt wæs gōd cyning!" The founder of the Danish line was a
good king — and how could the poet of *Bēowulf* offer a more
laconic or more telegraphic eulogy of his reign? Since the Norman Conquest, as handbooks regularly point out, the usual
adjective pertaining to kingship has been the French *royal*.
Writers who have wanted to emphasize it somewhat have been
able to substitute the Latin cognate, *regal*. But whenever
they have wanted to be truly emphatic, they have turned back
again toward Old English with *kingly*. Our language owes
its strength to such concrete roots, which in turn are closely
associated with work and daily experience — not to mention

the unmentionable, the Anglo-Saxon terms for bodily functions. Whereas, virtually by definition, its loan-words are bookish and more abstract. Though they add touches of coloring,
they effect a distance; they neutralize the immediacy of the
situation at hand. Thus genteel refinement flinches at *naked*
but tolerates *nude*; and when Nathaniel Hawthorne wrote
smell, Mrs. Hawthorne changed it to *odor*, presumably miti-
gating the offense. Distance, of course, is not without enchantments of its own; and Latin, surviving in tags and formulas, remains the ever impressive parlance of learning and
liturgy. With Dr. Faustus drawing his magic circle, it re-
asserts the power of incantation, not less impressive for not
being understood.

Madame de Staël dramatized European culture as a perennial rivalry between Nordic and Mediterranean factors.
This conception would apply to the history of English style.
Latin, the ecclesiastical tongue, and French, the courtly
tongue, joined forces against the vernacular, which was bound
to triumph but which was marked and shaped by the struggle.
One of its characteristic marks is the so-called doublet, the
transitional arrangement that first appears on legal documents, where a foreign term is coupled with the native
synonym as a gloss: for instance, *lord and master* or *goods and
chattels*. Sir Thomas Browne would avail himself of this
doubling as a conscious stylistic device, in balanced conjunc-
tive phrases which are almost signatures: "name and appella-
tion," "enigmas and riddles," "low and abject condition."
Shakespeare inclines toward doublets especially in the turgid
verse of his middle period, as when the Prologue to *Troilus and
Cressida* speaks of "corresponsive and fulfilling bolts." Such
reduplications have given foreigners the impression that English is redundant, that it says the same thing in different
ways. But if you say it in a different way, is it still the same
thing? Is there, in fact, such a thing as an exact synonym?
Does not each alternative rendering express another nuance,
introduce a new possibility, and thereby contribute to the incomparable expressiveness of our language?

Oscar Wilde declared of *Hamlet*: "The world has become

sad because a puppet was once melancholy." Thereupon William Butler Yeats accused Wilde of affectation, assuming that *melancholy* was no more than a studied avoidance of repetition, an elegant variation upon *sad*. That may be; and yet the shift of phrasing, which Wilde justified by euphony, might well betoken a deliberate contrast between the immediate reality of this sad world and the distant artificiality of that melancholy puppet. The feeling against big words is a deeply rooted manifestation of xenophobia; there is even another big word, *cacozelia,* to stigmatize this peculiar vice of style. Shakespeare plays with it in the scene between Hamlet and Osric. More broadly in *Love's Labor's Lost,* amid a plethora of stylistic tricks, the sum of three farthings is vastly augmented by being referred to as a "remuneration." The humanists of the Renaissance mocked the *stila pedantesca,* the intrusion of Latinisms in everyday discourse, which has its Shakespearean spokesman in Holofernes. Scholars like Roger Ascham warned against inkhorn terms, against mixing imported wines with the local beer. Macaronics at the other extreme, classical verses inflecting vernacular words, were easily achieved in the Romance languages but went counter to the *Sprachgefühl* of English. Attempting them in Anglo-Scottish hexameters, Drummond of Hawthornden produced barbarous hybrids like *"sweepare flooras"* and *"milkare cowæas,"* precedents for the jocular antipathy of generations of British schoolboys.

From the first, there were purists who opposed the adaptation of Latinate and Romance forms into English. The measure and intonation of the folk ballad were continued with the Elizabethan fourteener: "And straight I callèd unto mind that it was Christmas day." Spenser expressly cultivated archaisms, "old and unwonted words" from the Middle English store. But others were swayed by the spirit of illustration, in Dante's sense of making the vulgar idiom illustrious, decorating the vernacular with importations from the Continent. The resulting language, Early New English, is a hodgepodge or — as the Elizabethans liked to denominate it — a gallimaufry. Yet it could maintain "a disorderly order," as Spenser's apologist, E. K., aptly insisted, in a paradoxical phrase which Cervantes soon would hit upon under other circumstances. "Even so do the rough and harsh terms enlumine and make more clearly to appear the brightness of brave and glorious words. So oftentimes a discord in music maketh a comely concordance." It is this unexpected harmony, this *discordia concors,* that distinguishes the tone of English poetry. The phenomenon is not altogether unique: a modern Russian poet like Mayakovsky can gain like effects by echoing the Old Church Slavonic, and I have been told that the underlying Sanscrit gives Bengali poetry the kind of stratification that Latin gives English.

Nevertheless, the more flexible structure of English makes possible a uniquely variegated texture. The comparative freedom of its syntax was guaranteed through its formative centuries by the total absence of grammars, dictionaries, and academies. France, in this respect, was at the opposite pole. There the academic authorities managed to fix the language and crystallize the style. It has therefore never returned the hospitality that England has accorded to French words and phrases. English sounds strange when cited in a French context; and that strangeness combines a certain exoticism with a certain — shall we say? — *snobisme.* Mallarmé conveys the notion that he has already crossed the Channel, when he exclaims: *"Je partirai! Steamer balançant ta mâture . . ."* But, in an English poem, the noun *steamer* would hardly sound so poetic. Ironically enough, the normal word that Mallarmé was replacing, partly on metrical grounds, is one of the few English words that French has completely naturalized: *paquebot.* But French too stands out strangely, in much the same fashion, when the contextual language is German. One of the humorous lyrics of Heinrich Heine reduces this juxtaposition to absurdity by rhyming pairs of affected gallicisms, such as *kapabel* and *spendabel.*

Since English is closely related to German and French, it can receive its relatives on both sides; but we should be mistaken if we believed that it invariably assimilates; now and then it exploits the remote and mysterious connotations of

foreign phraseology. When Keats celebrated a lady whom —
even in English — we would describe as a *femme fatale,* he
described her by another French epithet: *La Belle Dame sans
Merci.* He borrowed his title from an Old French poem by
Alain Chartier, which he had already alluded to in "The
Eve of Saint Agnes." But Keats's romantic ballad resembles
Alain's medieval allegory less than it does a fourteenth-cen-
tury dialogue wherein each stanza terminates with the refrain,
Quia amore langueo. The difference is that between sacred
and profane love, since the Middle English poem symbolizes
Christ's lament for his sister, man's soul. So far I have been
citing borderline cases to define the borders of our subject.
Let us next consider a central example, a touchstone for the
type of verbal interplay to which our eyes and ears should
now be almost morbidly alerted. This is the initial quatrain
of a fifteenth-century dirge, which has haunted its readers and
hearers for reasons that we should be in a position to analyze:

> This ae night, this ae night,
> *Every night and all,*
> Fire and sleet and candle-light,
> *And Christ receive thy soul.*

Here we are made aware of the Northern dialect only by the
use of "ae" for *one* and, as the manuscript spelling would indicate, the pronunciation of "soul" to rhyme with "all." Were
we to read on, we should find that the second and fourth
lines repeat themselves as an unchanging refrain, framing the
succession of particulars within a rhythm of larger generality.
Leaving this formula aside temporarily, we find that the first
and third lines make no declaration; the first, with heavy re-
currence, designates a time; while the third sketches a background, with a sequence as bare and impressionistic as a
Japanese *haiku.* *Fire* — the primordial element, and the warning of what lies ahead, Purgatory — is pure Saxon, like *earth*
and *water,* but unlike the intangible element, *air,* which
happens to be Greco-Latin. The interlinking substantive, *sleet,*
is something of a crux; we are tempted to accept the denotation that comes first to mind and view it as a force of outer

nature, storm contending with fire as on the heath in *King Lear*. Other readings would make it a provincial variant of *salt*, or else *fleet* meaning house-room, either being pre-requisite for a wake. In either case, the derivation is elemental. With the compound *candle-light*, which incidentally com-pounds Romance with Saxon, we definitely find ourselves in-doors and about to witness a rite. The litany appropriately conforms to the Latin: *Christus recipiat*. But the final syllable is personal, existential, and again Germanic.

Latinity confers an aura which is religious or — at any rate — spiritual and transcendent, as against what is immediately felt, the corporeal and the material. Never has this distinction been more trenchantly preserved than in Hamlet's dying in-junction to Horatio, who has also proposed to die:

> Absent thee from felicity a while,
> And in this harsh world draw thy breath in pain. . .

The two worlds could not be set farther apart than they are by the opposing vocables of these two successive and parallel lines, the second metrically no longer than the first, but vo-cally and typographically prolonged by the weight of its in-dividual syllables. The afterlife, though euphonious, is vague and opaque; the present, though painful, is near and vivid, here and now as against what is far away, what was long ago, or what will be millennial. A French translation can catch the delayed impact of the first line: *"Diffère encore l'instant de ta béatitude . . ."* But, having enunciated what might be an Alexandrine, André Gide trails on in conventional prose, with a series of clichés and abstractions which bring nothing home to the spectator: *". . . et, dans ce monde affreux, réserve avec douleur ton souffle . . ."* Shakespeare's exploitation of such contrasts is so habitual and so ingenious that a whole treatise would scarcely do it justice; but it can be succinctly exemplified by a line which leaps to memory, Othello's greet-ing to his assailants: "Keep up your bright swords, for the dew will rust them." The oblique threat is strikingly pro-jected, in a pair of antithetical images, by means of ten monosyllables which reflect the noble simplicity of Othello's character.

The contrasting aspect of it comes out subsequently, with his locutions of military pomp and circumstance. Recounting his adventures as he has told them to Desdemona, he tells us — at a third remove — of *moving accidents* and *disastrous chances,* of *portance* and *redemption* et cetera. Would Desdemona have become so enthralled, we wonder, if he had spoken of large caves instead of *antres vast?* Shakespearean characterization seems to fluctuate between a mode of formality and a vein of sincerity: compare the stilted repartee of Juliet answering Paris with her private confession to Friar Lawrence a moment later. Again, compare Othello's moments of raging and ranting with his monosyllabic reiteration as he enters the fatal bedchamber: "Put out the light, and then — " And then the literal act becomes a symbolic image, an omen of impending tragic catastrophe, the extinction of life itself: ". . . and then — put out the light." This transference from the plane of action to the plane of imagination reaches its dramatic height in the scene where Lady Macbeth makes a matter-of-fact statement in few and ordinary words: "A little water clears us of this deed." Whereupon Macbeth's hyperbolic reply, with its expanding polysyllables, is not only a realization of blood-guilt but a reversal of the natural order, a disproportion stretching toward infinity. The crucial line contains eleven feet, four words, one pentasyllable, one tetrasyllable, two monosyllables:

> No. This my hand will rather
> The multitudinous seas incarnadine,
> Making the green one red.

English verse derives its sonority from the drama, from the fact that it was spoken — not to say vocalized — on the Elizabethan stage; and there the primary contribution was Marlowe's. If his lines are mighty, as Ben Jonson has so widely proclaimed, it is because Marlowe undertook to fill them with "high, astounding terms." Since these were polysyllabic, they accelerated the pace of blank verse; and since they bore geographical and mythological allusions, they extended and colored its imaginative sweep. In them a sesquipedalian nomenclature seems to herald a heroic world. The actual motive that animates Tamburlaine is the reverberation of exotic place-names, the vista of fabled capitals. Overhearing the name of Persepolis, he addresses his lieutenants, two of whose names — plus a conjunction — round out a pentameter:

> Is it not brave to be a king, Techelles?
> Usumcasane and Theridamas,
> Is it not passing brave to be a king,
> And ride in triumph through Persepolis?

When Théophile Gautier singled out a favorite alexandrine from *Phèdre* as the most beautiful verse in French poetry — *"La fille de Minos et de Pasiphaé"* — he may have meant that, because the operative words are proper names which have overtones but not meanings, we are more free to enjoy the sheer sensory pleasure of their sounds. Association still accounts for much of the emotional impact, when Othello cries: "O Desdemona, Desdemona! dead!" But James Thomson found that imitation, leaving out the meaningful syllable, was a dangerous game: "O Sophonisba, Sophonisba! O!" The pathos was leveled to bathos when Fielding, choosing a cacophonous name for his heroine, prompted Tom Thumb to lament: "O Huncamunca, Huncamunca! O!" What's in a name? A great deal when John Webster, with a Marlovian flourish, invokes "the honor of Vittoria Corombona." But taken in its place, approached via the previous line, the gesture is less romantic and more realistic, more Italianate in the Machiavellian sense:

> . . . And by close pandarism seeks to prostitute
> The honor of Vittoria Corombona.

The sibilants add a sinister touch of onomatopoeia, even as they do when Shakespeare's Cleopatra imagines that her snake is hissing at Caesar "ass unpolicied." But Webster was also capable of Shakespearean straightforwardness, as in the famous response to the death of his Duchess of Malfi: "Cover her face; mine eyes dazzle; she died young."

There is an ancedote contrived by O. Henry in which an author and an editor disagree as to the way people talk in the throes of emotion. Both are tested, with symmetrical irony, when their wives run away. The naturalistic author, who has always asserted that crisis is met by prosaic understatement, embarks upon a rhetorical tirade beginning: "My God, why hast thou given me this cup to drink?" The sensationalistic editor, who believes that sordid actuality should be clothed in orotund utterance, can only ask: "Ain't that a hell of a note?" The issue still is moot, even in the theater, and in the latter-day renewal of poetic drama: between the high-flying verbiage of Christopher Fry, in one direction, and in the other T. S. Eliot's highly successful efforts to disguise verse as prose. Whether a mode of writing should be eloquent or plain has generally depended upon its subject-matter, and whether that was highly or lowly placed. Ancient rhetoric drew sharp distinctions accordingly between the grand manner and the humble style, which have been handed on in classicized cultures, notably the French. The intermixture of styles is characteristically English, and so — as we note — is the intermixture of words. This is also the case with the Old Testament, as Erich Auerbach has demonstrated in *Mimesis*. The process of realism undercuts the sublime and exalts the vulgar.

The neoclassical period, which likewise practiced experiments trivializing the heroic and glorifying the trivial, was dogged by uncertainties as to whether a style was suited to its subject. Critics like Voltaire professed disgust at the vulgarity of the sentinel's description in the first scene of *Hamlet*: "Not a mouse stirring." French classicism would have amplified that report with a majestic resonance: "*Mais tout dort, et l'armée, et les vents, et Neptune.*" Keeping to the same canon of decorum, Dr. Johnson rejected the domesticity of Macbeth's "blanket of the dark." Hence he abstracted the unwelcome concreteness by emending to "blank height," which has a ring of pseudo-Miltonic sublimity. If Milton himself seems all but unapproachable, it is because — scorning any middle flight — he created his rarefied atmosphere largely through the cult of the Latinism. Many of his sonorities might be echoes from the dramatists. "Damasco or Morocco or Trebizond" — this is the tune of Marlowe, but the metrics are subtler, more diverse in their enjambments and cesuras:

> . . . when Charlemagne with all his peerage fell
> By Fontarabbia.

Occasionally the amplification conveys an air of fussy technicality rather than stately grandeur, as in that clinical passage where Milton lists "Convulsions, epilepsies, fierce catarrhs," and goes on with a diagnosis of cramps and other symptoms which reminds us that, after all, he was a contemporary of Molière. He displays his remarkable skill at combining, varying adjectives to reveal mixed emotions, employing oxymoron to take back what he gives away, almost teasing as the ambivalent Eve yields to Adam

> with coy submission, modest pride,
> And sweet, reluctant, amorous delay.

Milton's timing, the way in which he measures his words against his lines, is invariably interesting. A single line from *Samson Agonistes* comprises four verbs, the first of four syllables, the second of three, the third two, the fourth one: "Solicited, commanded, threatened, urged." Despite his polysyllabics, he offers one noted exhibit of ten low words all creeping in a single line; but where the upshot would be dullness for Pope, here it intensifies Milton's vision of hell, and works out an inner pattern of vowels and consonants:

> Rocks, caves, bogs, fens, caves, dens, and shades of death —
> A universe of death.

The lengthy general noun subsumes the numerous particular ones. This tempo, which could be stated musically as *rubato,* retards the voiced monosyllables and speeds up the slurred polysyllables, recovering on the swings what it loses on the roundabouts. "Slow, slow," a song of Ben Jonson's commences; and it attains that slowness by stringing together ten one-syllable words, eight of them strongly accentuated: "Slow, slow, fresh fount, keep time with my salt tears." The more words included in any metrical unit, the more pauses it will entail and the longer it will take; this is the converse of Marlowe's rapidity, and both effects are attainable in English through the variance between meter and accent. One French poet, Jules Laforgue, has wistfully commented on "the singular abundance of monosyllables in English," and invidiously compared this with "the horrible length of German words" — he was evidently thinking of compounds.

We forget that *fall* has a name which mirrors its beauty until we see Shakespeare completing the metaphor, *fall of leaf.* But though it is standard American and accords with our Saxon names for the other seasons, though Hopkins revived it and Yeats penned "The Falling of the Leaves," the term that has prevailed in England is the Gallic *autumn.* Though *autumnal* may be the word for Donne, monosyllables are the backbone of plain style. In the moving farewell of Chidiock Tichborne, written at the Tower of London on the eve of execution, eighteen decasyllabics comprise 180 words. Among the Elizabethan sonnets, that most quoted from Drayton imparts its refreshing quality in three opening lines which are purely monosyllabic:

> Since there's no help, come, let us kiss and part;
> Nay, I have done, you get no more of me,
> And I am glad, yea, glad with all my heart. . .

The *yeas* and *nays* and repetitions enhance the conversational rhythm, which will not be interrupted by an occasional dissyllable in the succeeding lines. But the informal conversation of the octave is arrested by a formal picture in the sestet, where Love figures on its deathbed attended by personifications like Faith and Innocence. Alexander Pope, on at least one occasion, begins a poem no less conversationally: " 'Shut, shut the door, good John,' fatigued I said." When he quotes himself, "Shut, shut the door, good John," he has been speaking to his servant. The tone changes with the Gallic disyllable *fatigued,* and he is now writing his "Epistle to Dr. Arbuthnot."

It is significant that their common friend, Swift, was suspicious of monosyllables; for, in his own unquotable line about Celia, he has notoriously justified his suspicion.

We have been assuming a rough correspondence, neither complete nor precise, between length — whether a word has one or several syllables — and source — whether it is Germanic or Latinate. The Danish philologist, Otto Jespersen, has argued that English might have become a monosyllabic language like Chinese, were it not for the continual transfusion of foreign borrowings. Clearly the shorter words preponderate because they are called in so often to perform the functional duties and make the auxiliary connections. This preponderance, by putting a limitation on the number of rhymes most available, has specifically increased the problems of writing poetry in English. Its positive lesson, for poetic technique, has been to encourage the development of unrhymed or blank verse. Negatively, the "sure returns of still expected rhymes" have made such banalities as *breeze* and *trees* hard to avoid, and therefore to be avoided by all serious poets. With the exhaustion of obvious combinations, the search for others leads farther and farther afield, culminating perhaps in the farthest-fetched periphrastics of Ogden Nash. Rhyme itself, we must stop to remember, was an importation in England; and doggerel — the desperate endeavor to rhyme, if need be, at the expense of every other consideration — has been a periodic symptom of the need for readjustment. Thus John Skelton, who could handle the aureate Chaucerian stanza, chose to drop back into Old English measure, breaking its double line into verses of two stresses each, held together not by alliteration but by a continuing rhyme on a forced beat:

> For she is somewhat sage,
> And well worn in age;
> For her visage,
> It would assuage
> A man's courage.

During Skelton's time, around 1500, the phonetic transition to modern English took place; and its decisive consequence for prosody was the disappearance of the final *e*. This reinforced the iambic impetus of the language, which has favored the end-beat more and more: *courage,* pronounced as an iamb by Skelton, would have been an amphibrach to Chaucer — three syllables, the middle one long, as in French. The same shift turned trochaic dissyllables into monosyllables: *sage* and *age* had two syllables for Chaucer, with the acent on the first. Where trochees abound in German — *"Die Kleine, die Feine, die Reine, die Eine"* — their English equivalents seldom carry the extra syllable: "The small, the fine, the pure, the one." Another reason for the dearth of unaccented terminal syllables is that English has fewer suffixes than the more inflected languages; nor has it that inclination toward diminutives which helps to make Italian or Russian so fertile in rhymes. Hence it cannot afford to alternate masculine and feminine endings, as continental poetry so consistently does. Not only is it deficient in rhymes, but any attempt at a rhyme of two or more syllables has a weakening, a relaxing, or else an explicitly facetious effect. The Hudibrastic, with its prosy delivery and its anticlimactic jingling, heavily relies on the Latin suffix:

> He'd run in debt with disputation,
> And pay with ratiocination.

But this is too easy; and it does no more than hasten the trend toward *vers de société*. Self-conscious rhyming of this sort is most effective when it enforces agreement on slightly recalcitrant materials, as when Byron yokes Latinisms together with proper names: *laureate* and *Tory at / Last*. Is high seriousness, then, incompatible with the feminine ending? Not in Goethe's *Faust,* where a typical chorus chants:

> [Wir] führen, beim Saüfeln der Nächte
> Durch liebliches Wellengeflechte,
> Unsichtbar dem neuen Geschlechte,
> Die lieblichste Tochter heran.

Bayard Taylor, who is by no means the worst of the fifty-odd English translators, shows us why such passages cannot be

satisfactorily rendered in their original meters, as well as why
the suffix -*ation* cannot be taken seriously:

> By the murmurs, the nightly vibrations,
> O'er the waves and their sweetest pulsations,
> Unseen to the new generations,
> The loveliest daughter we lead.

This cries aloud for music by Sir Arthur Sullivan. Notice too
how the condensation of the English language forces Goethe's
translator — and Dante's even more — to insert extraneous matter, if he is working line by line, in order to compensate for
the surplus of syllables in the German or the Italian. In view
of these difficulties, Emile Verhaeren affirmed that it was quite
natural for English and American poets to practice free verse,
but that it would be pointless in languages where rhyme was
copious and convenient. His dictum reëchoes ironically in the
epoch of Paul Claudel, Saint-John Perse, Paul Eluard, Francis
Ponge, and René Char, when *vers libre* is the rule among
French poets and only the most light-minded persist in traditional metrics. Meanwhile Anglo-American poets have been
reviving the strictest of the old forms; but they have eased their
task and enlarged their verbal repertory by utilizing off-beat
stress and allowing assonance to serve for rhyme.

The progress of poetry has its saturation points, when the
existing potentialities all seem to have been tried. Concurrently it has its atavistic reversions, its fondness for archaisms,
its intermittent yearnings to regain lost strength by touching
the soil like the mythical giant of old. The most sophisticated
poets, sooner or later, recapitulate the most primitive patterns of their craft. Here I should like, with your indulgence,
to cite the first stanza of Gray's "Elegy Written in a Country
Churchyard," not for the elegance of its pastoral mood but
for the way it harks back to the Anglo-Saxon:

> The curfew tolls the knell of parting day,
> The lowing herd winds slowly o'er the lea,
> The plowman homeward plods his weary way. . .

This third line would perfectly satisfy the requirements of
Old English versification with its repeating double beat and

its alliterated pairings, *plowman plods* and *weary way*. Though Gray was writing in heroic quatrains, it is frequently true of all iambic pentameter that at least one of its five feet is weaker than the others. Dispensing with an adjective in each of these three lines, as George Saintsbury has done with heroic couplets from Pope, we could reduce them to tetrameter with no loss to grammar and not much to meaning:

> The curfew tolls the knell of day,
> The herd winds slowly o'er the lea,
> The plowman homeward plods his way. . .

It is surprising how little we miss those flat adjectives. Our trifling experiment, for what it may be worth, confirms the richly detailed studies of Josephine Miles, which have traced the role of the adjective in superimposing an ornamental style on English poetry. We could proceed through the "Elegy," pruning nearly every line of a foot and sometimes two. By alternating trimeters, we could even reduce the heroic quatrain to ballad measure, which would bring out the homely character of Gray's nonadjectival vocabulary:

> The curfew tolls the knell of day,
>   The herd winds o'er the lea,
> The plowman homeward plods his way,
>   And leaves the world to me.

In the interests of balladry, I have unfairly deprived Gray of his darkness. Leaving him to share the world with it, we may continue with our logomachy.

The battle — or is it a game? — is carried on in imagery as in meter. In this regard our most striking object-lessons are those provided by the Metaphysical School, whose conceits and paradoxes and intellectual twists hinge, more often than not, upon verbal incongruities. The discourse of Donne is the *sermo pedestris* of satire, oscillating between the poles of the general and the specific, basically colloquial with pedantic marginalia. His lyrics, as he confesses, are lectures on "love's philosophy." He can conceive of love, in the course of a single line, as both an insect and a sacrament: "The spider, love, which transubstantiates all." The theological verb changes everything, sublimating the pejorative noun; and the ensuing contradiction in terms is indeed that yoking of opposites which has come to be regarded as the essence of Metaphysical style. George Herbert utilizes the same means to achieve an entirely different end: to simplify the theme of religion rather than to elaborate the theme of love. Though the vocabulary of theology is Latinate, preachers score their points with Biblical words, as in Abraham Lincoln's climactic triad: "We cannot dedicate, we cannot consecrate, we cannot hallow . . ." So with Herbert, who sets forth abstract virtues as concrete details in the construction of a metaphorical church:

> Mark you the floor? That square and speckled stone,
> Which looks so firm and strong,
> Is Patience.

The rare use of the rare expression, the single comprehensive word embedded in a context of plainer style, is habitual with the seventeenth century. Listen, expecting to be surprised, to Herrick:

> Whenas in silks my Julia goes,
> Then, then, methinks, how sweetly flows
> The liquefaction of her clothes.

Here the force of the word is stronger than the force of the metaphor; and the philological surprise creates what the Metaphysicals considered a "strong line" — that form of *curiosa felicitas*, of lapidary composition, in which an unusual key word turns out to be the strategic factor that holds all the other pieces together and triumphantly completes the jigsaw puzzle. Marvell's conjunction of "vegetable' and "love" is another example. There is a better one in the same poem, where the key word closes a couplet and rings out all the more emphatically because of its pyrrhic ending and weak rhyme:

> And yonder all before us lie
> Deserts of vast eternity.

That last word, so chilling to the skeptic, has an intimate significance for the mystic — for Henry Vaughan and, in a wholly different gyre, for Yeats. Ultimately, for Blake, it is the *logos,* the word that stands for what cannot be put into words but can be defined by the poet's gesture of reaching out to grasp the ineffable, to

> Hold infinity in the palm of your hand,
> And eternity in an hour.

And this time the last word shifts back into the area of concreteness. To move, as so much modern poetry does, from a sense-impression to a psychological reflection, is to pursue a parallel movement of phraseology, which Emily Dickinson typically expresses in a distich where the rhyming word is the whole line:

> To be a flower is profound
> Responsibility.

The romantic fusion of feeling and thought, as Wordsworth envisaged it, was a reconciliation between the language of poetry and the language of prose; but in his attack upon the poetic diction of the eighteenth century, he was not necessarily repudiating the Latin tradition; it is for inversions and archaisms that he criticizes Gray, whose English was not so Latinized as Wordsworth's own critical prose. His balladmonger simplicities —

> I've measured it from side to side:
> 'Tis three feet long, and two feet wide

— are counterweighted by his Miltonic intonations:

> Thou whose exterior semblance doth belie
> Thy soul's immensity.

The nimbus of circumlocution with which the poet surrounds the apostrophized child glimmers from the title of his ode, "Intimations of Immortality from Recollections of Early Childhood." Dryden, in a comparable situation, had selfrevealingly hailed his subject as a "young probationer / And candidate of Heaven," with the implication that immortal-

ity was — as, indeed, it may be — a form of preferment. Wordsworth is most himself and at his best when his verse is sus-
pended between two idioms, the Miltonic and the Biblical.
He joins the one to the other in those luminous verses from
"Tintern Abbey" where he evokes

> a sense sublime
> Of something far more deeply interfused,
> Whose dwelling is the light of setting suns.

Coleridge, who redrew the line between poetic and prosaic
style, paradoxically won his greatest success with a pseudo-
ballad, far more successful than any of Wordsworth's exercises in that genre. Yet, to complete the paradox, we may ask
whether Coleridge's hero would have cut so memorable a
figure, had he been introduced as an old sailor rather than as
an ancient mariner.

The interfusion works powerfully with Keats, poet of the
tangible and the palpable, who is no less a poet of dreams and
reveries. It is the charm that conjures up the vision of Ruth
amid the "alien corn," the strange and the familiar being instinctively juxtaposed in the Latin adjective and the Saxon
noun. The alternation continues in the lines that conclude the
last stanza but one of the "Ode to a Nightingale":

> The same that oft-time hath
> Charmed magic casements, opening on the foam
> Of perilous seas, in faery lands forlorn.

It would be tempting to discuss the pictorial suggestiveness of
this much admired passage, or to follow its patterned progression of consonants and vowels across the palate. But what
we should be noticing is how the word *forlorn,* so Keatsian
and so immutably English, is picked up at the beginning of
the last stanza; and how the continuation, looking back from
imaginary perspectives to first-hand realities, slowly drops into
a lilt of mourning:

> Forlorn! the very word is like a bell
> To toll me back from thee unto myself.

So Keats originally wrote; but in revision, as W. J. Bate points out, he slowed the cadence down to a dying fall:

> To toll me back from thee to my sole self.

Shelley is Keats's antithesis in style as in ideas; ethereal yet rationalistic, the heir of the eighteenth century in diction as in philosophy, he took a myopic view of nature. Nothing could be dimmer than that region where his unrecognized poets sit enthroned, "beyond mortal thought, / Far in the Unapparent." Though he did not hymn "congregated thrushes" as James Thomson had done, he could envision a "sanguine sunrise" — a sunrise which, by substituting a colorless Latin euphemism for the unspeakable Saxon *bloody*, leaves something to be desired in the way of pictorial vividness.

Shelley's vague radiance helps to explain the effort of Gerard Manley Hopkins to recover the buried Germanic strain, an effort somewhat ominously prefigured in the title of his most ambitious poem, "The Wreck of the Deutschland." This priest, who practiced austerity by eliminating the Latin, describes

> . . . How a lush-kept plush-capped sloe
> Will, mouthed to flesh-burst,
> Gush! flush the man, the being with it, sour or sweet,
> Brim, in a flash, full.

And here, compressed to the utmost density of alliteration, assonance, and internal rhyme, is practically the metaphor in which Keats embodied the pleasure of the senses — "him whose strenuous tongue / Can burst joy's grape against his palate fine" — reconsecrated now as a vehicle of religious ecstasy. Hopkins' diction is obviously far removed from the plain speech of common people, and seldom really close to the structure of Anglo-Saxon verse. Whether his unfamiliar words are archaisms or neologisms is at times in doubt. The remarkable compound, "Brim, in a flash, full," with its prepositional infix, seems Teutonic; but it also observes the classical rhythm of the Sapphic tag-line or Adonic, e.g. *"dulce ridentem.*" It is a nice question with Hopkins as with Chatterton, or with Hugh Macdiarmid's exhumations out of Sir William Craigie's Scottish dictionary, when the poetic becomes antiquarian and when the antiquarian becomes spurious. In the grand strategy of our war of words we may visualize the Germanic compounds of Hopkins standing at one extreme, while the Latin inflections of Milton stand at the other. Whereas Milton drew upon his Latin to discipline the vernacular of his day, the English of Hopkins' day had become so loosely Latinized that he sought to purify it by coming full circle.

"One of the most remarkable products of the Industrial Revolution," according to Lytton Strachey, was Lord Macaulay's style. Further advances of science and technology, influencing forensic and journalistic literature, have brought about a prose which is metallic and mechanical beyond the wildest innovations of Whiggery. Descriptive terms like *portable* and *compendious*, with which Crashaw brought off his most spectacular conceit, are now the stock-in-trade of advertising. The very forces that undermined the classics have not only deadened our linguistic awareness so that we lose sight of the metaphors implied by *disastrous, ruminate,* or *magnanimity*; they have inflated our language with pseudo-Latinisms of dubious currency, such as *electrocute, normalcy,* and *mortician.* These are identifiable at once as Americanisms; and our own polyglot brand of English is notorious for the welcome it offers to jargon.

> Into this neutral air
> Where blind skyscrapers use
> Their full height to proclaim
> The strength of Collective Man,
> Each language pours its vain
> Competitive excuse:
> But who can live for long
> In an euphoric dream;
> Out of the mirror they stare,
> Imperialism's face
> And the international wrong.

This might be labeled the international style, having been written in New York City on or about September 1, 1939, by an English poet who has become an American citizen; and Mr. Auden was consciously imitating a poem written in Ireland by Yeats for an earlier occasion, "Easter, 1916":

> Hearts with one purpose alone
> Through summer and winter seem
> Enchanted to a stone
> To trouble the living stream.
> The horse that comes from the road,
> The rider, the birds that range
> From cloud to tumbling cloud,
> Minute by minute they change.

Without glancing back at other poems of retrospection in the same meter, the song from Dryden's "Secular Masque" or Matthew Arnold's "Rugby Chapel," this confrontation reveals the extent to which differences of language may be differences of culture, separating the agrarian countryside from the metropolitan way of life. Happily, it is still possible to make poetry out of the very perception of these discrepancies, as E. E. Cummings does by counterpointing his super-colossal slogans against the timeless refrain of the weather: "sun moon stars rain." Similarly, Ernest Hemingway must deflate verbalisms to remind us how reality feels, since the very words we employ to communicate it — as they accumulate — get in the way.

Verbal inflation is a longstanding policy with Americans. Benjamin Franklin, in a letter to David Hume, wished that opacities like *inaccessible* might be replaced by self-explanatory coinages like *uncomeatable*. But James Russell Lowell remarked that the newspapers would not be content with *man fell* when they could print *individual was precipitated* — a remark which is well borne out by the professional verbosity of sports-writers. Edgar Allan Poe, who was something of a verbal counterfeiter, was so entranced by the Tennysonian adjective *immemorial* that he made it quite meaningless, as Mr. Eliot has lately made us realize. The propensity

of words to outrun their meanings, in what could be termed
a nice derangement of malapropisms, is a persistent feature
of American style which ranges from the *Congressional Record*
to the *Glossary of New Criticism*. In his lifelong quest for
self-expression, which he equated with national expression,
Walt Whitman saluted *camerados* everywhere with a word
which was not quite Spanish, and dubbed himself a *habitan*
— which is not even French Canadian — of all the capitals
of the world, adding perhaps a hint of Esperanto to the Latin
increment. Our late contemporary and debonair compatriot
on a grand tour, Wallace Stevens, incorporated all that took
his fancy into his text:

> The palais de justice of chambermaids
> Tops the horizon with its colonnades.
>
> If it were lost in Übermenschlichkeit,
> Perhaps our wretched state would soon come right.

Perhaps. At all events, rhyme and meter have done what
they could to resolve international tensions. More uncom-
promisingly cosmopolite and expatriate, Ezra Pound would
solve the problem drastically by writing *Cantos* which are
centos, poems pieced together from other works, a virtual
commonplace-book of choice passages from American, European, and Oriental sources. His multilingual method is pushed
to its consummation in the eight concluding lines of Eliot's
Waste Land, which consist — besides one line by Eliot — of
seven quotations in six languages. One of them, from the late
Latin *Pervigilium Veneris*, in replacing the Latin for swallow,
hirundo, by the Greek *chelidon*, passes on to us the re-
assurance that poetry has survived previous confusions of
tongues. But that way Babel lies — or its modern reconstruction, *Finnegans Wake*, a monument which we shall not go
out of our way to inspect at this late stage of our discussion.
Yet we may observe in passing that Joyce's double-talk is an
artificial exaggeration of the natural process we have been
following, that English offered a maximum of opportunity
for overlapping and interweaving other languages, and that
each manipulation of the texture enfolds another facet of

meaning. Joyce, however, will not give us a paradigm. It is
Eliot whose succinctness clarifies and illustrates the whole
story in four lines:

> Sweeney shifts from ham to ham
> Stirring the water in his bath.
> The masters of the subtle schools
> Are controversial, polymath.

In this final stanza of "Mr. Eliot's Sunday Morning Service,"
which shifts from the church to the bathroom and back again,
the distribution of words is a perfect equipoise between personal intimacy and scholastic detachment. If the first two
lines are vulgarly elemental, the last two are intellectually
speculative. The first and second might be taken to represent
that real thing, life itself such as it is; the third and fourth
that criticism of life, that problematic inquiry into it, which
is literature.

A Gallery of Mirrors

This lecture, presented on February 9, 1949, as "Some European Views of Contemporary American Literature," was the last of a series on The American Writer and the European Tradition, *sponsored by the University of Rochester and subsequently published by the University of Minnesota Press under the editorship of Margaret Denny and W. H. Gilman, after previous publication in the* American Quarterly, I, 3 *(Fall, 1949). To all these sponsors my grateful acknowledgments are due. It does not now seem necessary to reproduce a set of footnotes already printed twice, most of which refer to foreign periodicals eight or ten years out of date; but the account of them has not been modified, for the situation has not drastically changed. Comparable soundings, if taken today, would probably show the Franco-American entente less cordial and the Russo-American hostility less automatic.*

▀▀

I

Occasion to see ourselves, not merely as others see us, but as they reflect our own reflection of ourselves, through whatever glass, however darkly — such is the gallery of mirrors our subject opens before us. To traverse it, to glance in passing at its multiplied and refracted images, is not a proud but a chastening experience. Possibly it may lead us, via those corridors which our publicists are now contriving, into the midst of the American Century. Perhaps we can best comprehend the present vogue of American letters in Europe by remembering three brusque words used by Thomas Hobbes to account for the authority of the classics: "colonies and conquests." For, though we may well disclaim imperialistic or even commercial motives, we cannot disavow the situation that ties Western Europe to our country as no two continents have ever been tied before. Along with the Marshall Plan go jeeps and jukeboxes, CARE packages and foreign-language editions of the *Reader's Digest*; along with our products we export culture — "culture" not in Matthew Arnold's terms but in Ruth Benedict's patterns. All this helps to explain what European critics can justify no better than we could: why the world's best-seller, second only to the Bible, should be *Gone with the Wind*.

But this is the sort of tribute we cannot accept with much complacency. Culturally, even more than ideologically, we are unprepared for the role of hegemony that fortune seems determined to thrust upon us. Though we believe in our great literary tradition, we realize that its grandeur is far from Augustan. Its greatest works are so functionally adapted to the contours of the land itself that, in distant lands under different conditions, they may not serve as very usable models. Their characteristic virtues are critical, radical, pluralistic, exploratory — virtues which presuppose the settled existence of an older world. What Cooper did for Balzac or Emerson for Carlyle, what Poe did for Baudelaire or Whitman for Mayakovsky, what *Moby-Dick* did for Lawrence of Arabia was to challenge that presupposition. In the past, precisely because Europe was central and America was tangential, European horizons were broadened by American minds. The flight of imagination toward the new world, the fantasy of Châteaubriand or Kafka, the nightmare of Dickens or Céline, was always centrifugal. In recent years, for better or worse, the center of international gravity has shifted. Strategic considerations have converted the U.S.A. from a place of escape to a place of retreat, from a source of exoticism to a source of recovery.

It is not surprising, therefore, that professors of English at continental universities now convert themselves into professors of American; that brilliant European students take part in an American Seminar at Salzburg; that major European periodicals are crowded with announcements and reviews of American books; that translation is consummated by imitation, the sincerest acknowledgment of cultural ascendancy. It is not surprising, but it is somewhat embarrassing, since any movement so novel and far-reaching is bound to evoke more enthusiasm than discrimination. Thus André Gide, acting on André Malraux's advice, reads William Faulkner and Dashiell Hammett with equal attention; while an article in *Les Temps modernes*, after deploring the taste of French translators, dismisses Katherine Anne Porter and Kathleen Winsor in the same breath. European criticism has sometimes recognized the qualities of neglected American genius: for example, the English recognition of Melville. Yet often, as in the Russian cult of Jack London, a writer has been extravagantly praised for qualities which are not especially striking to other Americans. When the Russians admire Howard Fast, or the Germans exalt Thomas Wolfe, their reasons are not far to seek. The same play, Thornton Wilder's *Skin of Our Teeth*, has been welcomed in Catholic Bavaria for its rediscovery of original sin and condemned in Marxist Russia for its cyclical theory of history.

When Jean-Paul Sartre visited this country a few years ago, he clarified for readers of the *Atlantic Monthly* why his approach to American literature differed so very candidly from theirs. Why, he asked, read Henry James when Flaubert is accessible? European readers, weary of time, seeking perennial youth with André Gide, turn from the traditional to the contemporary. Local color, the Wild West, highways and byways of the Jack London territory, make a stronger impression on them than upon ourselves. My colleague, F. O. Matthiessen, reports that Czechoslovakian students see through *The Moon Is Down*, yet fail to notice the defects of *Cannery Row*. In other words, they know that John Steinbeck romances when he writes about Norwegians, yet eagerly swallow his romantic Californians. Although they may confound myths with documents, their real concern is with subject rather than style. As for the Scandinavians themselves, when the Swedish Academy awarded the Nobel Prize to Pearl S. Buck in 1938, it gratified a naïve documentary interest in still remoter areas of the world. Our two compatriots who preceded her, Sinclair Lewis and Eugene O'Neill, had almost been professionally American. "Books are not written to last in America," says

Denis de Rougemont, a Swiss who has taken up American journalism, "but to strike and agitate as quickly and fully as possible."

The figure of the American man of letters that emerges to sweep his European admirers off their feet is a reporter, a soldier, a sportsman, anything but a literary man. Par excellence he is Ernest Hemingway, and lets nothing intervene between actions, emotions, and the surface of his prose. Those who feel overburdened with the past, overconscious of artifice, cultivate in him — as Emilio Cecchi points out in his introduction to an Italian anthology of American stories — "the illusion of having finally hit upon a literature which has nothing to do with literature, which is not spoiled or weakened by literature." But Signor Cecchi, who is too well read to be taken in by that illusion, goes on to acknowledge Faulkner's literary debts to Anderson, Joyce, Conrad, and Flaubert. Conversely Mario Praz finds, in younger Italian writers like Elio Vittorini and Giuseppe Berto, an indebtedness to the proletarianizing influence of transatlantic fiction. The resulting synthesis may be what philosophers discern at the end of a historical cycle: an interfusion of decadent culture with barbarian energy. But there are at least as many interpretations as there are countries, and we can only take soundings here and there. Though we must not look for one consistent and comprehensive view, we may profitably ask what significant attitudes are manifested in England, France, and Russia.

II

First let us look toward England, where we stand in a special relationship — that relation between colony and mother country which latter-day history has all but reversed. The strongest continuity, which of course is our language, can be traced through successive editions of H. L. Mencken's rich compilation; the American language, having gradually attained its autonomy, has more recently asserted a counterinfluence over English speech. Similar trends are reported from the book market. Books that were sold on a scale of

100,000 copies or more during the nineteen-twenties and thirties in England seem to have mainly been of American authorship. The unanticipated British success of *Babbitt*, which started the trend, gave Sinclair Lewis the opportunity to unfurl a declaration of independence. But the literary revolution had already been fought and won when the copyright issue was settled, when Oxford presented its doctorate to Mark Twain, when England's foremost novelist was Henry James. Dean Inge was now ready to acknowledge the cultural dependence of the mother country. "The Americans are our masters," he announced; and though the prospect held little to cheer his native pessimism, it ironically answered the question raised by Sydney Smith a century before: "In the four quarters of the globe who reads an American book?"

But ironies work both ways, and in this instance the way was open for English writers in the United States, just as the Scots had sought their fortunes in eighteenth-century London. The visiting Englishman, with his certain condescension, is hardly a stranger to the American scene. Such transient Georgian relics as the Sitwells, however, are rare today. An Evelyn Waugh may return to England declaring that the good life is impossible in America; yet thereupon, declaring that Americans talk too much, he recrosses the Atlantic for another lecture tour. More common is the British novelist in residence, who oscillates between Hollywood and theosophy, thereby enjoying the worst of both worlds, like Aldous Huxley or Christopher Isherwood. When Huxley and Waugh satirize the American way of life, it somehow resists their satire — not because it is invulnerable but because it is fairly tough, while their techniques are too brittle, their values too sentimental. The turmoil that made our continent a haven for English-speaking culture has also enriched it with exiles from the European continent. The wave of the 'thirties swept home, with what they had picked up abroad, our expatriates of the 'twenties. The Americanization of W. H. Auden recharted the traditional direction that T. S. Eliot's British passport had pointed.

The effect of these migrations has not been, in any organized sense, to make this hemisphere the literary center; rather it has functioned as an agent for the decentralization and diffusion of European literature. When Auden arrived, he propounded the paradox that American gregariousness isolated the poet and left him to the lonely rigors of artistic creation. Cyril Connolly carries this paradox to the point of *non sequitur*: "The peculiar horrors of America — its brashness, music at meals, and racial hysteria — . . . force the onlooker into a rejection of the world . . ." Rejection perhaps, but more probably acceptance, or some far-fetched compromise between the yogi and the scenario writer. Connolly compares his own arrival, and Auden's greeting, to the encounter between the country-mouse and the city-mouse in Disney's film. Connolly's subsequent grand tour of America, undertaken on behalf of his magazine *Horizon*, seems to have comprehended nothing between the intellectual circles of New York City and the artists' colonies of California, between Auden and Henry Miller — the latter sheltered by "a romantic shack" from such peculiar horrors as fastidiousness would instinctively reject. Connolly is not an outgoing onlooker. When he mentions a widely circulated and highly extroverted book about a chicken farm, whether by Freudian lapse or typographical error, he calls it *The Ego and I*.

During the preceding year Mr. Connolly had been nettled by an American review, which — I regret to say — I happened to write. I only allude to it now because of his editorial retort, which, modestly if not quite candidly, concealed the fact that a book of his was the object of my criticism and conveyed the impression that I had attacked the corpus of contemporary British writing. Our cross-grained and cross-purposed repartee is somewhat less than the stuff of an international incident, and Mr. Connolly is no more willing than I to be bullied into assuming a chauvinistic position. But what should interest others is his willingness to go much farther than I in conceding the superiority of particular American writers, and even suggesting genetic or psychosexual reasons for British inferiority. "Well, there are three writers I envy America," he writes, "Hemingway as a novelist, Edmund Wilson as a critic, and E. E. Cummings as a poet. America possesses many more good writers, but those three have something which we are inclined to lack (perhaps because they are father's boys and our literature is apt to be made by those more influenced by their mothers): that is to say, they are illusion-free and unite a courageous heart-whole emotional drive to an adult and lively intellectual toughness." Later he sums up the distinction, as other British critics have done, in terms of comparative virility. *"Our impotence liberates their potentialities."*

To such opinions a vigorous dissent must be registered in the name of George Orwell. As a specialist in popular culture, Orwell does not feel the esthete's need to stand in awe before the semiliterate or the antiliterary; indeed he is not hesitant to play the moralist when he feels called upon. He agrees that the cultural impetus has been shifting to America, but he thoroughly deplores the shift; not the hypercivilized old world, but the barbaric new, is for him the breeding-place of decadence. He contrasts the old-fashioned boys' weeklies — which, for all their old-school-tie snobbishness, professed a code, a notion of "cricket," an ideal of "playing the game" — with the so-called "Yank mags" that invaded England during the war, "written in a jargon that has been perfected by people who brood endlessly on violence." As opposed to the schoolboy idealism of Raffles, the gentleman crook, Orwell instances a current shocker, *No Orchids for Miss Blandish*. Here, under the influence of a Chicago setting and a Faulkner theme, an English novelist has gone beyond mere materialism to "realism" in its Machiavellian implications — in other words, a fascist lust for power. The critics we next consider, the Russians, consider our writers fascists because they are not realistic enough.

III

With England our problems are those of emphasis and adjustment, within the framework of shifting but more or less familiar conditions. With Russia we have more fundamental grounds for cleavage — cultural and linguistic diver-

gences as wide as our two nations and the civilization that falls
between them, ideological differences which can be theoret-
ically transcended but interpose practical obstacles every day.
The key to the literary misunderstandings between the Russians and ourselves may be found in that ambiguous term
realism. Though we pride ourselves on being realistic — that is
to say, hard-boiled — our traditional fiction is didactic, allegorical, romantic. Our naturalistic school was a late development,
largely a conscious importation from Europe, notably from
France. Somewhat the same tradition of social protest and self-
criticism developed, despite the czars, in nineteenth-century
Russia. When the Soviets took over, and the opposition became
an orthodoxy, "socialist realism" became the party line. Marxist
criticism perforce supported the authoritarian regime, though
it remained severely critical of life and literature in other countries. Meanwhile, in democratic countries, realists freely continue to criticize life as they find it, thus supplying a dialectical
antithesis which very neatly fits the Marxian thesis.

The Russians admit no inconsistency in the fact that their
realism, which once protested, now glorifies. Not the literary
method but the social situation, they maintain, has been
changed by revolution into its opposite. They would point
to the pivotal example of Gorky as the realist who weathered
the change. Even his prerevolutionary drama, *The Lower
Depths,* contains a note of affirmation: "The word *man* sounds
proud! " Whereas, for the vagrants depicted by Eugene
O'Neill in *The Iceman Cometh,* a Soviet critic now declares
that the word *man* (*chelovek*) sounds "low and rotten." For
the Russians, it is not socialist realism but bourgeois realism
which has fallen away. In 1946 it was estimated that some
forty million copies of American books had been published in
Russia since 1917. Among them the strongly marked preference has been for writers who flourished during the muck-
raking years of the early twentieth century — most appropriately for Theodore Dreiser. The extraordinary vogue of Upton
Sinclair, which began when Tolstoy recommended *The
Jungle* to the Russian public, has reached the stage where a
current magazine calls him "the most important writer in

contemporary America." Lanny Budd to the contrary not-
withstanding, the same article insists that plutocracy is forcing Sinclair to publish his own books, and presents an account
of American publishing practices which is largely derived
from *The Brass Check* (1919).

Such American qualities as the Russians admire came to a
dead end, it would seem, in the books of our immediate contemporaries. In the Soviet Union, as in the United States, the
writer tends to be an unliterary man; the novelist is becoming
a superior journalist; and the most esteemed book is the plain,
unvarnished tale. But, unlike most of the Western Europeans,
the Russians believe that our recent writing has been sicklied
over with what they call *literaturshchina*, "literariness." Faulkner and Henry Miller reveal to them a kind of "witches' sab-
bath," which celebrates the decadence of our culture as well
as the decay of our society. Even the popularity of Steinbeck
and Erskine Caldwell, who were welcome and sympathetic
visitors to Russia a few years ago, has recently been attacked
in a public lecture. The lecturer, M. Mendelson, officially
accuses Caldwell of creating "monotonous biologically conditioned monstrosities" and Steinbeck of "insistently emphasizing the biological undertones." Such criticisms are quite
understandable; it is harder to understand why a Communist
critic, who presumably believes in scientific materialism,
should use the language of science so pejoratively. However,
the subject of biology, along with various intellectual questions, is currently under revision in the U.S.S.R.

The Marxists are more consistent when — with the literary
historian Startsev — they attack "the renegadism of liberal intelligentsia," the backsliding of American fellow travelers,
the rediscovery of so-called "spiritual values" by Lewis Mum-
ford and Van Wyck Brooks. Professional philistines like J.
Donald Adams are approvingly cited in the Soviet press
whenever they disapprovingly refer to the pessimism of our
more serious novelists. As for our poets, their pens are
weapons enlisted in the service of reaction, seeking to "dis-
arm people for the war against fascism and to spread cyni-

cism, defeatism, and other fascist ideas." E. E. Cummings is compared to Goebbels, while the poems of Robinson Jeffers belong to "the fifth column of literature." Fortunately, or unfortunately, there seem to be certain exceptions; but to name them here would be to do them a disservice, for their poetic virtues are measured solely by an ideology which would seem progressive to the Cominform and subversive to a congressional committee. Failure to adhere to party lines is as damaging in one moral climate as straight adherence is in another — if adherence, in these days of sudden twists and sinuous turnings, can indeed be straight. At the moment the odds are large that any American writer, judged by the canons of Soviet criticism, will be indicted as a lackey of capitalistic imperialism.

Can one culture ever have shown toward another, at the very same time, such eager attention and such uniform disapproval? Can it be that the Russians protest too much, or are we simply unused to the harsh accusations of Marxist controversy? After all, they have dealt no less harshly with many of their own leading artists, and they seem to regard the word *putrid* as the hallmark of critical acumen. When Ilya Ehrenburg denounces Western intellectuals as "idiots" and "dolts," he may be merely dodging the suspicion of cosmopolitan urbanity that some of his compatriots hold against him. At all events, unreasoning hostility seems to be part of a Russian counteroffensive, planned with an eye upon the friendlier reception that American writers are getting in Western Europe. "Along with the shopworn goods that are disposed of by the Marshall Plan," writes the Soviet critic, Ivan Anisimov, "America trades widely in its literature. Slavish criticism in France, as in other occupied countries, obsequiously praises the 'gifts' of American literature. These cheaply bought delights cannot conceal the fact that, under the guise of literature, America exports wastage, rottenness, lies." It confirms our lack of communication with Russia, as well as our present closeness to the French, that the latter should look for truth in this doubtful cargo.

IV

For, without a doubt, the conclusion of the war brought with it "a Franco-American cultural offensive," launched in the United States and profusely greeted in France. Though the currents of transatlantic influence now run eastward rather than westward, the two cultures still preserve their peculiar traits; it is simply that France, for so long the exporter of elegance, has begun to import a kind of American toughness. A French professor at Princeton University, Maurice-Edgar Coindreau, by his translations of Faulkner and other contemporaries, has decisively contributed to this movement. The publishing list of the *Nouvelle Revue française*, in its *Série noire*, carries each month the scarifying titles of California thrillers, *traduits de l'américain*. One of the most enterprising translators, Marcel Duhamel, after a performance of his version of *Tobacco Road*, was asked why he translated so many plays "from the American." He replied that he did so because it was easier than to translate plays from the French. Despite their zeal for immediacy and sensationalism, the importers have not neglected our older writers; witness the translation of *Moby-Dick* by Jean Giono and others, or such critical studies of Melville as Jean Simon's. Yet a recent French visitor, meditating for a moment at Concord, discerns the world of Damon Runyon in the village of Emerson.

It is we who are undiscriminating, not they, the French admirers of our literature argue. They appreciated Henry Miller before we did — before we do. We are too simple; he is too ambiguous for us, according to Maurice Blanchot. If we make the mistake of thinking him unambiguous, we read him single-mindedly and therefore low-mindedly; he is never really obscene, he is merely fantastic. Apology yields to eulogy in Henri Fluchère's preface to the French translation of *Tropic of Cancer*, where we are told that Miller is as subtle as Proust, as vigorous as Joyce, as comprehensive as Balzac, and as brutal as Shakespeare. Choice of phrase and clarity of thought, those virtues for which we traditionally admire

French criticism, fade and blur before the American onrush. Miller's expatriate Bohemianism, for another critic, fuses together the cosmic and the nostalgic: "Brooklyn calls Montparnasse, Montparnasse Brooklyn; Cancer answers Capricorn; the Pont de Sèvres evokes all the bridges in the world . . ." T. S. Eliot, at the other extreme, is beginning to draw upon his laureled head the scorn that stigmatizes an academic elder. He is more of an English gentleman than an American poet, says Jean de Bosschère, who goes on to accuse the Nobel Prize committee of betraying their obligation to poetry.

American writers on their native ground have again become a subject for observation by traveling French writers. Simone de Beauvoir notes, in her sharp-eyed book, *L'Amérique au jour le jour*, that "America is hard on intellectuals." It is instructive to match her impressions of the New York intelligentsia against Mary McCarthy's article, "America the Beautiful," where one such encounter is seen from the other side. Mlle. de Beauvoir was armed for something more positive; Miss McCarthy feels embarrassed at being so negative. If I may hark back to Connolly's fable, the roles of the country-mouse and the city-mouse are reversed. The absence of solidarity in American literary life seems particularly striking to Mlle. de Beauvoir's fellow Existentialist, Jean-Paul Sartre, who has been so active in Parisian coteries and artistic schools. The plight of the artist, isolated from society, yet engaged in a struggle for its freedom and his own, is typified for Sartre by Richard Wright. As a Negro, Wright cannot do otherwise; he cannot disengage himself, like Flaubert, to practice belles-lettres. What Europe means to Sartre on the plane of time, America means on the plane of space; Americans are "men on the loose, lost in a continent too big for them, as we have lost ourselves in history."

Sartre explains the widespread French imitation of modern American fiction as "the defense-mechanism of a literature which, feeling threatened because its techniques and myths were no longer enabling it to face the historical situation, grafted foreign methods upon itself, so that it could fulfill its function by new experiments." Thus in his novel, *Le Sursis*,

Sartre adapted a technique from Dos Passos — who had adapted it in turn from Joyce — for presenting the theme of disorder within an ordered structure. And in his play, *La Putain respectueuse*, he created a myth from the facts of the Scottsboro case, which not only dramatized an American dilemma, but stated the moral problem that Frenchmen faced during the years of collaboration and resistance. The word *south*, so rich in its European connotations, as Mlle. de Beauvoir points out, connotes the most tragic part of America, "the land of slavery and hunger." With its racial tension, its meaningless violence, its personal alienation, it could just as well be North Africa, as Albert Camus suggests in *L'Etranger*. And if, as Camus elsewhere suggests, the human condition is that of Sisyphus, going through his motions eternally and ineffectually, it is easy to understand French admiration for a novel about an American dance-marathon: Horace McCoy's *They Shoot Horses, Don't They?*

Anxiety within, absurdity without, the existential outlook, man's effort to control himself where he has lost control over his circumstances — is there anything in such a situation that confines it to one hemisphere or to the other? "What gives American literature the glamor it has for us today is not that it is more talented than ours," declares Maurice Nadeau, "but that it expresses more forcefully, more sincerely, and more brutally the despair of our time." Such considerations, matters not of kind but of degree, differentiate Sartre from Dos Passos, Céline from Miller, or Malraux from Hemingway. The new world speaks with characteristic liveliness; but it speaks of troubles that beset the old world; and to this extent our writers, at the midpoint of the twentieth century, have gone back upon the well-known optimism of their forerunners. Shortly after World War I, André Gide set down in his journal this sentence from Walter Rathenau: "America has no soul and will not deserve to have one until it consents to plunge into the abyss of human sin and suffering." At the end of the last war Gide told an imaginary reporter that America had abandoned its soulless contentment, its trust in material progress, and had taken the plunge.

V

We have sampled a small but, I believe, representative portion of the accumulating testimony. Within the three areas that have particularly concerned us, individual views have run closely parallel; but each of the three, collectively considered, registers a different attitude. Our literature is shared by England, repulsed by Russia, embraced by France. The only response that seems common to all is an inclination to see their problems reflected in our mirrors. The British lecturer finds new opportunities for satirizing Anglo-Saxon mores; the Russian Marxist pounces on further deviations from the party line; the French Existentialist is obsessed with the conditions of his own existence. Yet sometimes, when the angle of determination is known, the most oblique refraction can be the most revealing. We have much to learn from the exaggerations of our critics. The British remind us that our sudden international ascendancy is, more than a simple matter of bombs and loans, a cultural responsibility. The Russians can teach us something about ideology, that mysterious allegiance which unites some men while dividing others, which sets up barbed-wire entanglements between nations as well as classes. The French, enlarging our critical perspective, can lend a moral and universal scope to the social and regional issues confronting our writers.

Lest we confine ourselves to mere opinion — or, what is slighter, to my generalizations about the opinions of others — let me cite one startlingly concrete example. American novels are not merely imitated in Europe today, they are fabricated; and one of these synthetic products, perhaps by an oversight on the part of our customs authorities, is available for examination. Its very title is a commentary: *J'irai cracher sur vos tombes*. Its professed translator, Boris Vian, who writes for *Les Temps modernes* under the candid pseudonym of *Le Menteur*, appears to be its actual author. Its apocryphal author is one Vernon Sullivan, a Negro whose books are said to be unpublishable in the original American, but who has undergone the translucent influence of Faulkner,

Miller, and especially James M. Cain. His story is a night-marish fulfillment of the recurrent southern fantasy that every colored man aspires to rape the white man's daughters and sisters. The hero, who is also the narrator, has Scandinavian as well as Negro blood. His ambiguous blondness allows him to pass among the whites, where he sadistically revenges the lynching of a younger brother. His racial vendetta drives him across the limbo that separates existentialism from por-nography and leads him to be masochistically lynched in the end.

The book is not, in its own words, *"une réunion de l'école du dimanche."* To our language, our fiction, our jazz, M. Vian is nothing if not hep. His local color is vague, however; for though a reference to *le sénateur Balbo* presumably lo-cates the scene in Mississippi, the village rather untypically contains a bookshop, which is opened and shut by a typical Parisian *rideau de fer.* The bookseller offers a literary formula: "It's easy to be audacious in this country; you have only to say what anyone who takes the trouble can see." The assumption is that our most sensational novels are direct transcriptions from American life — an assumption disproved by the paradox of the book itself, which is based not on first-hand experience but sheer book-knowledge. Yet if an indige-nous school of writing can be so grotesquely parodied by a foreigner, it must show certain pervasive tendencies; if its twisted characters and brutal incidents are not social docu-ments, they must at any rate be psychological myths. The Negro is the dramatic protagonist because he is our displaced person; the conflict it dramatizes is what Gunnar Myrdal has termed our dilemma. Our tragic region is the South, even as our epic theme is the Civil War. Hence any resemblances be-tween our history and postwar Europe are more than coin-cidental.

The European success of *Gone with the Wind* has sig-nificantly coincided with a decade of invasion, occupation, displacement, dispossession, and reconstruction. The lost cause that appealed so strongly to readers in occupied countries, the implied analogy between the Yankees and the Nazis, are signs that life occasionally does better than literature. *Uncle Tom's Cabin,* sweeping across the Continent, was a happier omen, since it presaged liberation for the slaves; whereas Margaret Mitchell's *roman-fleuve* cultivates the unreconstructed nostalgia of the masters. More vital questions are raised by the continental reception of Steinbeck's *Grapes of Wrath.* Its translation was officially sponsored, in Nazi Germany and Fascist Italy, because its painful depiction of the underdog's plight was expected to make for anti-American propaganda. The expectation backfired in both countries, partly because of the disparity in standards of living. What most impressed Germans and Italians was that the Okies, however humble their lot, had their jalopies. To thoughtful readers it occurred that a civilization which allowed its writers to attack its defects possessed, at least, the redeeming virtue of self-criticism. To those of little faith, who loudly fear that we expose ourselves too vulnerably when we permit the exposures of our realists to circulate, that result should underline the distinction between critical and totalitarian realism.

"There is an American anguish in the face of Americanism," Jean-Paul Sartre has written. "There is an ambivalence of anguish which simultaneously asks 'Am I American enough?' and 'How can I escape from Americanism?'" If anything can redeem us, it is this hesitation between our optimists and our pessimists, our frontiersmen and our expatriates. Once we rush to the one extreme or the other, we are lost. On the one hand we have a unique background, which would be quite barren if it remained unique. On the other we are strengthened by a hybrid strain, the cross-fertilization of many different cultures. What is commonly regarded as peculiarly American is blatant and standardized: Ford, Luce, Metro-Goldwyn-Mayer. What is most original is most traditional: Melville. Moving, in T. S. Eliot's phrase, "Between two worlds become much like each other," these opposites are neutralized. As André Siegfried predicted many years ago, Europe is Americanized and America is Europeanized. Organization reconquers the old world, chaos is rediscovered in the new. Beyond the clamor, beneath the surfaces of the present, the past continues, and our brightest lights are those that keep burning underground. So a young English poet, John Heath-Stubbs, in a sonnet on Hart Crane, invokes America:

> . . a hollow land,
> Where with false rhetoric through the hard sky
> The bridges leap, twanged by dry-throated wind,
> And crowded thick below, with idiot eye,
> The leaning deadmen strive to pierce the dim
> Tunnels and vaults, which agate lamps illume.

Criticism in Crisis

Forty minutes is a generous allotment of time at a public meeting, but hardly enough to do justice to the development of criticism — or poetry or drama or fiction — over the past hundred years. Yet, in accepting the cordial invitation of Professor Victor Lange to take part in his program on "Changing Perspectives of Modern Literature" before the Comparative Literature section of the Modern Language Association on December 27, 1954, one accepted those succinct conditions. The best that I could do, under the circumstances, was to subdivide my subject into an arbitrary sequence of ten propositions — to nail, as it were, these theses on the door. They appear here with thanks to the editor, Chandler Beall, who printed them in Comparative Literature, VII, 2 *(Spring, 1956). A German version, translated by Heinz Politzer, is being published in* Die Neue Rundschau.

▀▀

1. The Nineteenth Century and After

"*Ce serait encore une gloire, dans cette grande confusion de la société qui commence, d'avoir été les derniers des délicats. — Soyons les derniers de notre ordre, de notre ordre d'esprits.*" The confusion has been even greater than Sainte-Beuve foresaw when he set down this reflection a hundred years ago, and those of us who are still occupied with the problems of criticism have abandoned any pretensions to his kind of elegant connoisseurship. He, and the kindred spirits that he invokes, enjoyed the privilege of living more at ease with their time and in closer touch with the past; the influx and reflux of subject-matter from both of those continual sources were rich indeed, yet not too overwhelmingly large to be breasted by a nicely discriminating eclecticism. Something like a synthesis could be effected between classical judgment and romantic appreciation, but it was too precarious and personal to outlast the middle years of the nineteenth century. Walter Pater, addressing himself to the next generation, exceeded Sainte-Beuve in his epicurean sense of the heightened moment and the coming deluge. The flood — by which I mean the uncontrollable flow of undifferentiated reading-matter — was destined to sweep away the surviving landmarks, so that when we take our bearings in this postdiluvian world, it is by means of such dead reckonings as I have been rash enough to venture here.

Not only have tastes changed, and changed utterly, but the concept of good taste has lost its validity, since that depended upon its appeal to universal standards. *Buen gusto*, the faculty of Renaissance man for judging aright, has gradually yielded to the sort of uncritical enthusiasm connoted by "gusto," or to the degustation of literary vintages that has its cellar-book in George Saintsbury's *History of Criticism*. Critics, falling back on impressionism, sought their own criteria in the range and perceptiveness of their individual impressions. Some of these were based upon a rounded cultivation which might well have passed for professional erudition among their successors; other instances have been so capricious that today the term "impressionist" has gone the way of "amateur" and "dilettante." Such terms, as long as they had a positive meaning, embodied the natural impulse of every man to be his own critic rather than to delegate another job to another expert. Their passing marks a final stage in the dissolution of that ideal which Nietzsche so poignantly and vainly evoked, the whole man. The century had its exemplary figure in Goethe; it also had its object-lesson in Coleridge. The philosophical fragments of his poetic ruins, shored in his *Biographia Literaria*, ironically emphasized the need for organic wholeness. Similarly, Nietzsche's desperate attempt to discover and affirm a set of modern values succeeded only in its negative impact, its iconoclastic critique of all traditions. The year of his death, 1900, bore witness not to the advent of the superman but to the heyday of the specialist.

2. *The New Alexandria*

Now decadence, the state of mind anticipated by Sainte-Beuve and consciously cultivated in the nineties, need not be critically inarticulate. On the contrary, that manifestation of it known as Alexandrianism is characterized precisely by the ascendancy of criticism over artistic creation. That we are living through such a period has been attested *a fortiori* by such creative writers as Thomas Mann. If the main effort of Matthew Arnold's day was already "a critical effort," as he never tired of repeating, then poet-critics have had increasing occasion to call each successive age an "age of criticism." The original Alexandria could never have vied with our epoch in its encyclopedic profusion of revivals, revaluations, exegeses, collections, editions, and manuals. Our relationship to the past is a gradual relinquishment rather than any sharp Nietzschean break; it involves many reasserted continuities and perhaps one consistent trend of reaction, which is suggested by the English title of Mario Praz's study of decadent themes — *The Romantic Agony*. The power of romanticism is felt in the very gestures of dissociation from it that every subsequent school has seen fit to make. Insofar as the romanticists stood in perennial opposition to classicism, all those who reacted against them joined forces in a sort of countermovement. Naturalism and symbolism, though they diverged to planes remote from each other, shared a predisposition for analysis. The antiromanticism of Irving Babbitt, T. E. Hulme, or the Action Française, while it could not activate a classical revival, could foster an approach to literature which is more rationalistic than intuitive.

The romantic movement provided a dialectical pattern, as well as an initial impetus, for the ever accelerating cycle of cultural movements that follows from generation to generation. Criticism, in each case, has been divided between the manifestoes of coteries and the strictures of academies. The party of innovation always tends to conceive itself as an "advance-guard," in terms of a military analogy which Renato Poggioli has traced to Proudhon, thereby indicating a historical parallel between literary and political radicalism. This kinship was acknowledged when modernism in the arts was described as *Kulturbolschewismus*: but the actual revolutions of our time have proved so grimly far-reaching that the later esthetic *-isms* seem comparatively attenuated and inconsequential. Futurism, as James Joyce predicted, had no future. When the modernist tired of playing the revolutionary, he could draw a further comparison between his work and scientific experiment. Here, too, he aligned himself with an intellectual élite as against an uncomprehending majority. Science, at least technology, has had its influence on the techniques of art, which have become abstracted and dehumanized — so Ortega y Gasset would maintain — to the point where they are bound to be unpopular. The critic is therefore led, by the complexities of his subject, to be what is popularly regarded as a highbrow. His exemplar is Paul Valéry's cerebral hero, M. Teste. His horizon is Valéry's awareness of tradition extending from its Mediterranean origins into our lives, and terminating in that crisis of intellect which transcends — and threatens to extirpate — criticism.

3. The Persistence of History

History is one *donnée* which we must take as it comes. Our consciousness of it, our retrospective acknowledgment that we are heirs of all the ages, is itself a heritage from the Renaissance. The historical method, devised and bequeathed by the romanticists to literary historians like Francesco De Sanctis and Georg Brandes, prompted them to interpret the unfolding of national and international culture on a scale commensurate with the grandeur of their themes. Such works have since been somewhat outdated by the more exhaustive researches they stimulated, which in turn have been reducing literary history to a mere sequence of monographs and compilations. Taine, who made criticism compatible with the fulfillment of the doctoral degree, was primarily interested in literature as a source of historical documentation; his emphasis on background, molded into an academic formula by

Gustave Lanson, deflected the attention of generations of students. So much of the extra-literary was brought into their frame of critical reference that the esthetic object was all but completely obscured; hence, upon recovering that object, some of the present generation have come to assume a fundamental incompatibility between the categories of literary history and those of literary criticism. Their willingness to make this assumption is strengthened by the demands and pressures of current history, along with the attractions of escaping into a bookish sphere from which such contingencies can be excluded by definition. But it is that very exclusion which imposes on bookishness its mode of unreality, and their refusal to face the collateral facts of scholarship runs the risk of ignoring the facts of life.

To put the matter more affirmatively, the sense of a living past — the ambiance of anything not contemporary — can only be reconstructed by the skilled application of relevant detail. For example, no phase of English poetry seems more vital to contemporary readers than the Metaphysical School. It would scarcely have this vitality if Sir Herbert Grierson had not been able to offer us Donne's poems in an authoritative text with an indispensable commentary. Footnotes are not — or should not be — excrescences; they are simply our means of removing, so far as we can, the encrustations of time. Since we cannot see things under the aspect of eternity, we do our best to understand the conditions of their existence in its relation to ours. By understanding the context in which a given work was originally framed, we can detach it without undue violence and bring it into the differing contexts of our own experience. Knowledge of history leads to control of history, according to the Marxists, who have amply proved that a little knowledge is a dangerous thing. Conversely, historical ignorance is a form of slavery; the greatest liberation the mind has known came when the humanists rediscovered the classics. What is historically unique in our epoch, André Malraux has discerned, is the accumulation of art-objects from all periods on a timeless plane in an imaginary museum. So we might speak of an imaginary library, where the whole continuum of man's recorded expression can be connected and placed in perspective.

4. The Autonomy of Art

Thus criticism learns to live with history. Writers, on the other hand, have felt more free to accept or reject the historical situation in which they have found themselves. Rejection has sometimes taken the form of social protest, particularly against the bourgeoisie; at other times, denying the claims of society altogether, it has professed an intransigent estheticism. Marxism, with Plekhanov, explains this second position as an aggravated consequence of the first; and there is certainly a temperamental linkage between the writer's sense of alienation and his intensified self-consciousness. The less secure his status, the more he is preoccupied with his craft; he makes common cause with the misunderstood practitioners of the plastic arts; in short, he identifies himself with the artist's role. This identification, since Flaubert, has been axiomatic. The novel has become not merely a demonstration of craftsmanship, but often a self-portrait of the novelist as artist and even a presentation of his artistic theories. The Petrarchan ideal of literary immortality and the Kantian idea of esthetic disinterestedness combined to make their highest claims when Proust defined the function of art as a Last Judgment. But such a view proceeded from a point of detachment which no longer seems attainable. Jean-Paul Sartre, turning away from the ultimate, sharply reminds us that we are immersed in the immediate. Literature cannot be pure, for the Existentialist, so long as life is not. So long as men are engaged in conflict, words will be used as weapons, and writers will bear a special responsibility.

In this respect, the wheel has come full circle during the past hundred years. Poetry had previously been attacked and defended on the grounds of morality or utility; the beautiful had seldom been allowed to stand without the support of the true or the good. The rallying cry of "art for art's sake" was a defense against more extrinsic requirements; in the hands of such masters of paradox as Théophile Gautier and Oscar

Wilde it became a counterattack on didacticism. Their endeavor was not to isolate art from other human concerns but to accord it a certain priority among them, and above all to keep the intrinsic standards of literary technique from being subordinated to the cross-purposes of journalism or propaganda. To go farther and assert that literature should be autotelic, having no aim beyond its own existence, is a jejune conception largely propounded by hostile critics. The most that responsible proponents have urged is that the practice of the arts be considered autonomous — which means respectively governed by laws of their own but, like other institutions, sensitive to social influences and adaptable to historical changes. Today the single dedicated exponent of *ars gratia artis* is the roaring lion that figures as a trademark for one of Hollywood's most venal producers of films. The metamorphosis of the phrase into Latin is an unexpected twist of pedantry, since it has no classical sanction whatsoever. It is invoked to justify sheer entertainment at a moment when, on a more serious level, esthetics and ethics seem again to be moving closer together.

5. Problems of Belief

The study of esthetics, during its second century, has not resolved the tautologies of its first; the career of the late Benedetto Croce may well stand as its monument in the commemorative sense of the word. As a unified field theory of the arts, it has operated on too general a plane to have thrown much light upon problems of form. Nor has it been successful in demonstrating that different artistic media produce the same kind of response, an emotion uniquely detached from other feelings. Literature appeals to so many values, esthetic and otherwise, that it requires a pluralistic approach. John Crowe Ransom once advertised for "an ontological critic," whose presumable task would be to furnish poetry with a philosophic excuse for being. No candidate has yet presented himself; and most other critics have been content to start where the philosophers, the scientists, or the theologians have left off. This has meant that art is ultimately looked upon as a vehicle, not as an article, of belief: whether of Anglicanism for T. S. Eliot or of Thomism for Jacques Maritain. All critics, to be sure, are sooner or later confronted with works based upon beliefs they do not share. To what extent is suspension of disbelief possible, and does it leave an adequate basis for criticism? Can doctrines be taken — along with poems — as "pseudo-statements," and tested by emotive or formal criteria rather than by correspondence with reality? And if they cannot, must not the critic brave the winds of doctrine, seeking his particular version of truth? And when he applies what he finds, then will he be just to anything that conflicts with his assumptions?

The circle is even more constricting when the logic is not religious but political. It revolves in the direction of censorship whenever critical judgment is adverse, and — even under more sympathetic conditions — toward the sort of moralistic bias that Tolstoy and the Russian critics have exercised. It varies greatly, as between a free society, where Sartre's commitment may be a courageous gesture, and an authoritarian régime, where Ilya Ehrenburg's stand is simply an act of conformity. Marxism has shown two faces: a historical method which is analytic, and a doctrinal position which is dogmatic. Its repudiation of traditional ideologies has rendered it especially alert to the explicit consideration of writers in terms of what they implicitly believe. As it has consolidated its own ideology, it has exacted a stricter adherence to ever tightening canons of correctness. Thus a literate and cosmopolitan Marxist — and such a one survives in Georg Lukács — can move freely amid the self-critical literature of the past and of the West, but finds himself entrammeled by the anticritical convolutions of the party line in Communist Hungary. The coexistence of opposing orthodoxies, making absolute claims to moral authority, constitutes — for those who adhere to neither of them — an argument in favor of relativism. But freedom from state control or from church discipline is not necessarily a warrant of the critic's professional independence. One of our liveliest journals of literary opinion flaunts the title, *Partisan Review*. Significantly, its twenty-year history has been a recantation of Marxist principles; such militance as it still musters is centered less on causes than on personalities.

6. The Role of Personality

At all events, our lives as individuals are circumscribed by forces of uniformity, if not of conformity. In retrospect, it might well seem that creative talents had found the widest scope for their individuality in the late nineteenth and early twentieth centuries. Remy de Gourmont broadened the definition of symbolism to the verge of anarchy, when he termed it "the expression of individualism in art." The life and work of André Gide have been a striking test of the lengths to which such freedom of thought and action could be pursued. The tendency toward autobiography, toward the poet who dramatizes his ego, and the novelist who lives his fiction, has been part of the romantic bequest. Antiromantic reaction, turning from the image of the artist to the sphere of his artistry, has attempted to scrutinize the latter with a technician's impersonality. The focal point of the scrutiny has been — in a phrase formulated by a half-forgotten classicist, Washington Allston, and promulgated by Mr. Eliot — "the objective correlative." This is a far cry from the subjectivity of authors who put their overt selves into their works, forcing their critics to become biographers, or from the preoccupation of so much American criticism with the circumstances that underlie an artistic career. Croce, who was a mind of the nineteenth century in his emphasis on self-expression and on the uniqueness of the individual, belongs to the twentieth in his distinction between practical and poetic personality — his insistence that, for critical purposes, the man is the style.

Paradoxically enough, at the very point when the biographical approach to literature seems rather outmoded, the study of biography itself has taken on the newer dimensions of psychology. A closely related field has opened up which ought not to be confounded with criticism, but which could not be neglected by anyone professing an interest in the imaginative process. Granted that the figure in the carpet, as a conscious product of craftmanship, cannot be reduced by psychoanalysis to a mere pattern of subconscious motivation. Nevertheless, since a work of art entails a whole complex of dynamic relationships, its genesis is a relevant fact about it and a probable clue to its significance. Freud, though he took a somewhat reductive view of the arts, was generous in his acknowledgment of the insights he owed to writers. Would that they were comparably rigorous in applying the concepts they have borrowed from him! Having exposed themselves on paper more fully and frankly than other men, they have incidentally built up a body of documents which the more specialized students of human nature can utilize as sublimated case histories. These can be obliquely illuminating; but, as most other cases are less self-revealing, such comparison becomes invidious; and the writer is treated as more neurotic than men about whom we know less, a scapegoat for Max Nordau's kind of pseudo-scientific philistinism. Psychologists may devote themselves more profitably, in the long run, to the configuration of types than to the individuation of personalities. Studies of Shakespeare's imagery have gone astray when they have been too personal in their premises, whereas such broader investigations as Gaston Bachelard's have revealed how much the poets draw upon a common imagination.

7. The Quest for the Archetype

Imagination, in its conveyance of universals by means of particulars, tends to stress the one or the other. We are now undergoing a transition between a lavish concern for the minutiae of a highly organized existence and a difficult adjustment to the exigencies of some more generalized outlook — in the most broadly programmatic terms, between realism at one extreme and symbolism at the other. The art of the recent epoch is strongly marked by the interplay of those tendencies, but there can be little doubt that its continuing direction is toward the primordial, the irreducible, the typical. What is surprising is to have reached this mainroad by way of such introspective and devious bypaths. Dreams, the wayward

projections of fantasy, were worlds of escape for poets like
Rimbaud; for his inheritors, the Surrealists, they have been
deliberate and preferable alternatives to reality. How they
are compounded of actual experience, and how pertinently
they comment upon it, critics have learned from psycho-
analysts. Jung's formula of the collective unconscious, though
it is a suggestive abstraction rather than a cultural fact, has
helped to explain how the dream recapitulates the myth;
while archeologists, anthropologists, and folklorists have
shown that myths use the same vocabulary of symbols and the
same repertory of motifs as dreams are made of. All this has
shed an illumination so dazzling that it has sometimes obliter-
ated the degrees of difference between mythology and literature, or — as with Friedrich Gundolf — between mythography
and criticism. Nowadays it is virtually taken for granted, in
some quarters, that dramas are rituals out of *The Golden
Bough.*

The scholar's inclination to see the varieties of human behavior reduced to a manageable number of patterns and
themes is not restricted to his perception of recurrent archetypes beneath the work of modern writers. By tracing a succession of literary commonplaces or *topoi* through the Middle
Ages, Ernst Robert Curtius has reaffirmed the continuity of
the classical tradition. The "unit-idea," as explored by
Arthur Lovejoy, has given an integrating principle to other
historians of philosophy. Both of these methods move through
history toward a plane of timelessness, where all ideas and
topics are at one with their prototypes, and where the scholar-
critic gains — as it were — the presence of the past. But it is
quite another thing for the creative writer to confer a mythical kind of pastness upon the present. He can, if his name is
William Butler Yeats, make himself "a coat of old mytholo-
gies," but he cannot improvise a myth by an act of the will.
The archetypal is that which precedes the imaginings of the
poet and preëxists in the mind of his audience. Had Dante
not written his letter to Can Grande, his project would still
have had its rationale in scholastic thought and its iconog-
raphy in medieval cathedrals. For Yeats, discarding one set

of legends after another, it was necessary to synthesize *A Vision* explaining his poetic intentions to the even more syncretistic Ezra Pound. A homogeneous system of symbology guided Dante, and his readers after him, through the *selva oscura*. Lacking such guides, we lose ourselves among the confused sounds and shadows of Baudelaire's *forêts de symboles*.

8. *The Dark Forest*

Because we lack evidence of another world coexisting in parallelism with this one, we perceive no systematic series of correspondences between the two. Yet the habit of scanning a literal text for a symbolic meaning may perhaps reflect some dissatisfaction with immediate realities and some aspiration toward less worldly ideals. This is an Alexandrian mode of thought; it was also the state of mind of the pious Christians who allegorized the pagan classics. The method of prefiguration, instead of reverting to the archetype, superimposed a later significance upon its original analogues; but its arbitrary cross-references, which Erich Auerbach has so aptly elucidated, had a certain relevance and consistency. Latter-day interpretations of symbolism, having no single frame of reference, often derive from a work neither more nor less than the preconceptions they read into it; hence, in the arcane instance of Mallarmé, there are as many readings as interpreters. Here, and elsewhere, the hieratic qualities of the writer himself have been matched by the hierophantic attitude of his critics. Not to be outdone by the ancients, many of the moderns seem to invite hermeneutics — which, without special italics or apologies to the French, we now call explication. This invitation has engendered schools of explicators, who have set a standard of subtle ingenuity which has proved so intimidating to younger writers that many of them have turned critic, devoting their creative abilities to symbolistic reinterpretations of the world's great books. But there are courageous exceptions: notably William Empson, who can return from criticism to poetry, not impossibly animated by the hope of inventing an eighth type of ambiguity.

The problem of meaning is serious, however, on both sides and at every level; at the level of communication, it may be the crucial issue before civilization today. Consequently so percipient a critic as I. A. Richards has shifted his attention from writers to readers, and has brought the focus of semantics, pedagogy, and educational psychology to bear upon the reading process itself. The fact that basic literacy has been undermined accounts, on the other side, for the tenuous atmosphere in which some writers have been working. Obscurity, for them, has been associated with absence of recognition; whereas, to an unrecognizing public, it has seemed a cult of unintelligibility. In the ensuing confusion of tongues, much of the blame has fallen upon the interpreters, some of whom are themselves so bedeviled by language that their best effort at clarification turns out to be *obscurum per obscurius*. Others, disaffected from criticism, have gathered the emoluments reserved for men of letters who confirm the unlettered in their *haine de la littérature*. But literature is perdurable enough to survive both critical malpractice and public depreciation; and after all, to paraphrase Archibald MacLeish's famous distich on the art of poetry, existence is even more important than interpretation. The object-in-itself is so central, it has lately been argued, that we ought not to concern ourselves with the author's intention — a useful caveat against taking the word for the deed. But critics will want to reconsider thoughtfully before adopting a principle which would dismiss from their canon the *Prefaces* of Henry James.

9. The Revival of Rhetoric

A complementary argument would insist that it is fallacious to judge a literary work by its effects. Yet judgment is nothing more than considered effect, and effect nothing less than spontaneous judgment. To ignore the reader's response, along with the writer's aim, is to pass over questions of meaning and dwell upon problems of form. These have been, most appropriately, the locus of critical examination. The question-begging dichotomy of form and content, which confused substance with essence and artistic technique with external decoration, has outlived what usefulness it may have had for critics more concerned with ideology than with art. The category of content is misleading because literature can never be self-contained; its expressiveness springs from its innate capacity for leaving the page, entering our minds, and mingling with other matters; its verbal constructs are esthetic objects not in themselves, but by virtue of sounds and associations, metaphors and conventions. That is why a text cannot meaningfully be uprooted from its context, and also why critics are so readily sidetracked by extraneous considerations. As long as it takes these essential factors into account, recent criticism is richly justified in concentrating upon their artistic assimilation and formal arrangement. If the watchword, "New Criticism," has become a misnomer, it is because the activities thereby denoted have been so various, so widely diffused in America and England, and so comprehensively adumbrated on the Continent. Slavic formalism, the French *explication de texte*, and the German school of Romance philologists have still one precept which we flout at our peril: stylistics must be firmly founded upon linguistics.

It is commonly agreed, by both the New Critics and their fellow travelers, that they have most effectively dealt with poetry. With more extended and heterogeneous forms, they have kept fairly close to the texture, while the structure has remained as elusive as ever. Kenneth Burke has made this latter province his own, and has imported more or less pertinent notions into it from many other disciplines. Less fruitfully, in transposing rhetorical terms to social and psychological situations, he has blurred the distinctions between rhetoric and reality. The classical rhetoricians, though they were more rigidly categorical in their analyses of tropes and devices, had the advantage of a more exact terminology. Our up-to-date rhetoricians, in the very act of discerning the niceties of style, compound a jargon which might give occasional pause to a sociologist. Opaque phraseology can never be a substitute for clear thinking; and glossaries will not create a universe, where there is a chaos, of discourse. Modern rhetoric, if it is not to be logomachy, must meet the challenge of the larger structures with more concreteness and discrimination. The very existence of genres was questioned by Croce, and almost discredited when Ferdinand Brunetière tried to fit them into a Darwinian scheme of evolution; yet the working hypothesis is borne out by the development of drama, as retraced by scholars over the past fifty years. The completion this year of Arnold Toynbee's studies in the morphology of civilizations should encourage students of comparative literature, by establishing a point of convergence where the structural is reconciled with the historical, and where form is seen to be shaped by growth.

10. The Academy and the Market Place

Not the most tenacious champion of the moderns against the ancients, at this late date, would interpret the history of literature as a realization of the idea of progress. We cannot say that art, with all its ups and downs, is progressive; yet to the vast extent that it is cumulative, the knowledge of art — namely criticism — progresses. This knowledge, I hasten to add, is collective in character; for there can be no rivalry, in humanistic stature, between our contemporaries and certain great critics of a hundred years ago: last of their line, according to Sainte-Beuve. If our purview extends beyond theirs, it is owing in large measure to their achievements and those of others. Ours, for better or worse, come somewhat closer to the more organized inquiries of science; we have gained something in professional objectivity, while losing a good deal in personal breadth. Few of our critics feel called upon to set up as ideologues, unlike so many of their nineteenth-century predecessors, who were likewise politiques et moralistes. The shaping of public opinion today has become a high-powered technological enterprise in which old-fashioned literary attainments play little part. Edmund Wilson declares, with considerable authority, that the days of the critical free-lance are over, and that younger talents are now being forced to choose between journalistic commercialization and academic domestication. The choice may not be quite so clear-cut in England, we gather from a current article by V. S. Pritchett;

but when Mr. Pritchett goes on to lament the gravitation of criticism to the universities, as if it were some sort of new departure, he betrays the incompleteness of his own education.

Since the time of Aristotle, more often than not, the critical function has been connected with the pedagogical and the scholarly. It does not follow that this connection has been invariably fruitful; indeed the regressions to Aristotelianism, which still has exponents after some 2400 years, have been periodic symptoms of sterility. The emergence of the critic as reviewer, commenting on books as they come along rather than lecturing about them afterwards, coincided historically with the rise of periodicals in the eighteenth century. The decline of reviewing in the twentieth, to a level where it is hardly distinguishable from publishers' advertising, will probably end by depriving responsible criticism of any popular forum. Craftsmen, the writers themselves, will doubtless go on contributing the most valuable insights into their craft; but, because it is for them to speak the first word, the last must be spoken by critics. Critics, in their resistance to the market place and their return to the academy, have lately been joined by many creative writers. What the term "creative" signifies in the academic curriculum, and whether it always outranks "critical" in the esthetic hierarchy, are moot questions which we may see resolved. Those who criticize are those who cannot create, it used to be said by — among others — Bernard Shaw, who disproved the maxim by switching in mid-career from dramatic criticism to dramaturgy. Among all those who live by the printed word, such differences are far less strategic than their shared and jeopardized commitment: which is now, or never, the critique of forces encroaching not only upon the creation of literature but upon the preservation of culture itself.

APPENDIX

James Joyce et l'Idée de Littérature Mondiale

At the invitation of Professor Jean Wahl, this lecture was offered to the Collège Philosophique at Paris on May 10, 1953. It appears in the Revue de métaphysique et de morale, *LXI, 3–4 (July–December, 1956), with its title philosophically transposed to* James Joyce: un individu dans le monde. *I apologize for the French; I should have to apologize still more, if I repeated in English so much that I previously tried to set forth. The French translation of my book on Joyce made me painfully conscious of many practical difficulties, but also eager to see the gap bridged from the other side, as it were. I hoped this attempt would make up, in closeness to its subject-matter, for what it might lack in mastery of its medium. At all events, as a classroom exercise in the idea of world literature, it may illustrate some of the problems it seeks to formulate.*

▼▼

La notion qui nous occupe ici, l'idée de littérature mondiale, est plus facile à illustrer qu'à définir. Lorsqu'elle fut énoncée par Goethe, c'était un idéal plutôt qu'une réalité. Sommes-nous maintenant plus proches ou plus éloignés de sa réalisation? Nous sommes habitués aujourd'hui à considérer la peinture et la sculpture, tous les objets d'art du monde, comme s'ils coexistaient sur un même plan d'expérience esthétique. Mais cette idée d'un musée imaginaire, où l'on est libre de flâner entre les chefs-d'oeuvre, nous est plus accessible et plus attrayante que celle de quelque bibliothèque alexandrine, sur les rayons de laquelle les chefs-d'oeuvre recueillent la poussière. Nous pouvons imaginer tous les livres à la fois, une totalité et une continuité qui englobe toutes les littératures dans leur ensemble; mais il est plus difficile d'imaginer comment les lecteurs et les critiques, voire même les savants ou les bibliothécaires, pourraient se mouvoir avec aisance à travers une telle collection. La connaissance de tout ce qui a été pensé, dit, écrit, et publié partout depuis toujours, voilà peut-être une définition littéraire de Dieu. Ce dieu inconnu est qualifié par Joyce de "lecteur idéal souffrant d'une insomnie idéale" ("*that ideal reader suffering from an ideal insomnia*"). Celui qui s'adresse à cette intelligence supérieure, faute de l'audience de ses compatriotes ou de ses contemporains, a quelque chose d'un fou et en même temps d'un prophète: d'un fou qui discute avec lui-même, d'un prophète méconnu dans son pays.

Souvent l'écrivain, mécontent de son époque, s'en remet à la postérité; mais quand arrive la postérité, elle verra dans son mécontentement même une expression typique de cette époque. En outre l'écrivain, égaré dans son propre pays, peut trouver une consolation dans la maxime de Chamfort: "L'étranger, cette postérité contemporaine." C'est bien la maxime que Joyce a relevée dans son carnet, lors de son premier voyage sur le continent. La France surtout, pour les écrivains étrangers, a été cette postérité contemporaine. La position de l'Angleterre est moins centrale et plus complexe, l'anglais étant la langue littéraire de tant d'autres races et d'autres pays. A cet égard, rien n'est plus frappant que le rôle joué par les irlandais dans la littérature anglaise: la satire d'un Swift (irlandais naturalisé), l'éloquence d'un Burke, la métaphysique d'un Berkeley, et toute la lignée des auteurs comiques jusqu'à Bernard Shaw. Peut-être parce qu'ils avaient à dépasser les limites du provincialisme, ils ont pu atteindre l'originalité de conception et l'ampleur de perspective. Or, l'homme de lettres peut-il faire du monde sa province avant d'avoir réglé ses comptes avec sa terre natale? Dans quel sens peut-il dire, comme Peer Gynt: "Je suis norvégien (ou français, ou anglais, ou irlandais, ou américain, le cas échéant) de naissance, et cosmopolite d'esprit"? J'ai choisi à dessein cet exemple un peu ambigu, parce qu'il nous rapproche de notre sujet.

André Gide, ce maître de l'ambiguité, peut nous aider à résoudre la question, quand il signale que l'écrivain le plus universel est parfois aussi le plus national. On peut changer de langue: beaucoup d'écrivains, sans être nés en France, écrivent en français — ce n'est pas à moi de juger de leur succès. Avec plus de peine, on peut aussi changer de culture: Joseph Conrad présente le cas remarquable, un polonais qui est devenu un des meilleurs écrivains anglais de sa génération.

Mais une des qualités les plus remarquables que Conrad ait apportées à l'Angleterre, c'était précisément ce qu'on appelle l'âme slave. Quoi qu'il en soit, pour le meilleur ou pour le pire, il semble qu'on ne puisse pas échapper aux données élémentaires de la nationalité. Citons un autre cas slave: celui de Tolstoï, qu'on a quelque peu critiqué parce qu'il emploie si souvent le français dans le *Guerre et la paix*. Il a pu répondre à ces critiques — qui ne touchent évidemment pas la traduction française — que tel était l'usage dans certains milieux qu'il décrit. Ce qui est plus important, c'est que le contraste linguistique renforce le conflit fondamental du roman entre les artifices de la cour et la sincérité de la campagne, entre l'armée napoléonienne et le peuple russe, enfin entre la guerre et la paix.

Aujourd'hui nous pourrions bien nous souvenir, avec regret, des temps où la civilisation n'était pas divisée par le nationalisme, où la nationalité n'était pas encore devenue un principe d'individuation entre les cultures et les langues. Alors il n'y avait qu'une culture, qu'une langue, pour les hommes de toutes les nations et de toutes les races, quand ils voulaient communiquer sérieusement: c'était le latin. Combien avons-nous perdu en perdant cet humanisme d'autrefois, qui était un passeport pour le monde des idées, un droit d'entrée pour la plus grande des organisations internationales: la République des Lettres! Dante pourtant, que Joyce a appelé "le premier des européens," était le dernier des latinistes, lui qui abandonna le latin pour la langue vulgaire. Bien qu'il ait projeté une vision plus universelle qu'aucun poète a évoqué après lui, cette vision se compose de particularités. Son pélérinage imaginaire à travers le monde futur est fondé sur son propre voyage dans le monde réel. Exilé de sa Florence natale, il a pu situer ses amours et ses haines dans le Ciel ou dans l'Enfer, tels qu'ils les a connus sur la terre.

La littérature occidentale, dans son développement postérieur, a fait tant de conquêtes — la conscience de la personnalité, le culte de la nature, la découverte de domaines nouveaux, la perception de la couleur locale — elle a tant gagné que nous n'avons pas trop déploré la disparition de cette vieille latinité. L'accumulation même de traditions rivales nous avertit de plus en plus de nos devoirs et de nos privilèges, nous qui sommes les héritiers de toutes les époques. A défaut d'un guide clairvoyant, comme le fut Virgile pour Dante, notre époque trouve son poète caractéristique en T. S. Eliot, et son poème caractéristique dans la *Terre vaine*. Ce poème, à vrai dire, est moins épique qu'encyclopédique; en célébrant Londres il célébre aussi, comme le suggère le poète, Alexandrie; c'est un monument constitué par les ruines des autres monuments, les fragments de toutes sortes d'écoles et de styles. Le prince déshérité à la tour abolie, de Gérard de Nerval, fournit à Eliot un des huit derniers vers, qui comporte d'ailleurs six autres citations, dans six langues différentes — ce qui ne garantit pas l'universalité du texte. Si nous n'arrivons pas à le comprendre après avoir étudié le commentaire polyglotte que nous offre l'auteur lui-même, aussi bien que les travaux érudits d'anthropologie et d'autres disciplines auxquels il nous renvoie, si nous n'arrivons pas encore à le comprendre, peut-être est-ce notre meilleure réponse; car l'absence de compréhension est le véritable thème de l'ouvrage.

De la République des Lettres à la Tour de Babel, voilà la distance que nous avons parcourue. L'histoire littéraire est remplie de malentendus, de migrations et de déplacements, soit sociaux, soit psychologiques. En fait, on prétend parfois que ce sont là les conditions nécessaires à la sensibilité artistique, que l'artiste (et c'est seulement depuis Flaubert que l'homme de lettres se trouve dans la catégorie des artistes) doit être une sorte de "personne déplacée." Ce processus d'aliénation, intensifié par les gestes individuels du mouvement romantique, a été consommé par les événements politiques de ces dernières années. De nouveau, comme dans l'antiquité, le conteur a appris à plier sa tente et à suivre une étoile nomade, ainsi que le dit Thomas Mann dans une phrase émouvante. Mais l'exemple le plus significatif, parce qu'il est tellement exemplaire, parce qu'il se propose expressément à notre attention, c'est le cas extrême de James Joyce. Jusqu'un certain point, il a écrit sa vie; comme peu d'autres il a vécu son oeuvre; comme Flaubert surtout, il a été animé moins par les circonstances extérieures que par une exigence personnelle. Ce n'est pas par hasard qu'on retrouve, entre les lectures favorites du jeune Joyce, la *Tentation de Saint-Antoine*, aussi bien que les *Poètes maudits* de Verlaine.

Dans son île natale, l'Irlande, aucun de ses livres n'a pu être publié, et même à présent, certains d'entre eux sont interdits. En Angleterre et aux Etats-Unis ils ont attiré la censure, et de nombreux exemplaires d'*Ulysse* ont même été brûlés. *Ulysse* a été publié pour la première fois à Paris, il y a maintenant plus de trente ans, grâce au courage et au jugement de Mlle. Sylvia Beach, la propriétaire américaine de la librairie anglaise, Shakespeare & Co. Elle a aimablement autorisé beaucoup d'entre nous à participer à cette conspiration en faveur des lettres anglo-saxonnes, en nous permettant d'acheter ce livre Rue de l'Odéon pour le passer clandestinement à la douane britannique ou américaine. C'est Valéry Larbaud qui a initié les premiers lecteurs d'*Ulysse* dans une conférence qu'il a faite ici lors de sa publication. Quand un éloge de Joyce parut dans la *Revue des deux mondes*, le critique anglais Edmund Gosse adressa au rédacteur une violente protestation. D'autre part, le critique français Louis Gillet, auteur de cet éloge, nous a dit qu'à ce moment-là il n'était pas permis de mentionner les noms de Proust et de Gide dans une revue française respectable. Peut-être Joyce n'était-il pas le seul à se trouver plus estimé à l'étranger, "cette postérité contemporaine."

Toute la carrière littéraire de Joyce s'est passée en exil sur le continent. Les années irlandaises du début, ses années d'adolescence, lui ont donné toute la matière de ses oeuvres. Tout vient de Dublin, tout y retourne. Il aimait à nommer sa cité natale "la septième ville de la Chrétienté," et dans une lettre à Italo Svevo, il nomme les six autres, en partant de Clapham Junction, morne petite banlieue de Londres, et terminant par San Giacomo in Monte di Pietà — probablement un mont-de-piété protégé par son saint patron. Pour lui, dans sa vie d'expatrié, son oeuvre équivaut à une sorte de rapatriement. Cette double tendance, centrifuge et centripète à la fois, se précise brusquement quand le héros de son roman-confession écrit son nom sur la page de garde de son livre de classe:

> Stephen Dedalus

Et puis, son cours élémentaire:

> Classe des Eléments

Et puis:

> Collège de Clongowes Wood
> Sallins

Comté de Kildare
Irlande
Europe
Le Monde

Et enfin:

L'Univers

Voici le moi du jeune garçon qui, de son île, regarde le cosmos. Mais en renversant la hiérarchie, si nous le considérons du point de vue cosmique, il semble un peu égocentrique, ce garçon:

L'Univers
Le Monde
Europe
Irlande
Comté de Kildare
Sallins
Collège de Clongowes Wood
Classe des Eléments
Stephen Dedalus

D'une certaine manière, dans toute littérature il s'agit des rapports réciproques entre l'individu et l'univers, et entre l'univers et l'individu. L'essentiel est que la communication soit possible dans les deux sens. L'étape la plus essentielle de cette série, point de départ et point d'arrivée de Joyce, il la caractérise dans ses cahiers par cette phrase: "L'Irlande, une arrière-pensée de l'Europe."

Les Irlandais, cette race rebelle de bardes et de guerriers, avaient été constamment déçus dans leurs espoirs nationalistes. Mais leur lutte traditionelle avec l'Angleterre n'est pas plus féroce que la querelle de certains Irlandais avec l'Irlande. Joyce naquit et grandit pendant les années les plus décourageantes, entre la défaite du mouvement autonomiste et la révolution qui aboutit à la république d'Eiré. En conséquence, son caractère fut marqué par sa réaction contre toute activité politique. Comme Milton, presque comme Homère même, il passa une grande partie de sa vie dans un état de demi-cécité. En revanche, son oreille était extraordinairement sensible à la musique, à la poésie, aux résonnances de la voix humaine. A l'université, il manifesta de telles dispositions pour les langues, qu'on espéra qu'il y retournerait comme professeur en langues romanes. Son unique pièce, *Exilés*, reflète sa décision de cultiver son Irlande en Europe, au lieu d'apporter la culture européenne en Irlande. Dans la mesure où il pouvait gagner sa vie, il enseigna l'anglais dans les pays de langue italienne et allemande, souvent dans la babel des écoles Berlitz. Malgré son incomparable maîtrise de l'anglais, il persista à le considérer comme une langue étrangère. Bien qu'elle ait été empruntée à l'Angleterre, cette langue a été cultivée de nos jours en Irlande avec plus d'entrain, de lyrisme, d'imagination, et d'humour, et a même produit une nouvelle floraison presque élisabéthaine.

Joyce se détacha des activités littéraires et linguistiques qui se poursuivaient sous l'égide de la Renaissance irlandaise. Bien qu'il fut fasciné par la riche tradition du folklore national, il ne fut jamais nationaliste. Selon son expression, il était "bien trop irlandais" pour regarder le comportement des autres irlandais comme bizarre ou pittoresque. Il prévoyait avec raison que ce mouvement dégénérerait en un sectarisme étroit. Tandis que ses camarades étudiants s'appliquaient à renouveler les langues celtiques, il se tournait délibérément vers les langues scandinaves. Son but était de lire dans l'original l'écrivain vivant qu'il admirait le plus: Henrik Ibsen. Il écrivit même une lettre en norvégien, pour saluer Ibsen à la fin de sa carrière, qui était le début de la sienne. Son premier article fut un compte-rendu de la dernière pièce du dramaturge, *Quand nous nous réveillons d'entre les morts*. La dernière oeuvre de Joyce serait, en quelque sorte, sa propre version de *Quand nous nous réveillons d'entre les morts*. L'iconoclastie d'Ibsen, répondant à l'esprit moderne, renforçait et confirmait Joyce dans sa lutte contre les trolls du préjugé, de la médiocrité et de l'insularité — et spécialement contre les jésuites, qui furent ses maîtres au collège et à l'université. Comme étudiant, il publia un pamphlet acerbe, dirigé contre le Théâtre littéraire irlandais (plus connu aujourd'hui sous le titre Abbey Theatre) auquel il reprochait de présenter trop de pièces d'un intérêt purement local et insulaire, et pas assez de pièces de provenance étrangère.

Pendant cette période de formation intellectuelle et d'éducation sentimentale, qu'il a brossée dans son roman semi-autobiographique *Portrait de l'artiste jeune par lui-même*, il se tourne vers le continent. Contemplant le ciel, il voit "des nuages nomades qui voyageaient vers l'ouest, venant d'Europe." Il entend en esprit "une musique confuse de souvenirs et de noms." L'ambiance de la grande littérature lui paraissait très éloignée de la vie quotidienne qui l'entourait. Le vol des oiseaux lui semblait un présage de sa propre délivrance. Son nom même prédisait son destin; car Dédalus était cet artisan légendaire qui inventa non seulement le fameux labyrinthe (comme Joyce, à sa façon, devait le faire plus tard) mais aussi une paire d'ailes. Mais le jeune artiste, prêt à essayer ses ailes, ressemble moins à Dédalus, le père, qu'à Icare, son fils dans le mythe antique. Peut-être rencontra-t-il le danger, comme Icare, dont la chute est le symbole tragique de l'orgueil intellectuel. La formation religieuse de Joyce le disposait aussi à voir la perte de sa foi dans la chute de Lucifer, et sa propre révolte contre son milieu dans le grand refus de Lucifer: *"Non serviam!"*

La première fois que l'âme s'essaye à voler, explique Joyce, des filets sont tendus pour l'attraper. En Irlande, au début du vingtième siècle, ces filets étaient figurés par l'Empire britannique, l'Eglise catholique et la Famille bourgeoise. En France, au milieu du dix-neuvième siècle, Flaubert conseillait aux artistes de renoncer à leurs obligations envers leur classe, leur croyance et leur patrie, en faveur d'un plus haut engagement, l'engagement à l'art. Joyce se révèle, sous le visage de Stephen Dedalus, attiré par la religion et même par la prêtrise, mais suivant à la fin une vocation artistique, et sacralisant les chose ordinaires, comme Flaubert. La vocation de Joyce, telle que l'énonce Stephen, est de "fabriquer dans la forge de son âme la conscience incréée de sa race." Ce large dessein n'est pas incompatible avec le patriotisme; pour y parvenir en s'exprimant soi-même, le jeune artiste doit quitter son île pour le continent, se dégager absolument de la septième ville de la Chrétienté. Dostoïevski, en visite chez Tourguénieff à Bade, lui conseilla de se procurer un télescope et de le braquer sur la Russie; les irlandais en voyage n'avaient pas besoin de recommander à Joyce de diriger son regard télescopique vers sa terre natale. Dans un monde plus vaste, Stephen Dedalus se souviendra de la Classe des Eléments; si provinciale, si paroissiale qu'elle parût, c'était sa province, sa paroisse, et il en a fait la nôtre. Le régionalisme se transcende, quand un auteur élargit sa région particulière au point qu'un étranger s'y sente chez lui.

Le chef de l'école littéraire irlandaise, le plus grande poète anglais de notre siècle, William Butler Yeats, raconta une curieuse histoire, l'*Adoration des Mages*, dans laquelle les trois Rois d'Orient voyagent vers l'ouest, vers le Paris actuel où, dans les conditions les plus obscures, le Messie parait, le Christ renaît. Cette conception exerça une influence déterminante sur Joyce, la conception de Dieu se manifestant dans les rues d'une cité moderne, comme dans l'Epiphanie. Et si cela pouvait avoir lieu à Paris, pourquoi pas à Dublin? Qu'est-ce que Dieu, demande Stephen, sinon un cri dans la rue? Ainsi Joyce a cherché et gardé ses observations et ses impressions des moments fugitifs sous le nom d'*Epiphanies*. Celles-ci sont semblables aux moments privilégiés de Proust, où tout le secret de la vie se dévoile dans un geste fortuit ou dans une phrase banale. La valeur de la vision, comme nous le voyons dans le cas d'Henri Pichette, dépend du talent du visionnaire. Peut-être Joyce cherchait-il ici cette *quidditas*, cette quiddité, cette essence même dont parlent les philosophes scholastiques, conjonction du temps et de l'espace où le particulier devient l'universel. *Ulysse* mentionne un certain manuscrit, dont les copies devaient être envoyées dans toutes les bibliothèques du monde, y compris celle d'Alexandrie, après la mort de son auteur. Les manuscrits de Joyce, sauvés des allemands par le grand sacrifice de son meilleur ami Paul Léon, ont été exposés à Paris il y a quelques années. Celui des *Epiphanies* repose maintenant dans une bibliothèque à Buffalo, New York, et nous pouvons espérer qu'il sera prochainement imprimé. Mais la formulation de l'épiphanie annonce déjà la série d'esquisses métropolitaines recueillies dans le livre *Gens de Dublin*.

L'oeuvre principale de Joyce, *Ulysse*, est l'élaboration — et peut-être l'ultime élaboration que le roman puisse supporter — de cette attitude envers la vie, de ce sentiment de l'épiphanie. *Ulysse* continue la tendance à l'autobiographie, en suivant Stephen Dedalus, qui est revenu de Paris à Dublin au lit de mort de sa mère. Provisoirement, il est suppléant dans un collège de garçons; mais son chapeau du Quartier Latin annonce, comme un symbole débonnaire, que ses liens sont bristés, que ses voeux sont confirmés. A ce moment il décide de quitter l'Irlande, pour créer sa conscience. *Ulysse* n'est pas seulement cette création même, c'est la commémoration du jour où Joyce est arrivé à cette décision: le 16 juin 1904. Heure par heure, minute par minute, nous vivons cette journée à travers les idées et les sensations des personnages qui marchent dans la ville. Vous pouvez suivre l'histoire sur la carte, sans la carte vous ne pouvez guère la suivre. Rue par rue, maison par maison, la ville a été reconstruite en centaines et en milliers de petits détails que vous pouvez vérifier dans les journaux et les annuaires. De sorte que Joyce avait peur d'être surnommé "le Zola irlandais," mais il s'avance bien au-delà des limites du naturalisme. En principe, il serait toujours possible d'appliquer à un autre jour, dans une autre ville, une documentation aussi étendue et aussi minutieuse; tous les détails seraient différents, mais le résultat serait à peu près le même. Le but du roman exprimé par Balzac, "de faire concurrence à l'Etat-Civil," a été réalisé et dépassé. Le romancier a rivalisé le recensement, et il a gagné.

Qu'a-t-il gagné? Une place précaire dans les rangs des journalistes. Il serait accablé par l'entassement de "petits fais vrais," s'il ne leur imposait pas une portée générale, s'il n'orientait pas son réalisme vers un symbolisme. Le titre *Ulysse* indique le mythe qui sert à nous conduire au coeur du labyrinthe. Chaque chapitre de cette *Odyssée* moderne est parallèle à un épisode de l'épopée d'Homère: par exemple, la Caverne des Vents est le bureau d'un journal, dont le rédacteur est le sosie d'Eole. Chaque chapitre a son propre style, qui convient à son contenu: dans celui-ci, toutes les figures de rhétorique sonts désignées et utilisées pour démontrer l'art du journalisme. Une suite de manchettes, peu homériques, interrompt de temps en temps la narration, et arrête le déroulement de la conscience, nous rappelant que les nouvelles d'hier sont aussi démodées que la guerre de Troie. Notre Ulysse moderne, cet ingénieux qui a connu tant d'hommes et de villes, ce héros habile, fatigué et viellissant, s'accommode très convenablement au rôle d'un agent de publicité, petit employé d'un journal. Leopold Bloom est l'homme de la rue, homme de bonne volonté, citoyen moyen; et comme pour suggérer que l'homme moyen est en exil spirituel, Joyce en a fait un juif, qui pourrait habiter n'importe quelle capitale d'Europe. Type urbain et international, singulièrement insignifiant, et surtout dépourvu d'héroïsme, semblerait-il. Son épopée ne tourne que trop fréquemment au burlesque, et toutes ses aventures sont des mésaventures.

Mais l'aventure qui couronne les autres, qui place en effet une couronne d'épines sur son front, se passe dans un bistrot, pendant une brûlante discussion politique. En s'efforçant de maintenir la paix, Mr. Bloom devient, comme d'habitude, un souffre-douleur. L'analogie homérique est celle du cyclope Polyphème, personnifié ici par un ivrogne nationaliste; sa colère se transforme soudain en anti-sémitisme, aux dépens de l'infortuné Mr. Bloom. Joyce nous laisse entendre que son bouc émissaire, mieux qu'Ulysse ou même le Juif Errant, pourrait être le Messie. En un mot, nous pourrions être témoins de l'Epiphanie. Ainsi Joyce pose à son tour la perpétuelle question, soulignée par Dostoïevski dans sa légende du Grand Inquisiteur: qu'arriverait-il si Jésus-Christ revenait sur la terre aujourd'hui? serait-il encore une fois lapidé et crucifié? Stephen, qui joue un rôle secondaire, en témoignera; au moins nous donnera-t-il un aperçu de la vision. Il avait cherché son père comme Télémaque chercha le sien, Ulysse. Mais l'artiste et le citoyen, quand ils se rencontrent enfin, n'ont pas grand' chose à se dire. Bientôt ils se quittent pour suivre leurs chemins respectifs.

Ithaque, le foyer domestique, n'est qu'une déception, une terne maison dans une rue sans couleur — en réalité, ce fut l'endroit de Dublin où Joyce conçut sa doctrine personnelle de l'épiphanie. Il y abandonne son héros pour se concentrer sur son héroïne, une Pénélope qui n'est rien moins que fidèle. Son infidélité, qui est une humiliation finale pour son mari, est pour elle une source constante de renouvellement. Elle représente l'Eternel Féminin, et son dernier mot, le dernier mot du livre, est "oui" — affirmation qui répond au refus de Stephen dans le Portrait de l'artiste. A la fin, c'est Stephen, plutôt que Bloom, qui est le vagabond. Le retour de Bloom est l'occasion du départ de Stephen, départ qui donnera maintes fois à son esprit l'occasion de revenir à Dublin. "Heureux qui comme Ulysse a fait un beau voyage," dit votre poète; mais son poème est l'expression de la nostalgie, plutôt que de l'attirance des pays lointains. Il a envie d'achever ses voyages et de se reposer sereinement, non pas à l'ombre des monuments romains, mais dans son petit village sur le Loir. Le retour du voyageur resta imaginaire pour Joyce, et Paris fut la montagne d'où il contemplait sa Terre Promise.

Ulysse embrassait son sujet d'une manière tellement compréhensive et systématique qu'il parvint à l'épuiser; et, avec lui, il faillit épuiser le genre même du roman. L'Irlande, dans l'intervalle, devait changer et évoluer. Tandis que le temps dépassait ce lieu dans l'espace que Joyce avait fixé pour l'éternité, il y a presque cinquante ans, il s'intéressait de plus en plus au changement, à l'évolution, à la quatrième dimension. Le jeune artiste, Stephen Dedalus, regardait l'histoire comme un cauchemar dont il essayait de se réveiller. Dans sa maturité, Joyce médita la philosophie de l'histoire, surtout la théorie des cycles du philosophe napolitain Jean-Baptiste Vico. Celui-ci a braqué son télescope sur la marche de l'humanité et lui promet, malgré bien des fluctuations de fortune, un progrès à longue échéance. La dernière oeuvre de Joyce, pendant les dix-sept ans qu'il mit à l'écrire, s'entitulait *Work in Progress* ("Oeuvre en marche"). Ce qui pouvait succéder à *Ulysse* tiendrait moins du roman que de l'épopée. Ce serait une oeuvre régionale, Joyce ne pouvait faire autrement; mais elle serait maintenant historique, aussi bien que géographique; il chercherait à saisir le flux de la vie, plutôt que sa cristallisation, le fleuve aussi bien que la cité. Au-delà de l'histoire il y a toujours la nature, le phénomène continu de l'existence, les fleurs comme les a évoquées Edgar Quinet, dans une phrase qui est une des clefs de la pensée de Joyce:

Aujourd'hui comme aux temps de Pline et de Columelle, la jacinthe se plaît dans les Gaules, la pervenche en Illyrie, la marguerite sur les ruines de Numance; et pendant qu'autour d'elles les villes ont changé de maîtres et de noms, que plusieurs sont entrées dans le néant, que les civilisations se sont choquées et brisées, leurs paisibles générations ont traversé les âges et sont arrivées jusqu'à nous, fraîches et riantes comme aux jours des batailles.

De toute façon, après tant de batailles, l'histoire irlandaise approchait d'une réussite tardive avec le soulèvement de Pâques, 1916. On peut réduire l'énorme complexité de la *Veillée de Finnegan* en signalant que son thème majeur est le soulèvement de Pâques, dont la beauté terrible est aussi le thème le plus passionnant de Yeats. Pour Stephen Dedalus, la requête de sa mère de faire ses Pâques symbolisait tout avec quoi il pensait avoir rompu. Maintenant, par le symbolisme du hasard, l'insurrection nationaliste arrive à une date qui coïncide avec la fête de la Résurrection chrétienne. Il y a d'autres analogies, que les anthropologues peuvent signaler: les rites de la végétation, les cultes d'Osiris et d'Adonis, et toutes les incarnations du dieu mourant qui se sacrifie et revient de nouveau à la vie. *Finnegans Wake* est, en vérité, le titre d'une chanson irlandaise du music-hall américain: l'histoire d'un ouvrier maçon qui tombe de son échelle, et qui est tenu pour morte. La veillée a lieu autour du corps, avec les consolations habituelles de la boisson; une goutte de whisky, qui tombe sur lui, provoque un miraculeux réveil. Le titre rappelle aussi une légende plus noble, car Finn se réveille encore *(Finn wakes again)*. C'est le réveil de Finn, le héros de l'Irlande antique, le Fingal dont les exploits ont été célébré par le barde Ossian, et qui dort parmi ses paladins sous quelque colline enchantée.

Joyce identifie cette colline avec Howth, promontoire au nord de la baie de Dublin, ce qui est, pour les gens de Dublin, la tête d'un géant endormi, dont de corps s'étend à travers la ville et le long du fleuve. Les initiales H. C. E., dérivant de l'épithète "Howth Castle and Environs" (Howth, le Château, et les Environs), et figurant à chaque page du livre sous des formes variées, sont celles du protagoniste, sur un plan vulgaire la patron d'un bistrot. Sa femme, un de ces caractères maternels comme Joyce aimait à en tracer, s'identifie à la Liffey, fleuve qui traverse Dublin, par les initiales A. L. P., mises pour Anna Livia Plurabelle. Son monologue, dans lequel les noms de tous les fleuves du monde sont entrelacés, est le plus grand tour de force entre tant d'autres. Même si vous ne lisez pas le livre, vous devez entendre le disque que Joyce lui-même a enrigistré de ce passage. Son héroïne est toutes les femmes, comme son héros est tous les hommes. La dialectique de leurs deux fils, Shem et Shaun, résout l'éternelle contradiction entre le "non" du *Portrait de l'artiste* et le "oui" d'*Ulysse*. Et nous rencontrons beaucoup d'autres personnages, dont les métamorphoses réunissent les légendes et les mythes du monde entier dans une seule construction imaginaire, d'après Joyce un "monomythe." Si gigantesque et éclectique qu'il nous paraisse, ce n'est qu'un rêve, une fantaisie d'ivresse dans l'esprit d'un cafetier qui a fermé son cabaret pour la nuit, bu ce qui restait dans les verres, et qui est tombé ivre-mort sur le plancher. Voici son cauchemar.

La nuit prête ses contours à la *Veillée de Finnegan* comme le jour avait prêté les siens à *Ulysse*. Là nous étions invités à entrer dans la conscience des personnages, ici nous sommes confrontés avec le courant de l'inconscient. Le langage d'*Ulysse* n'est pas aussi décourageant que le lecteur pourrait le croire au premier abord; nous sommes rebutés moins par le style que par les allusions et les associations d'idées. Nous apprenons à lire *Ulysse* en contrôlant ses méthodes psychologiques et ses données topographiques. Dans la *Veillée de Finnegan* le langage, comme le pigment de certaines peintures, n'est pas tellement le moyen, que la substance même de l'ouvrage. Il y a très peu de narrations et de descriptions; le livre doit être lu comme de la poésie — ou, mieux, de la musique, une musique des idées. A l'orchestration des thèmes, échos, réverbérations, pastiches d'un nombre infini de sources, s'oppose en contre-point le jeu continuel des mots. Le vocabulaire hétérogène de l'anglais est macaroniquement enrichi des emprunts à toutes les langues indo-européennes, et bien d'autres — sans compter les néologismes de Joyce, ou surtout les mots-valises à la manière de Lewis Carroll. Il n'est pas surprenant que le maître maçon Finnegan, qui est d'ailleurs constructeur de villes, prétende avoir construit la Tour de Babel.

Le calembour est pour Joyce un procédé pour avancer un accord phonétique là où il n'y a qu'un désaccord sémantique. Et voilà le hic: encore la difficulté de communication. Dès le début, l'intérêt de Joyce pour l'expérience stylistique en fait un auteur difficile. Son malentendu avec le public a été ratifié par la censure. La générosité d'une bienfaitrice anglaise le libéra de la nécessité de plaire à d'autres lecteurs qu'à lui-même. Pendant dix-sept ans, il fut libre de se laisser aller à sa virtuosité technique, d'ensevelir sa signification sous un monceau d'ingéniosités, de sceller ses réflections et ses réactions dans un sanctuaire hermétique. Renonçant à tout espoir d'être beaucoup lu, il limita son auditoire en élargissant son orientation. Un sort ironique veut que son oeuvre, qui contient tout, ne puisse s'adresser qu'à des spécialistes, qui déjà l'entourent de thèses et de monographies. Joyce lui-même reste un écrivain pour les écrivains, qui en effet assimilent et vulgarisent ses expériences spécialisées. Ici et là, dans la *Veillée de*

Finnegan, il s'arrête et se demande pourquoi il écrit ce livre monstrueux: *"Why?"* Il se répond alors: *"Such me."* Ce qui veut dire littéralement "tel moi" — c'est à dire, "je suis comme ça." Mais les deux mots correspondent aussi à l'expression argotique, *"search me"* — littéralement "cherchez-moi" ou encore "considérez l'auteur," mais plus justèment "je ne sais pas," avec une intonation cynique et un haussement d'épaules.

"Une centaine de soucis, une dîme de peines," gémit Anna Livia Plurabelle, "n'y a-t-il personne qui me comprenne?" Cependant nous écoutons cet.e musique confuse, et quelques sens émergent de la babel — du dialogue de Mutt et Jute, par exemple. Ceux-ci ne sont pas Mutt et Jeff, personnages comiques des journaux illustrés; ils ne sont pas non plus sourds-muets *(deaf-mutes),* bien qu'ils suggèrent quelque chose des deux. Ils évoquent plutôt notre surdité morale et notre mutisme spirituel, dans nos efforts pour communiquer entre nous. Voici un échantillon de leur dialogue. *"Phonio saxo? Spiggoty anglease?"* demande Mutt, l'indigène, à Jute, l'étranger, dans sa *lingua franca* personnelle. *"Tollerday donsk? Tolkatiff scowegian?"* Ne recevant aucune réponse, Mutt conclut que Jute est bel et bien un jute, un des Vikings conquérants de l'Irlande. Mais Mutt lui-même, au niveau inférieur, est le patron du bistrot; Jute en est l'habitué, qui frappe sur le comptoir et demande brutalement son verre de bière. *"Come on, fool porterfull,"* dit-il, *"hosiered women blown monk sewer."* Il commence par commander son *porter,* mais la phrase s'effondre dans un non-sens. Mais attendez. Ecoutez. Peut-être est-il normand. Peut-être parle-t-il français. Peut-être dit-il: "Comment vous portez-vous aujourd'hui, mon blond monsieur?" De nouveau il devient possible pour les branches de la même race, les membres du genre humain, de se comprendre l'un l'autre.

La littérature n'existe que par une telle compréhension, et le sort de la culture est symbolisé dans le livre de Joyce par une lettre: "écrite avec de la fumée, et obscurcie par le brouillard, et signée dans la solitude, et scellée pendant la nuit . . . C'était la vie, mais était-ce juste? C'était libre, mais était-ce de l'art?" Lettre envoyée du vieux monde au nouveau, ou est-ce du nouveau monde à l'ancien? En tout cas, elle est perdue dans un tas d'ordures — ou est-ce le dolmen de quelque héros enterré? Un jour l'archéologie la déterrera, et l'exégèse la déchiffrera. Ce message sera, Joyce nous l'a promis, "le testament de tous les morts à un certain nombre de vivants." Au cours de sa carrière, il avait rencontré deux écrivains plus âgés que lui, dont les oeuvres avaient été oubliées: Edouard Dujardin à qui il emprunta l'invention du monologue intérieur, et Italo Svevo qui fut son élève d'anglais à Trieste. Joyce contribua à rétablir le prestige littéraire de chacun d'eux; et chacun, par une bizarre coïncidence, en dédicaçant son livre à Joyce, le remercia d'avoir accompli le miracle de Lazare. Joyce n'était pas homme à laisser passer l'insinuation messianique de cette comparaison on ne peut plus flatteuse. Il était soulagé à la pensée d'une résurrection éventuelle de ses intentions ensevelies. Jusque-là, il est d'accord avec Gide et quelques autres évangélistes modernes: "Si le grain ne meurt . . ."

Et peut-être en est-il ainsi de la civilisation elle-même, selon la théorie cyclique de Joyce et de Vico. Nous traversons des temps troublés, comme diraient les irlandais; parfois nous avons l'impression de vivre au milieu d'une apocalypse. Nous avons témoigné: *"the dynamatisation of colleagues"* (la destruction par la dynamite des collèges et, bien entendu, des collègues), *"the reducing of records to ashes"* (les archives réduites en cendres, les livres brûlés), *"the levelling of all customs by blazes"* (le nivellement de toutes les coutumes par les flammes, et Joyce pense aussi aux douaniers — *customs officers* — qui ont jeté ses propres livres aux flammes). Mais le pire de tout ce que nous avons témoigné, et ici Joyce est prophète, c'est *"the abnihilisation of the etym"* — non seulement l'annihilation de l'atome avec toutes ses conséquences affreuses, non seulement la réduction de tout au néant, mais encore *ab nihilo*, du néant la signification (*etymon*), la recréation du monde par la parole. Comme Edgar Quinet l'a indiqué à Joyce, les paisibles générations des fleurs survivent aux jours des batailles. Chaque thèse a son antithèse, dans la *Veillée de Finnegan*: le thème de la destruction dans le thème de la création, le thème du sommeil dans le thème du réveil, le thème de la débâcle dans le thème du soulèvement. Le rêve de Finnegan est un cycle de mort et de résurrection, le voyage d'Ulysse est un cycle d'exil et de retour.

Ainsi le paradoxe de Gide, qu'un écrivain peut être à la fois le plus national et le plus universel, trouve en Joyce sa résolution. Si Joyce part du nationalisme pour arriver à l'internationalisme, il suit une autre voie que Dante; si Dante particularise les universaux, Joyce universalise les particularités. Dante avait rempli les conditions de la beauté, telles que les énumère Saint-Thomas d'Aquin: *integritas, consonantia, claritas.* Le problème, tel qu'il se présenta à Joyce, était plus compliqué: à partir des fragments créer une intégralité, à partir des désaccords une consonance, et à partir des obscurités une clarté. Il est peu étonnant qu'il ait caché sa lumière, et enterré ses intentions. Nous pouvons comprendre pourquoi il était obsédé par le destin qui le conduisait à écrire *Ulysse*, sa monumentale évocation de Dublin, dans trois autres villes d'Europe: Trieste, Zurich, Paris. A Paris, il vint d'abord comme étudiant en médecine, mais il était trop pauvre pour payer ses inscriptions, et presque même pour manger. Alors il s'asseyait "dans le silence studieux de la Bibliothèque Sainte-Geneviève où, à l'abri des péchés de Paris, il lisait, nuit après nuit" — je cite sa propre description — ". . . autour de lui, des cerveaux nourris et nourrissants . . . dans l'obscurité de l'esprit, l'éclaircissement tranquille de la pensée."

Bien des années plus tard, dans la *Veillée de Finnegan*, il regarde en arrière et se demande: *"Was Parish worth that mess?"* Question qu'Henri IV a résolue affirmativement: "Paris vaut bien une messe." Mais Joyce se demande aussi si cela valait la peine de recréer sa paroisse dans son oeuvre, tout en échangeant Dublin pour Paris. Ailleurs il se plaint: *"Trieste, ah Trieste, ate I my liver."* Plainte qui rappelle la ville austro-italo-slave, où il aurait été heureux d'avoir un morceau de foie à manger. Mais nous percevons encore un écho français: "Triste, ah triste, était mon livre." Pourtant le livre n'est pas triste, il est très drôle, en dépit de telles résonnances prométhéennes. La plus grande partie d'*Ulysse* a été écrite pendant la première guerre mondiale, à Zurich, qui à ce moment-là donnait asile au pacifisme de Romain Rolland, au dadaïsme de Tristan Tzara, au bolchévisme de Lénine, aussi bien qu'à la psychanalyse de Jung. Peu après la déclaration de la deuxième guerre, Joyce retourna malade à Zurich, où il mourut et où il est inhumé en terre neutre. Il n'est pas sans importance que son personnage autobiographique, Stephen Dedalus, joue le rôle de Télémaque, nom qui en grec signifie "eloigné de la guerre."

Son Ulysse contemporain, Leopold Bloom, est persécuté parce qu'il s'est fait l'avocat de la paix universelle. "Le contraire de la haine," dit-il, "je veux dire l'amour." Ceci en fait, pour le moment, un homme sans patrie. Mais Joyce savait, comme Marcel Proust, que l'homme de conscience est le citoyen d'une patrie perdue, qui vit de ces scrupules intérieurs, ces lois supérieures que les grands artistes ont pour tâche de découvrir. Il se pourrait bien que la République des Lettres soit aujourd'hui cette patrie perdue, étant donné la menace des guerres, la confusion des langues, les revendications contradictoires que les nations imposent aux écrivains. Il se pourrait bien que les écrivains n'aient plus les moyens d'être des artistes, qu'à l'idée même de l'art se substitue l'idée de témoignage dans les temps modernes, que l'homme de lettres désormais ne soit plus qu'un journaliste. Un autre artisan légendaire, Paul Valéry, renversant la fameuse définition que Clausewitz donne de la guerre, définit la paix: cet état où les instincts destructeurs de l'homme sont détournés vers la création. Les dernières générations ont bien peu connu de cet heureux état. Avec combien de force Joyce nous rappelle les pièges évités, les distractions repoussées, les obstacles surmontés par le talent créateur!

Index